The ABCs of Proposal Writing
& Conducting Academic Research
in Applied Linguistics

Seyyed Ali Kazemi, PhD
Leila Zarei, PhD
Mohammad S. Bagheri, PhD

PREFACE

The ABCs of Proposal Writing & Conducting Academic Research in Applied Linguistics has been designed to meet the needs of students attending graduate and postgraduate programs who do not have enough experience in writing theses, dissertations, papers, and articles.

The main incentive behind preparing this book, despite availability of different textbooks on the local and international markets, was compensating for lack of a comprehensive and learner-friendly textbook and helping those thesis/dissertation writers who want to manage the thesis/dissertation writing process effectively. This book provides novice researchers, especially in the field of applied linguistics, with a general picture of conducting academic studies and forms and then elaborates on details of related issues.

The book consists of *seven* valuable chapters each of which includes all necessary definitions and explanations to iron out ambiguities and clarify the subtleties in conducting a thesis. *Chapter One* helps researchers familiarize with different types of academic writing. *Chapter Two* introduces APA style to help researchers learn how to use the American Psychological Association citation and format style. *Chapter Three* is about two important sections of a thesis (i.e. Introduction and Literature Review). *Chapter Four* deals with the Methodology concerning participants, instruments, materials, and procedure. *Chapter Five* refers to Results, Discussion, conclusion, and implications. *Chapter Six* deals with planning a research study and it touches upon essentials of research methods in applied linguistics. *Chapter Seven* focuses on descriptive and inferential statistics in applied linguistics, and finally *Chapter Eight* provides the readers with a sample proposal and a sample article.

This book with its clear diction and thorough information may be used as textbook for courses like *Research Methods, Seminar,* and *Advanced Writing* in graduate programs of applied linguistics.

We would very much welcome the oral and written comments and constructive criticism with open arms. Correspondence concerning this book may be addressed to us at Kazemi.TEFL@Yahoo.com.

Seyyed Ali Kazemi, Leila Zarei, Mohammad S. Bagheri

CONTENTS

CHAPTER ONE
Different Types of Academic Writing
& Planning a Research Study

Introduction

This chapter familiarizes the readers, attending graduate programs without much experience in writing, with different academic writings ranging from articles to thesis/dissertation proposals and provides them with an overview of research methods in Applied Linguistics.

The first step in preparing any major project is producing an academic proposal. "A research proposal is a written plan for a project that will be submitted to others for evaluation. Writing the research proposal can be the most crucial and exciting step in the research process" (Ary, Jacob, Sorenson & Razavieh, 2010, 575). Its objective is to persuade a supervisor or academic committee that your topic and approach are suitable, so that you gain approval to conduct the actual research. As well as revealing your plan of action, an academic proposal should show your theoretical position and your relationship to past work in the research area. An academic proposal should have the following elements:

- A **rationale** for choosing the topic. It should indicate why the topic is important or useful within the course. It is logical also to show the limitations of your aims.

- A **review** of existing published work ("the literature") that is related to the topic. You need to tell how your suggested work will be made on existing studies and yet discover new territory (see more on The Literature Review).

- An **outline** of your intended approach or methodology with comparisons to the existing published work should indicate costs, resources needed, and a timeline of when you think to have things done.

This book discusses the ABCs of providing quality components of academic studies. **Title Page, acknowledgement, Table of Contents, List of Tables and Figures, List of Abbreviations, and Abstract** are examined in detail here as guidelines to make a systematic frame in writing process. Other components will be discussed in the following chapters. Different types of articles are introduced here to provide an overview of some concepts. Components of proposal writing are listed in this chapter to make the reader familiar with the procedures prepared in this book.

Five main stages in writing academic studies

Every student should have a general picture of the processes involved in conducting a term paper, an article, a thesis or a dissertation. There are five stages to conduct a research study. Inspired by Riazi (2000) and M. D. Gall, J. P. Gall, and Walter (2006), this book proposes a more comprehensive model as follows:

Stage one: Determining a significant research problem in order to improve knowledge or practice

This stage necessitates the following guidelines:

A. **Identify your research topic/question.** Your topic can emerge from a sense of curiosity, intuition and interest over a special problem that you think needs to be completed in the gap or absence of knowledge.

B. **Find out the difference between primary and secondary research.** Primary research indicates original research. It conveys that this knowledge is not produced in any other paper. Secondary research signifies that you need to read other experts' published papers to find out something new about your topic, to look over what others have said and written about it, and to draw a conclusion about your ideas on the topic.

C. **Identify your scope and time line.** The research scope has a particular meaning of knowing how much of your subject you will deal with. You must confine your reading and study to a particular aspect of the subject. Thinking about what specifically you want to cover is really necessary. Your academic research scope should not be too broad and not too narrow (in that it does not cover the significant requirement of a research scope).

D. **Write down a research question.** In your study, a research question will guide you a lot. It will become a **thesis statement** later. This question indicates what you want to find and what you are thinking about. It is not about a fact, but about an idea or opinion. The research questions should be written to be represented in your hypothesis. It should be the basis of your hypothesis. It is also possible to have a **theory-based research**, which consists of testing a hypothesis (guessing about the relationship between two or more variables). A hypothesis should contain a testable prediction about an observable phenomenon. There is possibility of disconfirming of evidence. Therefore, a theory is never proved. Theory-based research provides important findings and a rational basis for explaining the results of the research.

E. Be aware of finding useful and possible sources. There is useful information available on the Internet. You also need to use different types of resource books, magazines, journals, encyclopedias (probably not Wikipedia), <u>reference books</u>, newspapers, letters, <u>interviews</u>, blogs, etc. You can use an academic (school or university) library. Do not forget that you can't read everything on your topic. You also can't use every word you read in your paper. You need a background reading to learn about your question.

F. Start reading in detail. Your research question should be focused. It is good to find information that covers it, and describes, explains, analyzes, contrasts, or gives expert opinion on it. You are trying to make your own judgment, based on what you read from your sources.

G. Think about a method to take notes on what you read. Your notes should contain 1. Uncommon facts. 2. Unique, unusual, or startling quotes from experts. 3. Summaries of longer explanations.

- Recognize the difference between a direct <u>quote</u>, <u>paraphrase</u>, and <u>summary</u>.
- Cite exactly where the note came from in your source. You must know the exact location of using author, title, magazine, book, Internet page URL, date, volume number, etc.

H. Persist in considering new sources. You might need to find new information on a topic that is necessary to be read while you are reading. You might have to expand your research to check on details, possible errors, and corroborating or conflicting evidence.

I. Analyze your sources and keep your <u>research question in mind</u>. You should credit your source based on the author, location of publication, date, publisher, etc. You will analyze your research question later. Use your source material to help you establish your thesis (statement of opinion or belief) on that topic. You might change your question to fit what you are actually finding, after reading a lot.

J. Provide your tentative thesis. This is a single statement of your perspective on your research.

Stage two: Drafting and writing a research proposal in order to state all ideas on the paper

    A. Start writing your first draft. It is good to give the background and set the context for the topic at first. Then, you can explain, describe, give reasons, state causes or effects, or analyze parts of the topic. It is like a guide to avoid forgetting some points. It includes description of problem, record of research design (a plan outlining how and when each step of the project will be done), selection of a sample for data collection, data collection, and data analysis, rationale for the research project, literature review, and theoretical /conceptual framework.

    B. Start to <u>add quotes</u>, <u>paraphrases</u>, or summaries into your writing. You should be sure to introduce cited materials in an appropriate way (see a standard writing handbook), and mention where your citation will be. Based on what system you use, your (in text) citation will include a name, date, or page number.

Stage three: Conducting a pilot study in order to test a small scale of the procedure

A **pilot study** is a small scale preliminary study carried out to evaluate feasibility, time, cost, adverse events, and effect size to predict an appropriate sample size and improve upon the study design before the performance of a full-scale research project. Pilot studies show a basic phase of the research process. It can be done by a few participants for both quantitative and qualitative research. An exception is about developing an instrument such as achievement test or attitude test in which more participants are needed.

Stage four: Conducting the main study in order to analyze the actual data that is reported in the study

It is a challenging process, but it should be completed successfully. When you start to generate data, you may understand that the research project is not working as you had hoped. Do not worry about facing a problem. Research is unpredictable. Analyze the situation; think about what the problem is and how it arose. If a problem is unmanageable you should meet your supervisor as soon as possible. Give him/her a detailed explanation of the problem, and value their recommendations. Never try to neglect a problem, or hope that it will go away. It is worth remembering that every problem you encounter, and successfully solve, is useful information in writing up your research.

Stage five: Writing up the study and preparing the final report

A. **Finish writing your first draft, and then revise it.** Revising is checking the content of the paper, and assuring the thesis is developed, the content expresses your thesis, there is sufficient material, it is in a logical order, nothing off-topic is mentioned, and the writing flows smoothly. Editing is checking the writing details such as <u>paragraph</u> breaks, <u>sentence structure</u>, <u>punctuation</u>, <u>spelling</u>, citation formats, etc. At this stage your writing should be revised and edited by a supervisor or instructor. It can be accepted or rejected.

B. **Prepare the final draft.** Follow the format you are using. The most serious problem is <u>plagiarism</u> which is not citing the source of materials used. Your own thoughts are common knowledge, generally known to all, but any quote, paraphrase or piece of source must be cited. If a detailed research proposal has been written, much of the work of writing the study has been done. The personal computer and word processing have made manuscript preparation and revision much easier than it used to be. Researchers should have access to a word processor and to graphics software that allows numerical data to be graphed and mathematical equations to be represented. These are essential tools of the technical writer. All manuscripts must be checked for spelling (programs to check spelling are helpful), and all manuscripts must be carefully proofread before being submitted. Preliminary drafts should be edited by the advisor before the report is presented in final form. Your report should be written in your own words and follow appropriate citation style for any facts cited. Some universities provide students with a particular style manual while others refer students to a standard manual such as APA.

C. **Draw a conclusion.** The final stage should likewise include the key findings, conclusions and recommendations. The key findings must follow the logical sequence of the statement of the problem, while the conclusions must focus on the results of hypothesis testing. New ideas, tables or figures must be prepared in this final stage to complete the study.

Organization of reporting an academic research study

Front matter

Title Page
Preface and Acknowledgements
Table of Contents
List of Tables
List of Figures
List of Abbreviations
List of Appendices
Abstract

Body

General content of individual chapters of a (completed) study

Chapter One: Introduction (background)

General background information on the study
The research problem
Purpose of the study
Hypotheses or research questions
Scope of the study
Significance of the study
Definitions of key terms
Organization of the study

Chapter Two: Literature Review

Relevant review literature
Specific topics directly relating to the issue being investigated
Importance of the study based on previous research
The gap in the research that the study will fill

Chapter Three: Conceptual Framework and/or Methodology

Research design
Methods used to collect data
Research instruments
Methods used for analyzing the data
Demographic details (about who, how, when and why)
In ethnography, description of the setting and participants
Issues of ethics and consent

Chapter Four: Results

The findings of the study, described under themes that emerged from the data, under the research questions or under the data collection techniques that were used.

Chapter Five: Discussion and Conclusions

A re-statement of the research problem

A re-statement of results
Discussion of what was found in relation to previous research on the topic
Limitations of the study
Implications for future research
Consent

Back Matter

Bibliography (references)
Appendixes

(Adapted from Paltridge and Starfield, 2007)

Different types of academic writing

There are different types of academic writing which are classified as follows:

1. Articles in Scholarly Journals

Research articles should be published in a scholarly journal and not a newspaper or popular magazine. The authors should be experts in the field and not journalists. The article must include a reference list. If the article does not have these components it is not scholarly, and it cannot be a research article. The article should clearly mention that the author(s) conducted research, ran surveys, did experiments, collected data, or otherwise gathered material on their own or with a team of researchers. It must be original research carried out by the authors of the research article, and needs to be identified as such. A research article is different from a review article, which is a critical evaluation of material that has been previously published. This can be done to evaluate the state of the literature on a topic (which is a literature review), and to suggest steps for future research. The abstract often has clues. Look for a sentence that says something like "This study examines…". Such statements represent that the author probably conducted original research.

Experimental (empirical) articles deal with the developmental stages of conducting a scientific experiment. They are written by researchers in applied and hard sciences, and psychology. Their length can range from 3000 to 11000 words. They generally consist of the following stages in the research process.

- Introduction(the problem under investigation and emphasizing statements of the purpose of the investigation)

- Method(the method used to conduct the investigation)
- Results(considering the results found)
- Discussion(the interpretation and discussion of the result implications)

Sometimes *introduction* and *literature review* are merged into one part. *Discussion* and *results* can also be merged into one part.

Theoretical articles are those in which the author works upon existing research literature to advance theory in the related field or refine theoretical constructs. Researchers cannot experiment on divine and ethical matters like when they experiment on scientific issues. Different sections of these articles can be arranged based on relationship between events rather than chronology. They may consist of *Introduction*, *Argumentation*, and *Conclusion* (Ruiying & Allision, 2004).

Review articles are the critical evaluations of already published materials to trace the process of recent research toward a problem. They are arranged by relationship between events. They vary from 11000 to 15000 words with a long list of bibliographic works. They may have four sections: **history** (a historical view of the field), **theory** (a theory to solve a problem in the field), **Issue** (a problem in the field), and **recent work** (the existing state of the issue) (Swales, 2004).

- They define & clarify a problem.
- They summarize previous investigations to give the reader the information about current research state.
- They identify relations, contradictions, gaps, and shortcomings in the literature.
- They suggest the next steps in solving the existing problem.
- The sections of empirical studies are arranged **chronologically**, while the components of review articles are arranged by **relationship**.

Note: A **state-of-the-art review** mainly deals with the most current research in a given area or concerning a given topic. It often summarizes current and emerging educational trends, research priorities and standardizations in a particular field of interest. The review aims to provide a critical survey of the extensive literature produced in the past decade, a synthesis of current thinking in the field. It may offer new perspectives on an issue or point out an area in need of further research.

Note: It is required to be pointed out that different journals may need different formats. They usually provide their own templates to be followed.

2. Paper categories

A **term paper** is a research paper written by <u>students</u> over an <u>academic term</u>, accounting for a large part of a grade. Term papers are generally intended to describe an event, a concept, or argue a point. A term paper is a written original work discussing a topic in detail, usually several typed pages in length and is often due at the end of a semester. The best way to write a paper is selecting a category that is mostly related to your paper. Some papers have the features of more than one category. It is essential to choose your paper from one of the following classifications:

- Research paper
- Viewpoint
- Technical paper
- Conceptual paper
- Case study
- Literature review
- General review

Some papers fit into more than one category.

Research paper is a paper to report any type of research done by the authors. The research may embody research as follows:

- a research action
- an empirical, scientific or clinical research
- surveys or market research
- data testing
- the construction or testing of a model or framework

Viewpoint is dependent on the author's opinion and interpretation and also includes journalistic pieces. In general, Viewpoints are subset of articles that reflect a particular position adopted by a person or a group. A Viewpoint must be clearly expressed, and it demonstrates a thorough and broad understanding of the literature and practices in the field. The opinion expressed must be persuasive and it leads to insights and possibly new and interesting perspectives.

Technical paper deals with furthering the progress of science, usually by reporting new research. There are thousands of scientific journals in publication, and many more have been published at various points in the past to describe and evaluate technical products, processes or services.

Conceptual paper will not be based on research. It addresses a question that cannot be answered simply by getting more factual information. It develops hypotheses. It covers philosophical discussions and comparative studies of others' work and thinking. A purely conceptual question is one to which factual information is not even relevant.

Case study in the social sciences and life sciences is a descriptive, exploratory or explanatory analysis of a person, group or event. An explanatory case study is used to explore causation in order to find underlying principles. Case studies may be prospective (in which criteria are established and cases fitting the criteria are included as they become available) or retrospective (in which criteria are established for selecting cases from historical records for inclusion in the study). It describes actual experiences within organizations. In educational situation, it can be a description of a legal case or a hypothetical case study used as a teaching exercise.

Literature review is *not* an annotated bibliography in which you summarize each article/book that you have reviewed. While there is a summary of what you have read within the literature review, it goes well beyond merely summarizing professional literature. It is a comprehensive report based on a topic or research question and the existing literature available regarding that topic or question. It may be a selective bibliography providing advice on information sources. It may be comprehensive in that the aim is to cover the main contributors' ideas to the development of a topic and explore their different views. Literature review focuses on a *specific* topic of interest to you and includes a *critical analysis* of the relationship among different works, and relating this research to your work. The students critically analyze the method, results, discussion, and/or conclusions of a number of research articles (sometimes a specified number) and write a paper based on the articles' findings. For instance, the paper may address the following kinds of questions: Does the literature support the research query? Does the literature conflict with the query? Is there a combination of supporting and conflicting evidence? This type of paper can be used at both the undergraduate and graduate levels. It may be written as a stand-alone paper or to provide a theoretical framework and rationale for a research study (such as a thesis or dissertation).

General review is an attempt by one or more authors to sum up the current state of the research on a particular topic. Ideally, the author searches for everything relevant to the topic, and then sorts it all out into a coherent view. It covers those papers which deal with an overview or historical examination of some concept, technique or phenomenon. Such papers are likely to be more descriptive or instructional than discursive.

3. Thesis/Dissertations Proposal

A thesis/dissertation proposal is a document proposing a research project. A research project addresses a research problem. This problem is framed as a research question for which the thesis will offer a solution or answer. A thesis proposal seeks to convince a thesis supervisor or thesis committee that the research project is feasible and possible to be undertaken because it contains an important question for a particular field that should be researched, it is practical since the researcher has the know- how to approach and execute the project, he/she knows that there is sufficient data, and that he/she can do the project in the required timeframe.

Advantages of writing a strong thesis proposal

An intelligibly defined research problem (or question) is central to the success of a research project. It helps researchers to determine that their project is practical before they begin writing the thesis. In addition, if they take the time to clearly describe their project in their proposal, they will be capable of writing their thesis faster and more easily because they will have key elements. Also, the thesis proposal can be used as a guide to help you stay on track while writing your thesis.

A systems approach in proposal writing

A systems approach to proposal writing indicates representing the research project as a system made up of different elements. In a systems approach, each element is necessary to the system as a whole. If an element is removed, the system fails.

When writing each section, researchers should keep in mind the project as a whole and ask themselves: "What does the section contribute to the project? How is the section necessary to the project in general? And how would the project look without the section?"

Then, researchers should state a research question that drives the entire research project. It is important to state it clearly. Students often know what they want to discuss, but don't know how to make it into a research question. To identify the research question, it is useful to answer the following questions: "What is needed to be discussed? Why? Why is this significant? Why do you think you should discuss it in a thesis? What question activated the research?"

After making the research question, researchers must persuade their supervisor or supervisory committee that the research project is valuable. If there is lack of research on the topic the future implications should be considered to demonstrate the validity of the project. These are some related questions that should be answered based on providing sufficient rationale: "Why is it important to do a study on this topic? What new perceptions would this bring? What will be shown in a literature review? Have some studies been done which missed aspects of the problem you think are important? Would the results of such a study provide valuable information needed to solve a certain problem? Would the results provide possibilities for further research?"

Coping with anxiety in proposal writing

- Establish a writing schedule and begin by free-writing. Keep a small notebook with you to write down relevant thoughts.
- Write different parts of the proposal in different computer files.
- Start with more clear sections first, rather than with the most difficult parts like introduction.
- Be prepared to draft, redraft, and resubmit it.
- Think of the proposal as an introduction to your thesis—not a chapter. You are "bridging the gap" between existing work and your work.
- Bring to your mind that the proposal is not a contract that determines what your thesis will demonstrate. It is likely to modify and refine the scope, argument, and methods.
- Remember that the proposal helps you think in practical terms about how you like to research and write your thesis/dissertation.

- Ask your friends and classmates to exchange ideas, drafts, and experiences. Writing can be considered as a social activity.
- Consult with your advisor, ask to see past proposals, use other proposals to help you generate ideas, and do not plagiarize.

Research proposal format

It is believed that proposal of research studies can take different formats based on the nature of the problem as well as the design of the study. Some universities provide researchers with very specific instructions for the format of the proposals. Others give general guidelines considering form and content. So, there is no universally sanctioned correct format for research proposals. ***Students are strongly advised to consult their supervisor(s) and the department beforehand.***

General components of academic research

Academic research generally follows a similar format. Most universities provide detailed instructions or guidelines concerning the preparation of academic researches which will be considered in the following chapters. Such guidelines should be studied carefully before you begin writing the draft. Academic research can be qualitative, quantitative or mixed methods. There are some differences between the components of qualitative and quantitative research writing that will be mentioned in this chapter. The following outline contains the primary components of a research proposal *[2, 3, 4, 5, 9, 10, and 13 are parts of a completed thesis.]* For sections 1-5: Roman numerals are suggested: i, ii, iii, iv, v....

1. **Title Page**
2. **Acknowledgments**
3. **Table of Contents**
4. **List of Tables and Figures**
5. **List of Abbreviations**
6. **List of Appendices**
7. **Abstract**
8. **Introduction (Background)**
9. **Review of the related literature**
10. **Methodology**
11. **Plan of work**
12. **Results**

13. **Discussion, conclusion and implications**
14. **References**
15. **Appendices**

1. Title and title page
Title

The first aim of a title is to absorb the reader's attention and to draw his/her attention to the research problem being investigated. Since your title page provides the first impression for your audience of your proposal, your title should provide the focus of your investigation. Be sure that the title includes the key ideas and gives a glimpse of your research. Titles should be comprehensive enough to indicate the nature of the proposed work, but also be brief. The title summarizes the main idea or ideas of your study. A good title contains the fewest possible words that adequately describe the contents and/or purpose of your research paper. A working title should be provided by looking at the variables and deciding on the exact wording for your title when you are about to write your proposal. A good title should orient readers to the topic that you are going to research. It should also indicate the type of study that you are going to conduct.

Characteristics of an effective title in academic studies
- It indicates the subject and scope of the study accurately.
- It avoids using abbreviations (except standard ones).
- It contains words with high positive impression to stimulate readers' interest.
- It uses current nomenclature (the devising or choosing of names for things, esp. in a science or other discipline) from the field of study.
- It identifies key dependent and independent variables.
- It reveals how the paper will be organized.
- It suggests a relationship between variables to support the major hypothesis.
- The ideal length is 10 to 15 in informative words.
- It does not include "study of", "analysis of" or similar constructions.
- It is usually in the form of a phrase or a question.
- It uses correct grammar and capitalization with all first words and last words capitalized.
- All nouns, pronouns, verbs, adjectives, and adverbs that appear between the first and last words of the title are also capitalized.

- Rarely is a title followed by an exclamation mark.
- Generally the title should be informative, clear, concise, accurate, and eye-catching.

Choosing a Title

Choosing a good title is one of the most difficult tasks. Your title should be *as specific as possible*. Notice the titles used in the following examples:

[Specific] "The Effect of Using Translation from L1 to L2 as a Teaching Technique in the Improvement of Iranian EFL Learners' Linguistic Accuracy— Focus on Form"

[General] "The Effect of Using Translation from L1 to L2 on Language Learning"

The best way to structure your title is to look at your hypothesis and experimental variables. For example: "The Effects of [Independent Variable] on [Dependent Variable]"
Your title should serve as a mini-abstract of your investigation and *should put the most important words first*. Look at the following examples.
"Motivation in Students and Its Relationship to Learning Preferences"
It implies that the focus will be on "motivation."
"Learning Preferences in Students and the Connection to Motivation"
It implies that the focus will be on "learning preferences."

Note: If you are looking for a good topic, your own interest is important. In most studies, there is a "Suggestions for Further Research" section that you can study carefully to find an appropriate research topic.

Title of the research is the most important part of the research and it may attract readers' attention to the research or it might be misleading if it doesn't contain enough information about the study. **It is the immediate area for the readers to refer to and get the gist of what the whole research was about.** Avoid topics that cover too much material. It is better to narrow the topic down. Topics that are too narrow are problematic as well.
In writing a research paper and assigning a title for your research, you have to consider the three following requirements:
1. The title should indicate the **goal** of the research. Is it in the

area of testing? Is it in the area of teaching? Is it in the area of applied linguistics, language testing? , etc.

2. The topic of the study should **indicate** if you are doing it in the area of testing, it is focusing on alternative assessment or it is focusing on multiple-choice?

3. The title should be **self- explanatory** and **inclusive**. By looking at the title, the kind of study, the way of conducting, and the boundary of the research should be perceived. It should be as inclusive as possible while you keep the language as minimum as possible. It should have the combination of **economy** and **informativeness**. It has to be short, to the point, clear, and unambiguous.

Example: Direct vs. Indirect Measures to Testing University ESL Students

The **scope** of the study is indicated but the topic of study is not mentioned. Also, it is not self-explanatory and informative as it's expected to be. *It should be modified based on topic focus.* By looking at the title, the reader has to be capable of anticipating the boundaries of the research. With this limited linguistic term you cannot be capable of anticipating the boundary of the research. One question which might come up is: "What ESL context?" ESL context is as broad as it can be!

Modified: A Comparative Study of Direct and Indirect Scoring Measures for Testing Writing Language Proficiency of University Students

The expression "a comparative study" is added to show the research is comparative in nature. It is narrowed down by focusing on writing proficiency. It is focused on, one aspect of language, one part of language (here writing proficiency).

Example: Language Learning Skills

This title does not give required information. It is not self-explanatory. It indicates the focus but not very explicitly, because of these shortcomings, some questions can be raised: "What part of language? What mode of language? What skill? In what context?" This title is too economical to give information concerning context skills of language.

Modified: Language Learning Skills for Proficiency Test

Still this second modified title is deficient, it is not as informative as it should be, and it does not tell you about the context, so it needs more modification.

Further Modified: Investigating Reading Skill for Proficiency Test

It is narrowed down by focusing on reading skill. Here the part, the mode, the skill, and the context of language are all clear.

Title Page

The title page provides the first impression for the audience of your proposal. Your title page should contain a running head, title, author's name and school/university affiliation. When a title page is created, it is arranged in the following format:

In the Name of God

Islamic Azad University
Science and Research Branch- Tehran

M.A. Thesis in English Language Teaching

Subject
Construct Validation of Analytic Rating Scales in a Speaking Assessment

Thesis Advisor
Seyyed Ali Kazemi, PhD
Consulting advisor
Mohammad Alavi, PhD

By
Morteza Moradi

2012-2013

---

2. Acknowledgements

It is important to include an acknowledgement page in your research paper. To make an acknowledgement for a research paper, write down all the people that helped you with the study for example, colleagues, supervisors, advisors, reviewers, family and friends, etc. Acknowledge them in a statement of gratitude for their assistance in conducting the study.

Sample 1

I am profoundly indebted to all those who helped me pursue the present study. First of all, I express my gratitude to my thesis supervisor Dr. Shooshtari and my advisor Dr. Alipour, for their assistance and critical comments and discussions of some of the points raised in this study, without whose guidelines I couldn't have accomplished this task. To them, I am very grateful. I deeply appreciate the contribution of my teachers, Dr. Hayati, Dr. Bagheri and Mr. Tajalli who carefully read the earlier drafts of the thesis proposal and provided me with fruitful suggestions. I also appreciate the helpful comments provided by Dr. Yarmohammadi and Dr. Yamini during their classes. It was a pleasure working with all of them. Last but not least, I appreciate my family who encouraged me and sacrificed a lot for me.

Sample 2

I would like to thank the editors, Dan Douglas and John Read, for inviting me to write this article. Their support and comments on the formulation of the article are much appreciated. Also, I would like to acknowledge the invaluable input I received from the anonymous reviewers, whose questions and comments helped make this a better article. My utmost appreciation goes to Craig Deville, who, in playing "*the devil's advocate*", enabled me to sharpen and strengthen the arguments in the article. Additionally and as acknowledged in the article, some of the ideas presented here grew out of discussions we had in co-writing the Chalhoub-Deville and Deville (in press) article. Obviously, I remain solely responsible for the positions taken and any inaccuracies present in this article. Finally, I would like to recognize the support of the Lebanese American University which provided me with an office and additional resources while writing part of the article.

3. Table of Contents

A Sample Table of Contents (A completed Thesis)

4. List of Tables and Figures

Tables and figures help the author to show a large amount of information effectively to make their data more comprehensive. In APA chapter they will be discussed in detail.

List of Tables

List of Tables

page

A Sample List of Tables

List of Figures

List of Figures

page

A Sample List of Figures
5. List of Abbreviations

There should be a table to describe the significance of various abbreviations and acronyms used throughout the thesis.

Abbreviations	Meaning
CF	Corrective Feedback
EFL	English as a Foreign Language
ESL	English as a Second Language
FOF	Focus on Form
FOM	Focus on Meaning
IL	Inter-language

A Sample List of Abbreviations

6. List of Appendices

An **appendix** (one item) OR **appendices** (more than one item) is information that is NOT ESSENTIAL to explain your findings in the essay or report that you have written. However, this information may support your analysis and validate your conclusions. Some of the items may have been written by yourself or printed/photocopied from elsewhere, so there are special rules that you must follow.

When to use appendices

The body of the text should be complete without the appendices, and it must consist of all information including tables, diagrams and results necessary to answer the question or support the thesis. Therefore, you will need to know that appendices are used when the incorporation of material in the body of the work would make it poorly structured or too long and detailed. Appendices might be used for helpful, supporting or necessary material that would otherwise clutter, break up or be distracting to the text. Other people's work in the appendix will be referred to (e.g. see Appendix 3), not quoted (e.g. using short or long quotes) from the appendix. Appendices must be referred to in the body of the text, for example, "details of the questionnaire are given in Appendix B (on page 23)". **They are not included in the word count.**

Examples of items in appendices

Appendices may include some of the following:

- supporting evidence (e.g. raw data that is referred to in the text)
- contributory facts, specialized data (raw data appear in the appendix, but summarized data appear in the body of the text.)
- sample calculations (referred to in the text)

- technical figures, graphs, tables, statistics (referred to in the text)
- detailed description of research instruments (referred to in the text)
- maps, charts, photographs, drawings (referred to in the text)
- letters, copies of emails (referred to in the text)
- questionnaires/surveys (questionnaire/survey results appear in the body of the text)
- transcripts of interviews (summarized in the text)
- specification or data sheets (summarized in the text)

7. Abstract

The main purpose of an abstract is to provide readers with useful information about a document. Another main purpose of an abstract is to help readers to evaluate and select a document that they would find useful in their own research. An abstract is a concise summary of the research. It allows a reader to get the bare-bones of information about a document without requiring them to read the actual document. It is NOT, however, a simple summary of a document. Because an abstract is a description of an entire document, you can write an abstract only for a document that is complete.

Characteristics of a good abstract:
An effective abstract
- is accurate, clear, unified, coherent, concise, and able to stand alone.
- uses an introduction-body-conclusion structure in which the parts of the report are discussed in order: purpose, findings, conclusions, recommendations.
- follows strictly the chronology of the report.
- provides logical connections between material included.
- adds no new information but simply summarizes the report.
- is intelligible to a wide audience.
- doesn't quote but paraphrases.
- usually uses passive verbs to downplay the author and emphasizes the information.
- doesn't use abbreviations or acronyms.

Note: keywords should be mentioned below the abstract. Mentioning keywords is an essential part of writing an abstract. When retrieving information electronically, keywords act as the search terms. Use specific keywords that reflect what is vital about the study. Think of yourself as someone researching in your field, and then mention your key words.

Two types of abstracts
Informative abstracts
- include contents of reports.

- communicate purpose, methods, scope, **results, conclusions, and recommendations.**
- emphasize essential points.
- are short between 200 to 250 (depending upon the length of the original work they can be longer- from a paragraph to a page or two).
- let readers decide whether they want to read the report or not.

Descriptive abstracts
- tell the contents of the report.
- communicate purpose, methods, scope, but **NOT results, conclusions, and recommendations.**
- are under 100 words.
- Introduce the subject to readers, who must then read the report to learn study results.

The basic components of an abstract in any discipline
1. Motivation/Problem under investigation: Why do we care about the problem? What practical, scientific, theoretical or artistic gap is your research filling?
2. Methods/Data gathering procedures /subjects and their characteristics (i.e., number, type, age, sex, first language, proficiency level, and ethnicity) /approach/data analysis: What did you actually do to get your results? (E.g. analyzed 6 short stories, completed a series of 10 oil paintings, interviewed 35 university students)
3. Results/findings/product: As a result of completing the above procedure, what did you find/learn/invent/create?
4. Conclusion/implications: What are the larger implications of your findings, especially for the problem/gap identified in step 1?

Steps for writing effective abstracts
1. Reread your report with the purpose of abstracting in mind. Look specifically for these main parts: purpose, methods, scope, results, conclusions, and recommendations.
2. After you have finished rereading your report, write a rough draft without looking back at your report. Consider the main parts of the abstract listed in step 1. Do not merely copy key sentences from your report. Do not summarize information in a new way.
3. Revise your rough draft to
   - Correct weaknesses in organization and coherence
   - Add important information originally left out
   - Eliminate wordiness, and
   - Correct errors in grammar and mechanics.
4. Carefully proofread your final copy.

Abstract

_____
_____
_____
_____
_____
_____
_____
_____
_____
_____
_____
_____.

Keywords: _____, _____, _____, _____.

Sample 1
Second Language Teacher Education Today
Jack C. Richards

Abstract ■ Second Language Teacher Education (SLTE) is affected by two factors; a rethinking of its knowledge base and instructional practices as a response to changes in our understanding of the nature of SLTE, as well as external pressures resulting from the expanded need for competent language teachers worldwide. The impact of these two factors is seen in the growing professionalism of the field with the need for acceptance of standards, a rethinking of the knowledge base of the field, a move towards a sociocultural view of teacher learning, a focus on teacher cognition as the underpinning of teacher practice, acknowledgement of the role of teacher identity in teaching and teacher learning, implementation of collaborative approaches to SLTE, the need for greater accountability, as well as critical perspectives on teacher education. These factors are examined and their implications are discussed for theory and practice in SLTE.

Keywords ■ curriculum practices, sociocultural theory, teacher cognition, teacher education, teacher learning, teacher training.

Sample 2
Task Effectiveness and Word Learning in a Second Language: The Involvement Load Hypothesis on Trial Gregory
D. Keating

Abstract ■ This study tests the claim that word learning and retention in a second language are contingent upon a task's involvement load (i.e. the amount of need, search, and evaluation it imposes), as proposed by Laufer and Hulstijn (2001). Seventy-nine beginning learners of Spanish completed one of three vocabulary learning tasks that varied in the amount of involvement (i.e. mental effort) they induced: reading comprehension (no effort), reading comprehension plus target word suppliance (moderate effort), and sentence writing (strong effort). Passive and active knowledge of the target words was assessed immediately after treatment and two weeks later. In line with the predictions of the Involvement Load Hypothesis, retention was highest in the sentence writing task, lower in the reading plus fill-in task, and lowest in the reading comprehension task. However, when time on task was considered, the benefit associated with more involving tasks faded. The results are discussed in light of form-focused vocabulary instruction.

Keywords ■ active recall, incidental word learning, involvement load, passive recall, time on task

Length, tone, hedging, and headings

Length

Ideal length should cover the main points and supporting discussions clearly, briefly and directly. Restrict the discussion to the specific problem under investigation by omitting or combining tabular material and avoiding repetition. The active voice is recommended. Most dissertation proposals are about 20 pages. The tight focus should be developed on the research problem, in turn, focus the amount of time and space you spend reviewing relevant literature and discussing methods. Some advisors may require a more in-depth proposal, from 30-50 pages in length. Alternately, in some fields the proposal is the first three chapters of a dissertation (introduction, methodology, review of literature).

Tone

Tone refers to the writer's attitude toward his/ her writing, usually expressed most clearly in vocabulary choices and "hedging" considerations. It should be interesting and compelling. It should reflect the involvement with the problem.

Hedging

It is often believed that academic writing; especially scientific writing is factual and simply conveys facts and information. However it is now understood that an important feature of academic writing is the concept of cautious language, often called "hedging" or "vague language". It is necessary to make decisions about your attitude on a particular subject, or the strength of your claims. Different subjects prefer to do this in different ways. In Table 1.1. the necessary language used in hedging is displayed.

■ **Table 1.1.** *Language Used in Hedging*

1.	Introductory verbs	e.g. seem, tend, look like, appear to be, think, believe, doubt, be sure, indicate, suggest
2.	Certain lexical verbs	e.g. believe, assume, suggest
3.	Certain modal verbs	e.g. will, must, would, may, might, could
4.	Adverbs of frequency	e.g. often, sometimes, usually
4.	Modal adverbs	e.g. certainly, definitely, clearly, probably, possibly, perhaps, conceivably,
5.	Modal adjectives	e.g. certain, definite, clear, probable, possible
6.	Modal nouns	e.g. assumption, possibility, probability
7.	That clauses	e.g. It could be the case that . e.g. It might be suggested that . e.g. There is every hope that .
8.	To-clause + adjective	e.g. It may be possible to obtain . e.g. It is important to develop . e.g. It is useful to study .

Headings

Headings help the readers to get the main points considering the relative importance of the study.

- The heading system should be clear and logical.
- The sub-headings should be all at the same level and in the same font style.
- The wording of the headings and sub-headings should be alike.

Coherence, voice and visual aids

Coherence

Coherence reflects the property of unity in your writing that stems from the links among its underlying ideas and from the logical organization and development of its thematic content. It allows the readers to follow your writing. Coherence can be achieved through

- keeping the subject and verb together.
- moving from **"old"** (familiar) information to **"new"** information.
- putting the most important information at the end of the sentence (stress position).
- starting from sentences with **short, easily understood phrases**.
- using **transitional phrases** ("therefore," "however," "whereas") that indicate a shift in topic or emphasis.
- using **pronouns** to refer back to previously introduced information.

Voice

Choosing the "voice" of verb for a research paper – or for any form of writing – can be a tricky task. Voice in grammar can affect the way the verbs inflect, as well as where points of emphasis, intonations, and stress points may occur. In particular, voice affects the relationship between the action or the state that the verb expresses and the subjects or objects of that verb. Pay attention to the difference between "active" and "passive" voice.

Active: I will conduct the study during the fieldwork period.

Passive: the study will be conducted during the fieldwork period.

English teachers are interested in telling writers to avoid the passive voice. However, there are two reasons for using the passive voice construction:

1. The field may prefer its use, especially in describing research design and experimental activities.

2. The researcher needs to preserve coherence from sentence to sentence.

Visual aids

Incorporating visual aids is usually not mandatory for research papers; however, using non-text elements into the paper adds extra touches that help the paper seem more original. Depending on the topic, necessary visual aids should be used.

CHAPTER TWO
An Introduction to APA Editorial Style

Introduction

APA style is the official style which is used by the <u>American Psychological Association</u> (APA) and is usually used to cite sources in psychology, education and social sciences. The major guidelines for this format were laid out in a 1929 article published in *Psychological Bulletin*. These guidelines were finally expanded into the <u>Publication Manual of the American Psychological Association</u>. APA format may look difficult. But once you've familiarized yourself with the basic rules, it will become easier. You can refer to APA 6th edition if you need more information. This chapter contains detailed instructions for:

- Punctuation, Capitalization, Spelling, and Roman numerals
- Typology, Spacing, Pagination, Margin, Running head, and Italics
- Tables and Figures
- Numbers, Fractions, and Stylistics
- Grammar and Usage
- Abbreviations and Footnotes
- Proofreading marks
- Quotations and Summary (paraphrasing)
- In-text Citation References
- Reference list

Punctuation, Capitalization, Spelling, and Roman Numerals

Punctuation

In written English, punctuation is necessary to disambiguate the meaning of sentences. When speaking, we can pause or change the tone of our voices to reveals emphasis. When writing, we must use punctuation to show the places of emphasis. The following points help to clarify when and how to use various marks of punctuation.

How to use a full stop (.)
A full stop or (US) period is used
- at the end of a sentence that is not a question or an exclamation.
  There are certain criteria for evaluating hypotheses.
- in Latin abbreviations (*etc.,   et al., vs.*).
- in initials of names (*J. A. Collinson*).
- in reference abbreviations (*vol. 2, 1ˢᵗ ., p. 5*).

How to use a comma: a **(,)** indicates a slight pause and is used to divide a sentence into several parts so that it is easier to follow its meaning. It can be used

- in a series of three or more items before and/or.
  A research is systematic, logical, and generative.
- Before and after a clause that gives additional, but not essential information (nonrestrictive clause).
  The second rater, who was invited, revised the results.
- to separate two joined independent clauses(by a conjunction)
  APA format seems difficult, but a researcher needs basic rules.

How to use a semicolon: a **(;)** can be used

- to separate two independent clauses that are not connected by a conjunction.
  The advisor read my proposal; she has written a lot of books.
- to separate two elements that already have commas
  When your advisor comments on your proposal, he/she helps you continue the study; the advisor makes smooth the way for removing mistakes.

How to use a colon: a **(:)** can be used

- to exemplify, or extend the preceding material.
  These are our options: we make an observation and interview the students, or we take a quiz.
- to indicate ratio.
  ratio of girls to boys is 3:6

How to use a dash: a **(-)** can be used

- to show a sudden separation in the continuity of a sentence.
  These two groups—one control group and one experimental group are available.

How to use double quotation marks: **(" ")** can be used

- to bring quotations in text
  Assessment is "appraising or estimating the level or magnitude of some attribute of a person" (Mousavi, 2009, p. 36).
- to illustrate the title of an article or chapter when the title is mentioned in the text.
  Dörnyei (2003), "Research methods in applied linguistics"
- to introduce a word, phrase, comment as invented or coined expression for the first time
  It is a "mixed methods research".

How to use parentheses: **( )** can be used

- to introduce an abbreviation/acronym.
  analysis of variance in statistics (ANOVA)
- to set off independent elements.
  The study was scientifically important (see Table 1.5)
- to use for reference citation in the text.
  Lazarton (2005) also highlighted a major change in research.
- to show letters identifying items in series.
  The three most commonly used measures in descriptive statistics are (a) mean, (b) median, and (c) mode

How to use curly brackets: ({ }) can be used
- to show parenthetical material in parentheses.
  (The results for the experimental group {n=10} are also presented in Figure 2.3)
- to place material inserted in a quotation by another person other the writer.
  "when {his own and others' } behaviors were studied" (Hanisch, 1992, p. 24)

How to use a hyphen: (-) can be used
- to join two words together to make a new one. *Pre-test*
- to show that a word has been divided between the end of one line and the beginning of the next.
  Paired-samples t-tests (also known as "matched t-tests", "matched- pairs t-tests" or "pairs t-tests" are for research designs.

How to use ellipsis: (…) can be used
- to show omission
  Michigan asked, "When is it appropriate to use … in writing? People use it all the time and it seems like a way to make your writing more informal and conversational."

1. Capitalization

Capitalization is writing a word with its first letter as a capital (upper-case) letter and the remaining letters in small (lower case) letters.

You can capitalize
- the first word of a complete sentence.
- a word after a colon introducing a new independent sentence.
  The researcher gives a point estimate of the population mean: No clarification that has been proposed so far answers all questions.
- major words in titles of books, periodicals, and theses in the **body** of the study (All words that are four letters long or greater in the title of a source, all main verbs and linking verbs, both words in a

hyphenated compound, except conjunctions, articles, and short prepositions).

In his book, How to Write Research Proposals

- important words in article headings and subheadings.
- important words in table titles and figure legends (Only the first word and proper nouns in table headings and figure captions should be capitalized).
- trade names and proper nouns.
- specific nouns before numerals.

  In Table 3.1, Figure3.3, and Chapter 6

- volume number in reference list.

  Journal of Asian Studies, 55 *(2), 51-80*

- statistical symbols.   SEM
- titles of published and unpublished tests.

  Advanced Vocabulary Test

- in reference list, only the first word of a title of books and articles.

  Riazi, A. M. (2000). *How to write research proposals.* Tehran Rahnama Publication Press

2. Spelling

Spelling should be based on Standard American English as exemplified in *Merriam Webster's Collegiate Dictionary (2005)*. If a word doesn't exist in *Webster's Collegiate,* consult the more comprehensive *Webster's Third New international Dictionary (2002)*.

3.   Roman Numerals

Students should write in APA style with lowercase Roman numerals for the preliminary pages in a report. The title page of a report carries no number but counts as the first official page. The certification page, the abstract, the acknowledgements, the table of contents, the list of tables and figures, the list of abbreviations, and the list of appendices should carry Roman numerals.

Typology, Spacing, Pagination, Margin, Running head, Page number, and Italics

1. Typology, Spacing, Pagination, and Margin

In APA style, and in Microsoft Word, the term "spacing" has two different senses: (1) the vertical distance between the lines of a paragraph (line spacing), and (2) the vertical distance between paragraphs within a text (paragraph spacing).

All text in APA style should be Times New Roman standard font, set in 12 points (the font you are reading right now), 2 spaced (in some universities 1.5 is acceptable as well). A half-spaced on standard-sized paper with margins of 3 centimeters on all sides except for the left side, 4 centimeters.

2. Running head (page header) and page number

A running head is an abbreviated title about fifty characters or fewer, containing spaces between words, punctuation, and letters of your title in uppercase letters. It is asked by some journals to put a running head at the top of every page of your paper. The running head introduces the pages to the reader in case they get separated. In published articles it also identifies the article for the reader at a glance. A running head should be included in the upper left hand corner on all pages, including the title page.

The pages of your manuscripts should be numbered consecutively, beginning with the title page as a part of the manuscript header in the upper right corner of each page.

The first line of your title page should be left-aligned at the top of the page, using the following format: Running head: PAGE TITLE Your title, name and school should be double-spaced and centered on the page.

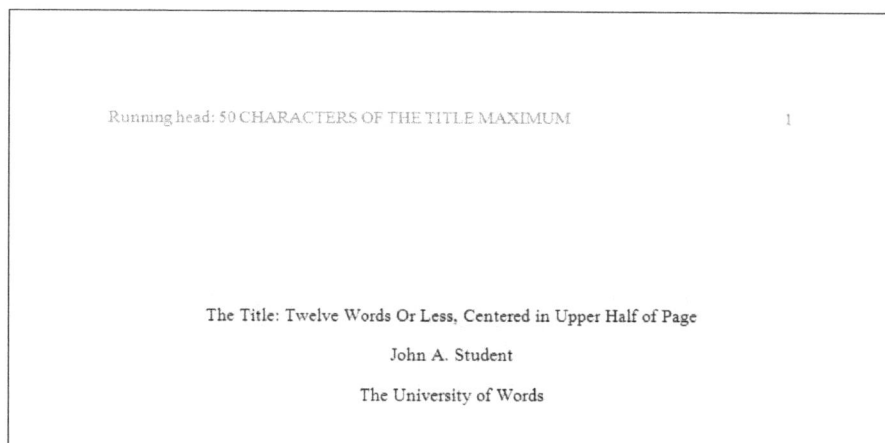

Running head: 50 CHARACTERS OF THE TITLE MAXIMUM   1

The Title: Twelve Words Or Less, Centered in Upper Half of Page

John A. Student

The University of Words

A Sample Running Head

3. Using italics

Italic type is a cursive typeface based on a stylized form of calligraphic handwriting in typography. Such typefaces often slant slightly to the right.

- titles of books, periodicals, videos, TV shows, and microfilm publications.
  Research Methods in Applied Linguistics
- species, genera, and varieties.
  Monacha
- introducing a new, technical, or key term for the first time.
  We compute a *post hoc* test.

- a letter, word, or phrase mentioned as a linguistic example.
  The letter *b*
- letters in statistical symbols or algebraic variables.
  $N = 325$
- some scales and test score.
  Ratio-scale
- in reference lists periodical volume numbers.
  Journal of Asian Studies, *55 (2), 51-80*

Tables and Figures

1. Tables

In APA paper format, tables are generally used to describe the results of statistical analysis and other quantitative data. However, it is important to mention that tables are not simply used to reproduce data that has already been presented in the text of the paper and not all data should be presented in a table. If you have little numeric information to mention, it should be described in the text of your paper. There is a sample table below:

Table 1

Correlations Between Measures

Measure	Second-order belief	Factual-deception	Self-presentation
Age	0.763*	0.631**	0.842**
Second-order belief		0.724**	0.775**

Note. *p < .01, **p < .001

A Sample APA Table

Basic Rules for Tables in APA Format

- All tables should be numbered (e.g. Table 1.1, Table 2.1, and Table 3.1) in the order in which they are referred to in text.
- Each table should have an individual title, italicized and presented with each word capitalized (except *and, in, of, with*, etc.). For example: *Correlations Between Age and Test Scores*
- Each table should begin on a separate page.
- Horizontal lines can be used to separate information and make it clearer. Do not use vertical lines in an APA format table.

- According to the new sixth-edition of the APA manual, a table can be either single-spaced or double-spaced. The key is to keep the table readable and the spacing consistent.
- A heading is necessary for each column of a table. All headings should identify item below them, not across from them. Table headings should be located flush right.
- Each column should be identified using a descriptive heading.
- All tables should be mentioned in the text of the paper.
- Tables should be last, after your reference list and appendixes.
- All tables should follow the same format.
- Any special or uncommon abbreviations mentioned in tables should be parenthetically explained in the table title.

2. Figures

There are many different types of figures with certain principles for all figure types. Standard figures argue the text and don't duplicate the text. They only convey essential facts and omit visual distractions. Their type, lines, labels, symbols, etc. are large to be read easily. They are carefully planned and prepared. Units of measures are provided. Axes are clearly labeled. Elements in the figures are labeled or explained.

Remember that the information value of the figure must be the most influential among other decisions like using of color, using of photographic images, or magnitude of cropping of a picture. Use parallel figures or figures of equal importance in equal size and scale. It is good to combine figures to facilitate comparisons between them and place labels for parts of a figure as close as possible to the components being identified.

Types of figures

- Graphs: usually displayed two quantitative indices as the y axis and groups of subjects displayed along the x axis.
- Charts: generally display non-quantitative information.
- Maps: generally display spatial information.
- Drawings: show information pictorially.
- Photographs: contain direct visual representation of information.

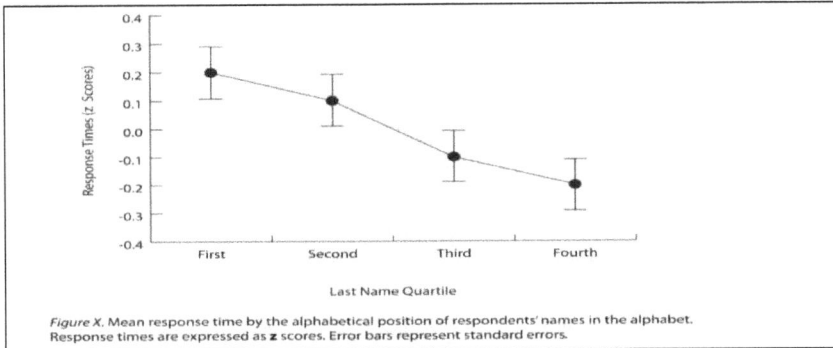

Figure X. Mean response time by the alphabetical position of respondents' names in the alphabet. Response times are expressed as **z** scores. Error bars represent standard errors.

A Sample APA Figure

Numbers, Fractions, and Stylistics
1. Numbers and Fractions

- Use words to express numbers below 10 that don't show measurements and are not grouped for comparison with number 10 and above.
  Three times, seven lists
- Place the decimal point on the line and use a zero before the decimal point when numbers are less than one.   0.5km   0.56cm
- Do not use a zero before a decimal fraction when it cannot be greater than one.

2. Stylistics

Writing in APA is not just simply learning the formula for citations or following a certain page layout. It also includes the stylistics of writing, from point of view to word choice.

Point of view and Voice: When writing in APA Style, you can use the first person point of view while discussing your research steps ("I examine...") and when referring to yourself and your co-authors ("We studied the literature..."). Use first person to discuss research steps rather than attributing the work to you. For example, a study cannot "control" or "interpret"; you and your co-authors, however, can.

In general, you should focus on the research and not the researchers ("The results imply... "). Avoid using the editorial "we"; if you use "we" in your writing, it should be clear that "we" refers to you and your co-researchers. It is a typical misunderstanding that focusing on the research requires using the passive voice ("Studies have been conducted..."). This is wrong. Rather, you would use pronouns in place of "studies" ("We conducted studies ...").

APA Style encourages the researchers to use the active voice ("We explained the results...") in their writing. The active voice is especially important in experimental reports, where the subject performing the action should be apparently identified (e.g. "We asked..." vs. "The participants answered...").

Clarity and Conciseness: Clarity and conciseness in writing are important while conveying research in APA Style. You shouldn't misrepresent the details of a study or confuse your readers with wordiness or unnecessarily complex sentences. For clarity, be specific rather than unclear in descriptions and explanations. Analyze details appropriately to provide sufficient information to your readers so they can follow the development of your study. To be more concise, particularly in introductory material or abstracts, you should remove unnecessary words and condense information as much as you can. Balance between the need for clarity and the need for conciseness. Study published articles and reports in your field show how to achieve this balance.

Word choice: You should be careful in choosing certain words or terms. Within applied linguistics, usually use words that have a remarkable effect on how your readers interpret your reported findings or claims. To improve clarity, avoid bias, and control how your information is given to the readers. Terms like "participants" or "respondents" (instead of "subjects") are better to be used to indicate how individuals were involved in your research. Use terms like "children" or "community members" to provide more detail about who was participating in the study. Phrases like "The evidence *suggests* ..." or "The study *indicates* ..." rather than referring to "proof" or "proves" are suggested because no single study can prove a theory or hypothesis. It is better to study the discourse of your field to see what terminology is most often used.

Avoid poetic language: Writing papers in APA Style is different from writing in more creative or literary styles in which poetic expressions and figurative language can be used. Such linguistic devices can take away your information from conveying clearly and appropriately.
You should

- reduce the use of figurative language in an APA paper, such as metaphors and analogies unless they are helpful in transferring a complex idea.
- avoid rhyming schemes, alliteration, or other poetic devices usually used in verse.
- use simple, descriptive adjectives and plain language that does not bring about the possibility of confusion in your meaning.

Grammar and usage

Incorrect grammar and inattentive organization of sentences confuse the reader and make ambiguity. There are some guidelines here:

- **Use the active voice.** The passive voice is preferable when the focus is on the object or recipient of the action rather than on the actor.

- **Choose tenses carefully.** The past tense can be used to talk about an action or condition at a specific, definite time in the past. *E.g. Armstrong (1994) showed similar results.*

- **Select the suitable mood such as the subjective in describing conditions.** The subjective can be used to describe conditions that are contrary to fact; do not use the subjective to describe simple conditions. *E.g. If the experiment were not conducted this way, the results could not be explained properly.*

- **Pay attention to the agreement of subjects and verbs.** The plural form of some nouns particularly those that end in the letter *a*, may seem to be singular and can cause problem. *E.g. The phenomena happen every 50 days.*

- **Bear in mind the agreement of pronouns and antecedents.** A pronoun must agree in number, gender with the noun it replaces. Use *who* for human beings and *that* or *which* for nonhuman animals or for things. Use neuter pronouns to refer to animals (*e.g. "the cat ... it"*) unless the animals have been named. When you use a participle as a noun, make the other pronoun or noun possessive. *E.g. I had nothing to do with their being the losers.*

- **Avoid misplacing and dangling, modifiers**. You can discard wrong modifiers by placing an adjective or an adverb as closed as possible to the word it modifies. E.g. *using this procedure, the investigator tested the respondents.* Place *only* next to the word or phrase it modifies. *E.g. these data provide only a partial answer.* Dangling modifiers have no referent in the sentence. By writing in the active voice, you can avoid many dangling modifiers. *E.g. using this procedure, I tested the respondents.* [I, not the participants, used the procedure,]

- **Choose relative pronouns and subordinate conjunctions carefully.** Confine your use of *while* and *since* to their temporal meanings. *E.g. Bragg (1965) understood that respondents performed well while listening to music.*

- **Express parallel ideas in parallel or coordinate form.** Be sure that all elements of the parallelism are present before and after the coordinate conjunctions (i.e., *and, but, or, nor*). *E.g. the technical terms were easy both to pronoun and to spell.*

- **Use adverbs as introductory or transitional words appropriately.** Adverbs modify verbs, adjectives, and other adverbs and convey manner or quality. Some adverbs, however, such as *fortunately, similarly, certainly, consequently, conversely*, and *regrettably* can also be used as introductory or transitional words. *E.g." It is a similar manner."* Some of the more common introductory adverbial phrases are *importantly, more importantly, interestingly*, and *firstly*.

- **Use good transitions to connect paragraphs and turn disconnected writing into a unified whole.** Readers can understand how paragraphs work together, reference one another, and build to a larger point through transitions. The important point to making good transitions is focusing on connections between corresponding paragraphs. Writers can develop important points for their readers by referencing in one paragraph the relevant material from previous paragraphs.

Abbreviations and Footnotes
1. Abbreviations

In APA style, abbreviations can be limited to instances when the abbreviation is standard and will not interfere with the reader's understanding and when space and repetition can be greatly avoided. Consider the followings while using abbreviations:

- The full term should be followed immediately by the abbreviation in parentheses the first time you use it. Standard abbreviations like units of measurement and states are not necessary to be written out. Abbreviations that are considered as words in *Meriam-Webster's Collegiate Dictionary* can be used without explanation (IQ, REM, AIDS, HIV).
- Periods or spaces are not used in abbreviations of all capital letters, unless it is a proper name *or* refers to participants using identity-concealing labels:
  MA, CD, HTML, APA
  P. D. James, J. R. R. Tolkien, E. B. White *or* F.I.M., S.W.F.
- When abbreviating the United States as an adjective, a period is used. (U.S. Helicopters or U.S. President)
- Latin abbreviations are used only in parenthetical material; in non-parenthetical material, the English translation of the Latin terms is used:
  (i.e.,) → that is   (etc.) → and so forth
  (cf. ---) → compare---   (e.g., ---)→ for example, ---
  Exception: et al.
- A period can be used if the abbreviation is Latin abbreviation or a reference abbreviation:
  etc., e.g., a.m. *or* Vol. 7, p. 12, 4th ed.
- When you abbreviate measurements do not use periods:
  cd, ft, lb, mi, min
- A period can be used when you abbreviate inch (in.) to avoid confusion.
- Units of measurement and statistical abbreviations can be used only when accompanied by numerical values:

7 mg, 12 mi, $M = 7.5$

- *Day, week, month*, and *year* should not be abbreviated.
- You can abbreviate hr, min, ms, ns, s.
- *S* can be added alone without apostrophe or italicization to make abbreviations plural: vols., IQs, Eds.
- Measurement units should not be abbreviated (12 m not 12 ms).
- The first and middle names of authors, editors, etc. should be abbreviated.
  Frase, L.T., Faletti, J., Ginther, A., & Grant, L. A.

Use the following abbreviations within citations as shown in the following table.

■ **Table 2.1.** *APA Abbreviation within Citation*

APA Citation Abbreviations			
Book Part	*Abbreviation*	*Book Part*	*Abbreviation*
Edition	ed.	Page(s)	p. or pp.
revised edition	Rev. ed.	Volume(s)	Vol. or Vols.
Second Edition	2nd ed.	Number	No.
Editor(s)	Ed. or Eds.	Part	Pt.
Translator(s)	Trans.	Technical Report	Tech. Rep.
No date	n.d.	Supplement	Suppl.

2. Footnotes

APA style does not suggest the use of footnotes and endnotes because they are often high-priced for publishers to reproduce. However, if descriptive notes are still needed for your document, APA describes the use of two types of footnotes: content and copyright.

When either type of footnote is used, a number formatted in superscript should be inserted following any punctuation mark. Footnote numbers should not follow dashes (—), and if they come in a sentence in parentheses, the footnote number should be inserted in the parentheses.

Scientists examined—over several years[1]—the fossilized remains of the wooly-wooly yak.[2] (These have now been transferred to the Chauan Museum.[3])

When using the footnote function in a word-processing program like Microsoft Word, put all footnotes at the bottom of the page on which they become into view. Footnotes may also come on the final page of your document (usually this is after the References page). Write the word "Footnotes" at the top of the page. Indent five spaces on the first line of each footnote. Then, follow normal paragraph spacing rules. Double-space throughout.

[1] While the method of examination for the wooly-wooly yak provides

important insights to this research, this document does not focus on this particular species.

Content notes

Content Notes provide additional information to your readers. When providing Content Notes, avoid wordiness and focus on only one subject. Try to limit your comments to one small paragraph. Content Notes can also direct readers to gain information that is available in more detail elsewhere.

[1] See Blackmur (1995), especially chapters 3 and 4, for an insightful analysis of this extraordinary animal.

Copyright permission notes

If you quote more than 500 words of published material or think you may be in the state of being violated of "Fair Use" copyright laws, you must receive the formal permission of the author(s). All other sources simply should appear in the reference list.

Follow the same formatting rules as with Content Notes for noting copyright permissions. Then, attach a copy of the permission letter to the document.

If you are reproducing a graphic, chart, or table, from some other source, you must make a special note at the bottom of the item that contains copyright information. You should also submit written permission along with your work. You can begin the citation with "*Note.*"

Note: From "Title of the article," by W. Jones and R. Smith, 2007, *Journal Title*, 21, p. 122. Copyright 2007 by Copyright Holder. Reprinted with permission.

Proofreading marks

These are standard symbols used to mark corrections and revisions on typographic proofs. Changes should be marked on the copy, using the appropriate symbols. For special or unusual changes such as underscoring, circle copy, and explain the changes in the margin. Make all corrections in red or similarly contrasting color.

	MARK IN TEXT	IN MARGIN	RESULT
new paragraph	to leave. Three days	¶	scheduled to leave. Three days later
no paragraph break	scheduled to leave. Three days later	run in	to leave. Three days
insert letter	lose change	o/	loose change
replace letter	laose change	o/	loose change
delete letter	loose your keys	⌖	lose your keys
delete letter/add space	lose/your keys	⌖ #/	lose your keys
delete word	three large tomatoes	⌖/	three tomatoes
insert word	three tomatoes	large/	three large tomatoes
close space	break through	⌒/	breakthrough
insert space	breakthrough	#/	break through
insert comma	three tomatoes stewed	⸲/	three tomatoes, stewed
insert period	three stewed tomatoes	⊙/	three stewed tomatoes.
insert apostrophe	Jackies honey chicken recipe	⸜/	Jackie's honey chicken
insert quote marks	Jackie's honey chicken recipe	⸜/⸝/	Jackie's "honey chicken"
transpose	he drives seldom after dark	tr/	he seldom drives
make uppercase	governor	cap/	Governor
make lowercase	Governor	lc/	governor
small capitals	Governor	sm cap	GOVERNOR
abbreviate	Governor	Gov./	Gov.
don't abbreviate	Gov.	sp	Governor
use figures	nine	9/	9
spell out	9	sp/	nine
insert hyphen	small business owner	=/	small-business owner
set in italic type	a true friend	ital/	a *true* friend
set in roman type	a true friend	rom/	a true friend
set in boldface	a true friend	bf/	a **true** friend
set in lightface type	a **true** friend	lf/	a true friend
en dash	1952 1960	N/	1952–1960
insert new text	Al hummed. Later	a tune/	Al hummed a tune. Later
let stand	a true friend	stet	a true friend
set flush left	⌐ Bob's bike	⌐/	Bob's bike
indent one em	Bob's bike	□/	Bob's bike
set centered	⌐Bob's bike⌐	⌐⌐/	Bob's bike
set flush right	Bob's bike ⌐	⌐/	Bob's bike
align	Decided to leave Three days later	align/	Decided to leave. Three days later

Citation
Quotations and summary/paraphrasing

A very important issue in academic studies is **citation. Citation is the opposite of plagiarism.** The content of what you say is not yours but comes from the works of others so you're borrowing the idea from another person.

Either you are making **a direct reference (quoting)** or you're making an **indirect reference (reporting)** and put it in your own morphological clothing, in both cases you are required to remain loyal to the works of others.

When you refer to the works of others, you're connecting your own work to the works of others. Since we're making claims in our studies and these claims have to be supported, one way of supporting our claims is referring to the works of others and using the ideas that have been developed by others. Through citation, you adhere to works of others and place yourself in a particular community. This way, you do a number of things:

- getting membership to a particular community
- getting acceptance from readers (convince my readers)

1. Quotations

Short quotations

When you **directly quote** 40 words or fewer from a work, you need to include **the author, year of publication, and the page number** for the reference (followed by "p."). The quotation should be introduced by a signal phrase that includes the author's last name followed by the date of publication in parentheses.

According to Ruspini (2002), "For most researchers, longitudinal research is still an unexplored land: fascinating but dangerous." (p.136-7).

Ruspini (2002) found " For most researchers, longitudinal research is still an unexplored land " (p. 136-7); what should teachers do to solve this problem?
If the author is not mentioned in a signal phrase, put the author's last name, the year of publication, and the page number in parentheses after the quotation.
She stated, "For most researchers, longitudinal research is still an unexplored land" (Ruspini, 2002, p. 136-7), but she did not offer any suggestion.

Long quotations

Put direct quotations that **are 40 words, or longer**, in a free-standing block of typewritten lines, and remove quotation marks. Start the quotation on a new line, indented 1/2 inch from the left margin (the same place you would begin a new paragraph). **Type the whole quotation on the new margin, and indent the first line of any subsequent paragraph within the quotation 1/2 inch from the new margin**. Double-spacing should be maintained throughout. The parenthetical citation should follow the closing punctuation mark.
Brown & Abeywickrama's (2010) study found the following:

> Human error, subjectivity, and bias may enter into the scoring process. Inter-rater reliability occurs when two or more scores yield consistent scores of the same test. Failure to achieve intra-rater reliability could stem from lack of adherence to scoring criteria, inexperience, inattention, or even preconceived biases. (p. 28)

2. Summary (paraphrase)

When you report (paraphrase) an idea from another work, you only have to make reference to the author and year of publication in your in-text reference.

Note: APA guidelines encourage authors to also provide the page number.

According to Ruspinsi (2002), longitudinal research is an exciting but difficult field for researchers.

Longitudinal research is an exciting but difficult field for researchers. (Ruspinisi, 2002, p. 136-7).

In-text citation

When you are using APA format, follow the author-date method of in-text citation. This means that the author's last name and the year of publication for the source should appear in the text, for example, (Brown, 2010), and the extended information on the source should appear in the reference list at the end of the paper.

Note: In APA style authors should use the past tense or present perfect tense when using signal phrases to describe earlier research, for example, Brown (2010) **found** or Brown (2010) **has found**...

1. Citing an author or authors

A work by two authors: Name both authors in one phrase or in the parentheses each time you cite the work. Put the word "and" between the authors' names within the text and use the ampersand in the parentheses.
Research by Brown and Rodgers (2002) supports...
(Brown & Rodgers, 2002)

A work by three to five authors: List all the authors in one phrase or in parentheses the first time you cite the source.
(Carter, Goddard, Reah, Sanger, & Bowring, 2001)

Six or more authors: Use the first author's name followed by et al. in the signal phrase or in parentheses.
Mendelsohn et al., 2010 argued...
(Mendelsohn et al., 2010)
Note: We don't use a period after *et* in *et al.*

Unknown author: Cite the source by its title in one phrase or use the first word or two in the parentheses. Titles of books and reports are underlined or italicized; titles of articles, chapters, and web pages should be in quotation marks.
A similar study was done on students learning to format research papers

("Using APA," 2001).

Organization or a government agency as an Author: Mention the organization in one phrase or in the parenthetical citation the first time you cite the source.
According to the American Speech and Hearing Association (2000),....
For the organization with a well-known abbreviation, include the abbreviation in brackets the first time you cite the source and then use only the abbreviation in later citations.
First citation: (Parent Teacher Organization, 2001)
Second citation: (PTO, 2001)

Two or more works in the same parentheses: When your parenthetical citation includes two or more works, order them the same way they appear in the reference list, separated by a semi-colon.
(Brown, 1995; Farhady, 2002)

Authors with the same last name: Use first initials with the last names to prevent confusion.
(M. D. Gall, 2006; J. P. Gall, 2006)

Two or more works by the same author in the same year: Use lower-case letters (a, b, c) with the year to order the entries in the reference list. Use the lower-case letters with the year in the in-text citation.
Study by Brown (2007a) illustrated that....

Introductions, prefaces, forewords, and afterwards: Cite the author and year as usual.
(Ary, 2002)

Personal communication: Like interviews, letters, e-mails, and other person-to-person communication, cite the communicator's name, the fact that it was personal communication, and the date of the communication. Do not mention personal communication in the reference list.
(E. Robbins, personal communication, January 4, 2001).
A. P. Smith also claimed that many of her students had difficulties with APA style (personal communication, November 3, 2002).

A class lecture, presentation, or discussion: Follow the guidelines for Personal Communication (citation does not appear on the References page)
In a lecture to an Educational Psychology class on April 2, 2009, R. Smith said...
OR
R. Smith (Educational Psychology lecture, April 2, 2009) discussed Piaget...

OR According Piaget's Theory of Cognitive Development..... (R. Smith, Educational Psychology lecture, April 2, 2009).

If the comment is from a fellow classmate, substitute the professor's name with the classmate's name, and use the word discussion or presentation instead of lecture.

If you wish to cite a general class discussion, include only the name of the course, discussion instead of lecture, and the date.

2. Citing indirect sources

When you use a source that was cited in another source, name the original source in your phrase. List the secondary source in your reference list and mention the secondary source in the parentheses.

Brown & Abeywickrama argued that...(as cited in Underhill, 1987, pp. 77-78).

Electronic sources: Cite an electronic document the same as any other document by using the author-date style.

Kenneth (2000) explained....

Unknown author and unknown date: Use the title in your phrase or the first word or two of the title in the parentheses and use the abbreviation "n.d." (for "no date").

Another study of students and research decisions discovered that students succeeded with tutoring ("Tutoring and APA," n.d.).

Sources with no page numbers: Include information that will help readers find the passage being cited. When an electronic document has numbered paragraphs, use the abbreviation "para." followed by the paragraph number (Hall, 2001, para. 5). If the paragraphs are not numbered and the document includes headings, provide the appropriate heading and specify the paragraph under that heading.

Note: The Find function can be used in a browser to locate any passages you cite in some electronic sources, like Web pages.

According to Smith (1997), ... (Mind over Matter section, para. 6).

Note: Do not ever use the page numbers of Web pages you print out because different computers print Web pages with different pagination.

Reference list (Bibliography)

Your references should be on a new separate page. Label this page "References" centered at the top of the page. Do not bold, underline, or use quotation marks for the title. The text should be double-spaced like all text in you writing. Each source you cite in the paper must appear in your reference list and each entry in the reference list must be cited in your text.

Basic rules of reference page

- You should indent all lines after the first line of each entry in your reference list. Indentation should be one-half inch from the left margin. This is called hanging indentation usually accomplished by using the TAB key.

Hanging indent

Dörnyei, Z. (2011). *Research methods in applied linguistics.* Oxford: Oxford University Press.

A Sample Hanging Indent

- Authors' names should be inverted (last name first); give the last name and initials for all authors of a particular work for up to and including seven authors. If the work has more than seven authors, list the first six authors and then use ellipses after the sixth author's name. After the ellipses, list the last author's name of the work.
- Reference list entries should be **alphabetized.** The last name of the first author of each work should come first.
- The same author with multiple articles, or authors listed in the same order, all entries should be listed chronologically, from earliest to most recent.
- The journal title should be presented in full.
- The punctuation and capitalization that is used by the journal in its title should be maintained. For example: *Quantitative, Qualitative, and Mixed Approaches* not *Quantitative, Qualitative, & Mixed Approaches*
- All major words should be capitalized in journal titles.
- When you refer to books, chapters, articles, or web pages, only the first letter of the first word of a title and subtitle should be capitalized, the first word after a colon or a dash in the title, and proper nouns. The first letter of the second word in a hyphenated compound word should not be capitalized.
- Titles of **books, journals, magazines, and newspapers** should appear in italics.
- Titles of longer works such as books and journals should be capitalized.
- The titles of shorter works such as journal articles or essays in edited collections should not be italicized, underlined. Do not put quotes around them.
- Earlier versions of APA format suggested only one space after each sentence but the new sixth-edition of the style manual now recommends **two spaces**.

Note: If you have a source that APA does not mention, APA suggests that you find the example that is most similar to your source and use that format. See page 193 of the *Publication Manual of the American Psychological Association,* (6th ed., 2nd printing) for more information.

1. Reference list: Author/authors

Single author: The author' initials should come after his/her last name.

Pallant, J. (2007). *A step-by-step guide to data analysis using SPSS version 15: SPSS survival manual.* Berkshire: Mcgraw-Hill.

Two authors: An ampersand should be used instead of "and." Their last names and initials should be listed.

Brown, J.D., & Rodgers, T.S. (2002). *Doing second language research.* Oxford, UK: Oxford University Press.

Three to seven authors: You should list by last names and initials. Put commas to separate authors' names. Put an ampersand before the last author' name.

Ary, D., Jacobs, L.C., & Razavieh, A. (2002). *Introduction to research in education* (6th ed.). Orlando, FL: Harccourt Brace Colledge Publishers.

More than seven authors: You should use ellipses after the name of the sixth author, and then list the last author named.

Gilbert, D. G., McClernon, J. F., Rabinovich, N. E., Sugai, C., Plath, L. C., Asgaard, G., . . . Botros, N. (2004). Effects of quitting smoking on EEG activation and attention last for more than 31 days and are more severe with stress, dependence, DRD2 A1 allele, and depressive traits. *Nicotine and Tobacco Research, 6,* 249-67.

Organization as author

American Psychological Association. (2003).

Unknown author

Merriam-Webster's collegiate dictionary (10th ed.).(1993). Springfield, MA: Merriam-Webster.

Two or more works by the same author: You should use the author's name for all entries and list the entries by the earliest year comes first.

Duff, P. (2002).

Duff, P. (2006).

Two or more works by the same author in the same year: You should arrange them in the reference list alphabetically by the title of the article or chapter and put letter suffixes to the year. Refer to these sources in your writing as they are written in your reference list, e.g.: "Brown (1981a) makes similar claims..."

Brown, H. D. (2007a). *Principles of language learning and teaching* (5th ed.). White Plains, NY: Pearson Education.

Brown, H. D. (2007b). *Teaching by principles: As interactive approach to   language pedagogy* (3rd ed.). White Plains, NY: Pearson Education.

Introductions, prefaces, forewords, and afterwards: You should cite Introduction, Preface, Foreword, or Afterword as the chapter of the book.

Funk, R., & Kolln, M. (1998). Introduction. In E. W. Ludlow (Ed.), *Understanding English grammar* (pp. 1-2). Needham, MA: Allyn and Bacon.

2. Reference list: Articles in periodicals

Authors should be named last name followed by initials. Publication year should go between parentheses, followed by a period. The first word and proper nouns in the title should be capitalized. The periodical title comes in title case, and should be followed by the volume number which is italicized with title. If a DOI (Digital Object Identifier) has been used in the article you should put it after the page numbers for the article. If no DOI has been used and you are using the periodical online, write the URL (Uniform Resource Locater) of the website from which you are getting the periodical.

Note: URL is an address used to show digital information on the Internet. URL's has information about the protocol, host server name, path to the document and the name of the specific document.

http://www.apa.org/monitor/workplace.html

Note: DOI is a system that provides identification for dealing with information on digital networks. Use the format doi:xxxx/xxxx.xx.xx

DOI: 10.3037/0278-7393.34.3.349

Author, A. A., Author, B. B., & Author, C. C. (Year). Title of article. *Title of Periodical, volume number* (issue number), pages.
    http://dx.doi.org/xx.xxx/yyyyy

Martin, R. (2001). Educational psychology in Newfoundland and Labrador: A thirty-year history. *Canadian Journal of School Psychology, 16*(2), 5-17. Retrieved from: http://cjs.sagepub.com/ on 10/10/2013.

Article in journal paginated by volume: It begins with page one in issue one, and continue numbering issue two where issue one ended, etc.

Harlow, H. F. (1983). Fundamentals for preparing psychology journal articles. *Journal of Comparative and Physiological Psychology, 55*, 893-896.

Article in journal paginated by issue: It begins with page one every issue in parentheses after the volume. The parentheses and issue number are not italicized or underlined.

Scruton, R. (1996). The eclipse of listening. *The New Criterion, 15*(3), 5-13.

Article in a magazine

Henry, W. A., III. (1990, April 9). Making the grade in today's schools. *Time, 135*, 28-31.

Article in a newspaper: P. or pp. precedes page unlike other periodicals. For single pages write p., e.g., p. B2; for multiple pages write pp., e.g., pp. B2, B4 or pp. C1, C3-C4.

Schultz, S. (2005, December 28). Calls made to strengthen state energy policies. *The Country Today*, pp. 1A, 2A.

Note: Because of issues with html coding, the listings below have brackets, which contain spaces. Use a space as normal before the brackets, but do not include a space following the bracket.

Letter to the editor

Moller, G. (2002, August). Ripples versus rumbles [Letter to the editor]. *Scientific American, 287*(2), 12.

Review

Baumeister, R. F. (1993). Exposing the self-knowledge myth [Review of the book *The self-knower: A hero under control*, by R. A. Wicklund & M. Eckert]. *Contemporary Psychology, 38*, 466-467.

3. Reference List: Books

Basic format for books

Author, A. A. (Year of publication). *Title of work: Capital letter also for subtitle.* Location: Publisher.

Note: List the city and the state using the two letter postal abbreviation without periods (New York, NY).

Calfee, R. C., & Valencia, R. R. (1991). *APA guide to preparing manuscripts for journal publication.* Washington, DC: American Psychological Association.

Edited book: State the editor(s) instead of author, followed by (Ed.) or, for multiple editors (Eds.).

Duncan, G. J., & Brooks-Gunn, J. (Eds.). (1997). *Consequences of growing up poor.* New York, NY: Russell Sage Foundation.

Edited book with an author or authors

Plath, S. (2000). *The unabridged journals.* K. V. Kukil (Ed.). New York, NY: Anchor.

A translation

Author, A. A. (Year). *Title of book.* (A.A. Translator, Trans.). Location: Publisher. (Original work published xxxx).

Freud, S. (1960). *Jokes and their relation to the unconscious.* (J. Strachey, Trans.). London, England: Routledge & K. Paul. (Original work published 1905).

Edition other than the first

Helfer, M. E., Kempe, R. S., & Krugman, R. D. (1997). *The battered child* (5th ed.). Chicago, IL: University of Chicago Press.

Article or chapter in an edited book

Author, A. A., & Author, B. B. (Year of publication). Title of chapter. In A. A. Editor & B. B. Editor (Eds.), *Title of book* (pages of chapter). Location: Publisher.

Note: After the book title, use "pp." it should be before the numbers: (pp. 1-21). This abbreviation, however, does not appear before the page numbers in periodical references, except for newspapers.

O'Neil, J. M., & Egan, J. (1992). Men's and women's gender role journeys: A metaphor for healing, transition, and transformation. In B. R. Wainrib (Ed.), *Gender issues across the life cycle* (pp. 107-123). New York, NY: Springer.

Multivolume work

Wiener, P. (Ed.). (1973). *Dictionary of the history of ideas* (Vols. 1-4). New York, NY: Scribner's.

4. Reference List: Other print sources

An entry in an encyclopedia

Bergmann, P. G. (1993). Relativity. In *The New Encyclopedia Britannica.* (Vol. 26, pp. 501-508). Chicago, IL: Encyclopedia Britannica.

Work discussed in a secondary source: You should list the source of the work discussed in:

Coltheart, M., Curtis, B., Atkins, P., & Haller, M. (1993). Models of reading aloud: Dual-route and parallel-distributed-processing approaches. *Psychological Review, 100,* 589-608.

Note: Write the secondary source in the references list; in the text, you should name the original work, and give a citation for the secondary source. For example, if Seidenberg and McClelland's work is cited in Coltheart et al. and you did not read the original work, list the Coltheart et al. reference in the References. In the text, write the following citation:

In Seidenberg and McClelland's study (as cited in Coltheart, Curtis, Atkins, & Haller, 1993), ...

Dissertation abstract

Yoshida, Y. (2001). Essays in urban transportation. *Dissertation Abstracts International, 62,* 7741A.

Dissertation, published
Lastname, F. N. (Year). *Title of dissertation.* (Doctoral dissertation). Retrieved from Name of database. (Accession or Order Number)

Dissertation, unpublished
Lastname, F. N. (Year). *Title of dissertation.* (Unpublished doctoral dissertation). Name of Institution, Location.

Government document
National Institute of Mental Health. (1990). *Clinical training in serious mental illness* (DHHS Publication No. ADM 90-1679). Washington, DC: U.S. Government Printing Office.

Report from a private organization
American Psychiatric Association. (2000). *Practice guidelines for the treatment of patients with eating disorders* (2nd ed.). Washington, DC: Author.

Conference proceedings
Schnase, J. L., & Cunnius, E. L. (Eds.). (1995). Proceedings from CSCL '95: *The First International Conference on Computer Support for Collaborative Learning.* Mahwah, NJ: Erl. baum

5. Reference List: Electronic sources (web publications)

Article from an online periodical: You should write all information the online host makes available, including an issue number in parentheses.
Author, A. A., & Author, B. B. (Date of publication). Title of article. *Title of Online Periodical, volume number*(issue number if available). Retrieved from http://www.someaddress.com/full/url/ on date/month/year.
Bernstein, M. (2002). 10 tips on writing the living Web. *A List Apart: For People Who Make Websites, 149.* Retrieved from http://www.alistapart.com/articles/writeliving on day/month/year.

Online scholarly journal article citing DOIs: Because of potentially changing URLs of online materials, APA suggests providing a DOI, when it is available. DOIs can provide stable, long-lasting links for online articles. They are unique to their documents and consist of a long alphanumeric code.

Article from an online periodical with DOI assigned
Author, A. A., & Author, B. B. (Date of publication). Title of article. *Title of Journal, volume number,* page range. doi:0000000/000000000000 or http://dx.doi.org/10.0000/0000
Brownlie, D. (2007). Toward effective poster presentations: An annotated bibliography. *European Journal of Marketing, 41,* 1245-1283.

doi:10.1108/03090560710821161

Wooldridge, M.B., & Shapka, J. (2012). Playing with technology: Mother-toddler interaction scores lower during play with electronic toys. *Journal of Applied Developmental Psychology, 33*(5), 211-218. http://dx.doi.org/10.1016/j.appdev.2012.05.005

Article from an online periodical with no DOI assigned: Online scholarly journal articles without a DOI need the URL of the journal home page.

Author, A. A., & Author, B. B. (Date of publication). Title of article. *Title of Journal, volume number.* Retrieved from http://www.journalhomepage.com/full/url/ on day/month/year.

Kenneth, I. A. (2000). A Buddhist response to the nature of human rights. *Journal of Buddhist Ethics, 8.* Retrieved from http://www.cac.psu.edu/jbe/twocont.html on day/month/year.

Article from a database

Author, A. A., & Author, B. B. (Date of publication). Title of article. *Title of Journal, volume number,* page range. Retrieved from http://www.someaddress.com/full/url/ on day/month/year.

Smyth, A. M., Parker, A. L., & Pease, D. L. (2002). A study of enjoyment of peas. *Journal of Abnormal Eating, 8*(3), 120-125. Retrieved from http://www.articlehomepage.com/full/url/ on day/month/year.

Abstract: If only an abstract is cited but the text of the article is also accessible, you should cite the online abstract like any other online citations. Then add "[Abstract]" after the article or source name. When the full text is not available, you can use an abstract that is available through an abstract's database as a secondary source.

Paterson, P. (2008). How well do young offenders with Asperger Syndrome cope in custody?: Two prison case studies [Abstract]. *British Journal of Learning Disabilities, 36*(1), 54-58.

Hendricks, J., Applebaum, R., & Kunkel, S. (2010). A world apart? Bridging the gap between theory and applied social gerontology. *Gerontologist, 50*(3), 284-293. Abstract retrieved from Abstracts in Social Gerontology database. (Accession No. 50360869)

Newspaper article

Author, A. A. (Year, Month Day). Title of article. *Title of Newspaper.* Retrieved from http://www.someaddress.com/full/url/ on day/month/year.

Parker-Pope, T. (2008, May 6). Psychiatry handbook linked to drug industry. *The New York Times.* Retrieved from http://well.blogs.nytimes.com on day/month/year.

Electronic books: For a book available in print form and electronic form, you should include the publish date in parentheses after the author's name. For references to e-book editions, assure yourself to include the type and version of e-book you are referencing (e.g., "[Kindle DX version]"). If DOIs are available, write them at the end of the reference.

De Huff, E. W. (n.d.). *Taytay's tales: Traditional Pueblo Indian tales*. Retrieve form http://digital.library.upenn.edu/women/dehuff/taytay/taytay.html on day/month/year.

Davis, J. (n.d.). *Familiar birdsongs of the Northwest*. Available from http://www.powells.com/cgi-bin/biblio on day/month/year.

Chapter/section of a web document or online book chapter

Author, A. A., & Author, B. B. (Date of publication). Title of article. In *Title of book or larger document* (chapter or section number). Retrieved from http://www.someaddress.com/full/url/ on day/month/year.

Engelshcall, R. S. (1997). Module mod_rewrite: URL Rewriting Engine. In *Apache HTTP Server version 1.3 documentation* (Apache modules). Retrieved from http://httpd.apache.org/docs/1.3/mod/mod_rewrite.html on day/month/year.

Peckinpaugh, J. (2003). Change in the Nineties. In J. S. Bough and G. B. DuBois (Eds.), *A century of growth in America*. Retrieved from GoldStar database.

Note: A chapter or section identifier should be used. You should provide a URL that links directly to the chapter section, not the home page of the Web site.

Online book reviews: In brackets, "Review of the book" should be written. Then you should give the title of the reviewed work. Put the web address after the words "Retrieved from," if the review is freely available to anyone. If the review comes from a subscription service or database, write "Available from" and provide the information where the review can be purchased.

Zacharek, S. (2008, April 27). Natural women [Review of the book *Girls like us*]. *The New York Times*. Retrieved from http://www.nytimes.com/2008/04/27/books/review/Zachareck-t.html on day/month/year.

Castle, G. (2007). New millennial Joyce [Review of the books *Twenty-first Joyce, Joyce's critics: Transitions in reading and culture, and Joyce's messianism: Dante, negative existence, and the messianic self*]. *Modern Fiction Studies, 50*(1), 163-173. Available from Project MUSE Web site: http://muse.jhu.edu/journals/modern_fiction_studies/toc/mfs52.1.html on day/month/year.

Dissertation/thesis from a database

Biswas, S. (2008). *Dopamine D3 receptor: A neuroprotective treatment target in Parkinson's disease*. Retrieved from ProQuest Digital Dissertations. (AAT 3295214) on day/month/year.

Online encyclopedias and dictionaries: When no byline (authors' names)is present, put the entry name to the front of the citation. Provide publication dates if present or specify (n.d.) if no date is present in the entry.

Feminism. (n.d.). In *Encyclopedia Britannica online*. Retrieved from http://www.britannica.com/EBchecked/topic/724633/feminism on day/month/year.

Online bibliographies and annotated bibliographies

Jürgens, R. (2005). *HIV/AIDS and HCV in prisons: A select annotated bibliography*. Retrieved from http://www.hc-sc.gc.ca/ahc-asc/alt_formats/hpb-dgps/pdf/intactiv/hiv-vih-aids-sida-prison-carceral_e.pdf on day/month/year.

Data sets: You should provide a Web address (use "Retrieved from") or a general place that houses data sets on the site (use "Available from").

United States Department of Housing and Urban Development. (2008). *Indiana income limits* [Data file]. Retrieved from http://www.huduser.org/Datasets/IL/IL08/in_fy2008.pdf on day/month/year.

Graphic data (e.g. interactive maps and other graphic representations of data): The name of the researching organization should be followed by the date. In brackets, write a brief explanation of what type of data and in what form it appears. Finally, you should provide the project name and retrieval information.

Solar Radiation and Climate Experiment. (2007). [Graph illustration the SORCE Spectral Plot May 8, 2008]. *Solar Spectral Data Access from the SIM, SOLSTICE, and XPS Instruments*. Retrieved from http://lasp.colorado.edu/cgi-bin/ion-p?page=input_data_for_spectra.ion on day/month/year.

Qualitative data and online interviews: If there is an irretrievable interview, cite the interview in the text (not in the reference list) and write the month, day, and year in the text. If an audio file or transcript is available online, use the following model, specifying the medium in brackets (e.g. [Interview transcript, Interview audio file]):

Butler, C. (Interviewer) & Stevenson, R. (Interviewee). (1999). *Oral History 2* [Interview transcript]. Retrieved from Johnson Space Center Oral Histories Project Web site: http://www11.jsc.nasa.gov/history/oral_histories/oral_histories.htm on day/month/year.

Online lecture notes and presentation slides: You should provide the file format in brackets after the lecture title (e.g. PowerPoint slides, Word document).

Hallam, A. *Duality in consumer theory* [PDF document]. Retrieved from Lecture Notes Online Web site: http://www.econ.iastate.edu/classes/econ501/Hallam/ index.html on day/month/year.

Roberts, K. F. (1998). *Federal regulations of chemicals in the environment* [PowerPoint slides]. Retrieved from http://siri.uvm.edu/ppt/40hrenv/index.html on day/month/year.

Non-periodical web document, web page, or report: If there is a page like http://www.somesite.com/somepage.htm, and somepage.htm doesn't have the information you're looking for, move up the URL to http://www.somesite.com/):

Author, A. A., & Author, B. B. (Date of publication). *Title of document.* Retrieved from http://Web address +on day/month/year.

Angeli, E., Wagner, J., Lawrick, E., Moore, K., Anderson, M., Soderland, L., & Brizee, A. (2010, May 5). *General format.* Retrieved from http://owl.english.purdue.edu/owl/resource/560/01/

Note: If an Internet document is more than one Web page, you should provide a URL that links to the home page or entry page for the document. If there isn't a date available for the document use (n.d.) for no date.

Computer software/downloaded software: It is not good to cite standard office software (e.g. Word, Excel) or programming languages. You should provide references only for specialized software.

Ludwig, T. (2002). PsychInquiry [computer software]. New York: Worth.

Software that is downloaded from a Web site should provide the software's version and year when available.

Hayes, B., Tesar, B., & Zuraw, K. (2003). OTSoft: Optimality Theory Software(Version2.1)[Software]. Available from http://www.linguistics.ucla.edu/people/hayes/otsoft/

E-mail: E-mails should not be included in the list of references. They can be parenthetically cited in the main text: (E. Robbins, personal communication, January 4, 2001).

Online forum or discussion board posting: You should write the title of the message, and the URL of the newsgroup or discussion board. Titles for items in online communities (e.g. blogs, newsgroups, forums) should not be italicized. If the author's name is not available, provide the screen name. Put identifiers like post or message numbers, if available, in brackets. If available, provide the URL where the message is archived (e.g. "Message posted to..., archived at...").

Frook, B. D. (1999, July 23). New inventions in the cyberworld of toylandia [Msg 25]. Message posted to
http://groups.earthlink.com/forum/messages/00025.html

Blog (weblog) and video blog post: You should write the title of the message and the URL. Titles for items in online communities (e.g. blogs, newsgroups, forums) should not be italicized. If the author's name is not available, provide the screen name.

J Dean. (2008, May 7). When the self emerges: Is that me in the mirror? [Web log comment]. Retrieved from
http://www.spring.org.uk/the1sttransport on day/month/year.

Psychology Video Blog #3 [Video file]. Retrieved from
http://www.youtube.com/watch?v=lqM90eQi5-M on day/month/year.

Wikis: Wikis (like Wikipedia, for example) cannot guarantee the verifiability or expertise of their entries since they are collaborative projects.

OLPC Peru/Arahuay. (n.d.). Retrieved April 29, 2011 from the OLPC Wiki:
http://wiki.laptop. org/go/OLPC_Peru/Arahuay

Audio podcast: If you can provide as much information as possible; not all of the following information will be available. Include possible addition identifiers such as producer, director, etc.

Bell, T., & Phillips, T. (2008, May 6). A solar flare. *Science @ NASA Podcast.* Podcast retrieved from http://science.nasa.gov/podcast.htm

Video podcasts: If you can provide as much information as possible; not all of the following information will be available. Include possible addition identifiers such as producer, director, etc.

Scott, D. (Producer). (2007, January 5). The community college classroom [Episode 7]. *Adventures in Education.* Podcast retrieved from
http://www.adveeducation.com

No page numbers: Some online sources do not have page numbers. For direct quotes, use a paragraph number, or cite the heading and the number of paragraphs following it.

(Basu & Jones, 2007, para. 4)

(Verbunt, Pernot, & Smeets, 2008, Discussion section, para. 1)

No author: You can use the first few words of the title instead. Within parentheses, use quotation marks around the title of an article, a chapter, or a web page; italicize the name of a journal, newspaper, magazine, or book.

("Study Finds", 2007)

(*College Bound Seniors*, 2008, pp. 42-3)

Note: For more information on citing sources within your paper, see pp. 174-79 of the *Publication Manual of the American Psychological Association*, 6th edition.

6. Reference List: Other non-print sources

Interviews, email, and other personal communication: You should not include any personal communication in your reference list. You can parenthetically cite the communicator's name, the phrase "personal communication," and the date of the communication in your main text only.
(E. Robbins, personal communication, January 4, 2001).
A. P. Smith also claimed that many of her students had difficulties with APA style (personal communication, November 3, 2002).

Motion picture: If a movie or video tape is not available in wide distribution, put the following to your citation after the country of origin: (Available from Distributor name, full address and zip code).
Producer, P. P. (Producer), & Director, D. D. (Director). (Date of publication). *Title of motion picture* [Motion picture]. Country of origin: Studio or distributor.

A motion picture or video tape with international or national availability
Smith, J. D. (Producer), & Smithee, A. F. (Director). (2001). *Really big disaster movie* [Motion picture]. United States: Paramount Pictures.

A motion picture or video tape with limited availability
Harris, M. (Producer), & Turley, M. J. (Director). (2002). *Writing labs: A history* [Motion picture]. (Available from Purdue University Pictures, 500 Oval Drive, West Lafayette, IN 47907)

Television broadcast or series episode
Writer, W. W. (Writer), & Director, D. D. (Director). (Date of broadcast or copyright). Title of broadcast [*Television broadcast or Television series*]. In P. Producer (Producer). City, state of origin: Studio or distributor.

Single episode of a television series
Writer, W. W. (Writer), & Director, D. D. (Director). (Date of publication). Title of episode [Television series episode]. In P. Producer (Producer), *Series title*. City, state of origin: Studio or distributor.
Wendy, S. W. (Writer), & Martian, I. R. (Director). (1986). The rising angel and the falling ape [Television series episode]. In D. Dude (Producer), *Creatures and monsters*. Los Angeles, CA: Belarus Studios.

Television broadcast
Important, I. M. (Producer). (1990, November 1). *The nightly news hour*

[Television broadcast]. New York, NY: Central Broadcasting Service.

A television series

Bellisario, D.L. (Producer). (1992). *Exciting action show* [Television series]. Hollywood: American Broadcasting Company.

Music recording

Songwriter, W. W. (Date of copyright). Title of song [Recorded by artist if different from song writer]. On *Title of album* [Medium of recording]. Location: Label. (Recording date if different from copyright date).

Taupin, B. (1975). Someone saved my life tonight [Recorded by Elton John]. On *Captain fantastic and the brown dirt cowboy* [CD]. London, England: Big Pig Music Limited.

Note: Although it is not possible to provide a full account of APA in this book, the most essential information of APA is included in this chapter. For more information you can either turn to the actual book (*Publication Manual of the American Psychological Association* (6th Edition)) *or* go to http://endnote.com/downloads/style/apa-6th-american-psychological association-6th-edition.

CHAPTER THREE
Introduction and Review of Literature

Introduction

The *Introduction Section* is considered as an important section of any study. Many people (even experienced ones) seem to have difficulties at providing a good introduction. The introduction has in fact probably been subjected to greater examination than other typical sections of the thesis. This may be because they are shorter and therefore more amenable to analysis than the other typically much longer sections, but whatever the cause, there is more research upon which to draw when we look at thesis introductions (Platridge & Starfeild, 2007). A very simple and efficient method for writing a good introduction is presented in this chapter. Generally, the introduction provides necessary background information to your study and provides readers with some sense of your overall research interest.

A literature review is another important section of any study. It indicates that you are familiar with the literature relevant to your topic. In addition, a literature review helps you to show the importance of your decision to conduct study and write on your topic with the approach you have chosen. These are some questions that will be answered in *Literature Review* section in this chapter.

- What kinds of literature do you have to write?
- What are general components of literature review?
- How and where can we access to the literature?

Introduction section (background)
The introduction section should contain the following components:
- General background information on the study
- The research problem
- Purpose of the study
- Hypotheses or research questions
- Scope of the study
- Significance of the study
- Definitions of key terms

Guidelines for writing a good introduction
- **Raise your problem in this part:** Your introduction is also called the anchor point of your research. Why is this research **important**?
- **Establish the context:** You should make your context clear in this part. (Background) What is the **context** of this research?

- **Introduce the problem**: If there was no problem, there would be no reason for writing a report, and definitely no reason for reading it. So, tell the reviewer why he/she should continue reading.
- **Give reasons for conducting the study:** Now propose a solution and outline the contribution of the study. Here you have to make sure you point out what the novel aspects of your work are. The rational for conducting the study should be stated. The significance of your study should be shown. Why is this study worth conducting?
- **Show that there is a gap:** There is a problem that has not been handled by other researchers in the field. A simple sentence like "So far nobody has investigated the link..." or "The above-mentioned solutions don't apply to the case ..." can sometimes be enough to clarify the point you want to get at. What is that we don't know?

An effective introduction should answer all the above questions in just a few pages by summarizing the relevant arguments and the past evidence, and give the reader a firm sense of what was done and why.

Swales and the CARS model

Swales analyzed the introductions of forty-eight articles in the natural and social sciences, and found that most of them contained an order of four rhetorical moves through which a researcher *creates a research space* for his/her work. Using these moves the writer

- establishes the field in which he or she is working,
- summarizes related research in the area of concern,
- creates a *research* space for the present study by indicating a gap in current knowledge or by raising questions
- introduces the study by indicating what the investigation being reported will accomplish for the field (Swale 2004).

Swales' model of rhetorical moves in research articles (CARS)

There are some "moves" and "steps" that many writers make in the introductions of their proposals. They allow researchers to indicate the precise contribution that their study will make to the disciplinary conversation. "Moves" have social and communicative roles while "steps" have linguistic roles (Swale, 2004).

Move one: Establish a research territory.

Step one: Centrality should be claimed.
Step two: Topic generalizations should be made.
Step three: Items of previous research should be reviewed.

Move two: Create a niche (/niːʃ, nɪtʃ/ *A hollow space*).

Step one: A) Counter-claiming should be made.

Step one: B) A gap should be indicated.
Step one: C) Questions should be raised.
Step one: D) a tradition should be continued.

Move three: Occupy the niche.
Step one: A) Purposes should be outlined.
Step one: B) Present research should be presented.
Step two: Principal findings should be announced.
Step three: Research Article structure should be indicated.

Research moves

Move one: Establish a research territory

- Researchers should show that the general research area is salient, central, engrossing, controversial, or appropriate to the matter at hand in some way (optional).
- Items of previous research in the area should be introduced and reviewed (obligatory).

Move two: Create a niche (/ni:ʃ, nɪtʃ/ *A hollow space*)

- The study should indicate a gap in the previous research, or expand previous knowledge in some way (obligatory).

Move three: Occupy the niche

- The nature of the present research should be stated and outlined (obligatory).
- Research questions or hypotheses should be listed (probable in some fields, but rare in others).
- Principal findings should be announced (probable in some fields).
- The value of the present research should be stated (probable in some fields).
- The structure of the research paper should be indicated (probable in some fields).

Sentence-level guidelines for writing introduction

Strong opening statements should be used.

Through stressing the growing amount of literature devoted to your topic you can claim centrality. Here are some examples of strong opening statements. Notice how many of them use the **present perfect tense** of the verb:

"There has been growing interest in . . . ,The possibility of . . . has raised interest in . . . , The development of . . . is a classic problem in . . . ,The development of . . . has contributed to the hope that . . . , The . . . has become a popular topic for analysis . . . , Knowledge of . . . has a great importance for . . . , The study of . . . has become an important aspect of . . .

A critical issue in . . . is . . . , (The) . . . has been studied in recent years, Many researchers have recently turned to . . . , The relationship between . . . and . . . has been investigated by many researchers, Many recent studies have focused on . . . , etc."

Negative openings should be used.

The best way to represent a gap in the current research is to use a *quasi-negative subject*. Consider the following uses of *little, few,* and *no/ none of*.

"However, little information . . . , little data . . . , little research . . . , However, few studies . . . , few investigations . . . , few researchers . . . , No studies/data/calculations . . . , None of these studies/findings/calculations . . . ., etc."

Obviously, not all research papers are expressed by indicating an obvious gap. You may prefer to avoid the quasi-negative comment altogether. A useful alternative *contrastive statement* might be used.

"The research has tended to focus on . . ., rather than on . . . , These studies have emphasized . . ., as opposed to . . . , Although considerable research has been devoted to . . ., rather less attention has been paid to . . ., etc."

Some writers might explicitly raise a question, a hypothesis, or a need in their introductions. Here are some examples.

"However, it remains unclear whether . . . , It would thus be of interest to learn how . . . , If these results could be confirmed, they would provide strong evidence for . . . , The findings suggest that this approach might be less effective when . . . , It would seem, therefore, that further investigations are needed in order to... , etc."

Special tenses and purpose statements should be used.

Some reference to the present text, such as the uses of *this, the present, reported,* and *here* can be used. If the conventions of the field or journal allow it, it is also common for authors to switch from the impersonal to the personal by using *we*.

"Was" or *"is"* are used in different situations. If you tend to refer to the type of text (paper, article, thesis, report, research note, etc.) you must use the present tense *is*. If you want to refer to type of investigation (experiment, investigation, study, survey, etc.) you can use either *was* or *is*, although there is an increasing tendency to use the present, perhaps because it makes the research seem relevant, fresh, and new. If you choose to refer to the type of text, you must use the present tense. If you choose to refer to type of investigation, you can use either *was* or *is*, although there is an increasing tendency to choose the present, perhaps because it makes the research seem relevant, fresh, and new.

Statement of the problem

Statement of problem may be used in your introduction or your purpose section, or it may come independently (it depends on the field). You can start your proposal with the statement of the problem, rather than a more general introduction. Regardless of placement, you need to obviously define the problem or knowledge gap that your project is responding to. A problem statement is necessarily a clear explanation of an issue that faces a group or individual. It is a description of a hardship or lack that needs to be solved or at least researched to see whether a solution can be found. It can also be defined as either *a gap* between the real and the desired or **a contradiction** between principle and practice.

You can consider making your problem "statement" as a question, since you really attempt to answer a question (or a set of questions) in your study.

The main goal of the statement of the problem is to change a generalized problem (something that disturbs you; a recognized lack) into a well-defined problem that can be resolved through focused research and careful decision-making.

Preparing the statement of the problem should help you easily identify the purpose of the project you will suggest. It will also perform as the basis for the introductory section of your final proposal; aim your readers' attention quickly in the issues that your proposed project will address and provide the reader with a brief statement of the proposed project itself. A statement problem should not be too long. One page is sufficient for a good statement of problem.

Historical and contextual backgrounds of the problem are needed since they contain a state of the art review of the field of study, containing past and current developments, controversies, breakthroughs and relevant background theory of the research topic. They show the gap between existing knowledge and the prevailing subject situation that needs to be filled.

Statement of the problem can be general or specific. The general problem should be mentioned in declarative form. The main problem should be consistent with the title of the study. The specific problem is a breakdown of the general problem, can be in question form or in declarative form. The questions must be clearly and logically presented and be connected to the title of the thesis or dissertation.

Statement of the problem should
- answer the question: "What is the niche that needs to be occupied?" and/or "What is the problem that can be solved?"
- state the problem distinctly early in a paragraph.
- limit the variables mentioned in stating your problem or question.
- address a gap.
- contain enough significance to lead to the existing body of research.

- be one that will direct more research.
- be practical to be investigated through data collection.
- be interesting to and convenient for the researcher based on his/her skills, time and resources.
- be ethical and moral.

Steps in writing the statement of the problem

A convincing statement of the problem contains four steps:

1. **Step one (the perfection)** tells off a desired goal or ideal situation; explains how things should be. It will build the ideal situation (what should be, what is expected, desired).
2. **Step two (the reality)** describes a condition that prevents the goal, state, or value in part one from being received or realized at this time; explains how the recent situation falls short of the goal or ideal. It will build the reality, the situation as it is and establish a gap between what should be and what is.
3. **Step three** connects steps one and two using a term such as "but," "however," "Unfortunately," or "in spite of".
4. **Step four (the consequences)** identify the way you offer to improve the current situation and move it closer to the goal or ideal.
   Use specific details to show how the situation in step two has little promise of improvement unless something is done. Then, emphasize the advantages of research by representing the consequences of possible solutions as well.

Purpose/Aims/Rationale/Research Questions

Generally, most proposals have an obvious statement of the research purposes, including an explanation of the questions the research tends to answer or the hypotheses the research advances. This may be used as part of the introduction, or it may be a separate section. Spend enough time brainstorming before and while you prepare the preliminary version of this section. When you start your research, you may find that your aims change in emphasis or in number. What is critical for you at this point is to specify for your readers and for yourself the exact focus of your research and to make known key concepts you will be studying.

A clear statement of purpose will

- give an explanation of the goals and research purposes of the study (what do you hope to find?).
- reveal the original contributions of your study by explaining how your research questions or approach are different from previous research (what will you add to the field of knowledge?).

- give a more detailed account of the points summarized in the introduction.
- cover a rationale for the study (why should we study this?).
- be clear about what your study will **not** inscribe (this is especially significant if you are applying for competitive funding; narrowly focused studies are more likely to win funding).
- describe the research questions and/or hypotheses of the study.
- include a subsection defining important terms, especially if they will be new to some readers or if you will use them in an unfamiliar way.
- state limitations of the research.
- provide a rationale for the particular subjects of the study.

Significance of the study

Some proposals have a separate section indicating the importance of the study. Significance of the study identifies who will take advantage of the results of the study. It is possible that specific institutions or groups of individuals or the researcher himself/herself will be benefited. These questions should be answered: What is the importance of the study? To whom is it significant? What benefit(s) will take place for each of them if the study is done?

A clear statement of significance may

- discuss the methodological and theoretical contribution you anticipate making to existing knowledge in your field.
- state the practical and theoretical importance of the problem and objectives of your study, given current knowledge and practices.
- explain the usefulness or benefits of the study to both the outside world and the research community.

Limitations and delimitations

Limitations deal with difficulties of your study, insufficiency of your study, and negative characteristics of your study. Limitations can define boundaries of the research to focus on the study. This part defines precise explanations and the rationale behind each limitation or exclusion beyond which the study is not dealt with. It discusses the nature of the study, its timeframe, its geographic locale, its duration. It represents the variables that should have been included in the study, and the reasons for their exclusion and how this is expected to affect the results of the study.

Limitations are shortcomings or conditions that cannot be managed by the researcher that limit your methodology and conclusions. Any limitations might affect the results of the study. In qualitative research these limitations can be the findings that cannot be generalized to the larger population. This is especially true when the definition of the population is broad (e.g. elderly bilingual women).

Delimitations are boundaries that you have in your research. So, you should narrow the research and consider: Is it a matter of boundary or manageability of the study?

If you have some **bias** in choosing the sample, it's a **limitation** of your research but if because of the **condition** you can't manage more than 25 samples it's your delimitation. **Delimitations are choices made by the researcher which should be mentioned to the reader reasonably.** Delimitations explain

- the things that are not done (and why you have chosen not to do them).
- the literature that will not be reviewed (and why not).
- the population/sample not studied (and why not).
- the methodological procedures, setting, instruments, and treatments that will not be used (and why you will not use them).

Example

Limitations and Delimitations of the Study

1. This project was limited to study the effect of using translation from L1 to L2 to improve the participants' linguistic accuracy; however, other aspects of language learning such as fluency and communicative use of language were not taken into account.
2. The participants of the study were in the age range of 13 to 24, therefore; the results might not be generalized to learners out of this age range.
3. In this study the practice of translation from L1 to L2 was done in written form; nevertheless, translation in spoken mode was not practiced.
4. In this study, Persian language was used in the form of translation from L1 to L2; however, other forms of using mother tongue in L2 teaching were not taken into account.
5. Among the participants who took part in this study, 6 out of 78 **participants did not go through all the steps of the study** Implementing Communication Strategies in Speaking Classes at the Foreign Language Center of ILI.

Basic elements of research

- **Hypothesis/Hypotheses**
- **Variables**
- **Scales**

Research question and Hypothesis
Research question

Characteristics of a good research question

A good research question must be researchable and suitable for the researcher. Its answer must contribute to the body of knowledge in education. It must lead to new problems and questions. Moreover, it must be ethical. Research should be cyclical and generative as well (Ary, Jacobs, & Razavieh (2011).

Some important factors to make a good research question are interest (the most important one), relevance, and manageability. A research question should be based on the researcher's interest. It ought to have relevance to the needs of people in the society and it should be manageable based on the availability of all facilities needed to conduct research, Farhady (2002).

Types of research questions

Types of research questions based on different areas of interest and the nature of variables:

Descriptive questions are asked to identify the frequency, duration and intensity of an event or a behavior. The researcher should be fond of asking about who, what, when, and where of an event or behavior. Descriptive questions are especially relevant in the area of second or foreign language acquisition /learning. Students interested in this area can formulate questions about topics such as the order of acquisition, the frequency of the occurrence of grammatical elements, the frequency of the errors made by first and second language learners, and the sequence of the elements learned in a particular language community.
"What is happening?"

Correlational questions are asked about the degree of relationship between two or more variables. Correlational questions are very common in the field of applied linguistics. Researchers are often interested in finding out the relationship between language abilities and some other mental factors such as intelligence, aptitude, knowledge, and so forth. They also ask questions about the relationship between students' abilities in different components and skills of the language. For example, they may ask questions about the relationship between the knowledge of vocabulary and grammar, the ability in speaking and writing, and so forth.
"What is the relationship between linguistic intelligence and speaking?"

Cause-effect questions are asked to find caused relationship between the variables. If your questions are cause- effect questions you want to find the effect of one variable on other variables. This type of question requires experimentation. It is usually asked in the form of

- What is the effect of explicit feedback on accuracy in speaking?

- What is the effect of practice in reading comprehension on language proficiency?
- What is the effect of playing music in class on the pronunciation accuracy of the learners?

When the research question of any type is formulated, it should be stated in a **hypothesis** form. Forming a hypothesis is of prime importance in the process of research.

In statistics section, you should choose statistical methods that are suitable to calculate the cause-effect relationship like *t*-test. Your question should be researchable; you should make sure that your research questions lead to empirical study. Avoid the expressions that show quality like "how". Instead, choose expressions that show quantity like "what". When you have formulated your question, then you should convert them to a number of hypotheses.

Hypothesis

After stating the problem, determining the variables and examining the relevant literature to the topic, the researcher is ready to state a hypothesis. The hypothesis states the expected answer to the research question. It is the possible/tentative answer to your research question and indicates the researcher's expectations about the relationship between variables within the problem. So, the statement made on the possible outcome of research is called a hypothesis.

Avoid bias in your research questions. You don't have to show any tendency on one answer, or the other. So, it is probably necessary to design null hypothesis.

The hypothesis is an influential tool in scientific inquiry. It makes the researchers able to relate theory to observation and observation to theory. In spite of the fact that hypotheses are proposed and serve several functions, they are not absolutely necessary. Hypotheses are tools in the research process, not ends. For example, qualitative research does not necessarily test hypothesis. But quantitative research requires hypothesis. There are two reasons for stating a hypothesis before data gathering.

- A valid hypothesis signifies that the researcher has sufficient knowledge in the area in which research will be conducted.
- The hypothesis can direct the collection and interpretation of data. It shows the researcher what procedure to follow and what type of data to gather. The hypothesis functions as a map for the researcher.

Since the relationship between the factors in a hypothesis is based on the researcher's expectations, this relationship can be stated in different forms.

Major forms of stating the relationship

1. **Null or non-directional hypothesis (H0):** If no direction can be anticipated between the two variables, no special direction is anticipated

and no special relationship is suggested.

Example: "There is no significant relationship between X and Y."

- **H0:** There is **no relationship** between sex and the degree of language acquisition of the learners. This is a null hypothesis which predicts no direction on the relationship between the two factors.

2. **Directional or alternative hypothesis (H1):** In this kind of hypothesis, the researcher predicts a direction, i. e., the existence of a relationship between two variables. (Positive or negative: they may or may not be included).

- **H1**: There is a **positive relationship** between sex and language acquisition.

This is an alternative to the null hypothesis expecting that being a boy or a girl increases language acquisition ability.

- **H1:** There is a **negative relationship** between sex and language acquisition.

This is another alternative to the null hypothesis stating that being a boy or girl decreases language acquisition ability.

It should be considered that there are options for researchers to choose one form of the hypothesis over the other. It is important to consider that selecting the hypothesis shouldn't be arbitrary. The best way for choosing a good hypothesis is studying the previous research reports attentively. If there is sufficient evidence in the literature to indicate the existence of a relationship between the two factors, the researcher may choose a directional hypothesis. However, if there are some contradictions among the findings of literature, the selection of a directional hypothesis is not proposed. It is more preferable to select a null hypothesis to conduct the study.

Your null hypothesis is either rejected or it is sustained. If your null hypothesis is sustained, it indicates that there is no relationship. If the null hypothesis is rejected, it represents that there is a kind of relationship which is either positive or negative (according to your statistics data).

Features of a good hypothesis

- *A good hypothesis should be a statement, not a question.* Your hypothesis is not the scientific question in your study. *The question should come first.* Before you make a hypothesis, you have to clearly identify the question you are interested in studying.
- A good hypothesis brings information to enable the researcher to make a tentative statement about variables.
- A good hypothesis is written in clear and simple language. Reading your hypothesis should tell what you thought was going to happen when you started your study.
- A good hypothesis stimulates a researcher to collect new knowledge. It allows researchers to verify theory.

71

- A good hypothesis defines the variables in easy-to-measure terms, like who the participants are, what changes during the testing, and what the effect of the changes will be.
- A good hypothesis gives the researcher a relational testable statement to collect and analyze data that will accept or reject the hypothesis. To confirm or reject your hypothesis, you need to be capable of doing an experiment and take measurements or make observations to see how your variables are related. You should also be able to repeat your experiment over and over again, if necessary. To create a "testable" hypothesis make sure you have thought about what experiments you will need to carry out to do the test, identified the variables in the project, and included the independent and dependent variables in the hypothesis statement.
- A good hypothesis gives the researcher direction to conduct the research. You may find many studies similar to yours. They can help you shape your project and hypothesis to conduct your research. Answering some scientific questions can involve more than one experiment, each with its own hypothesis. Make sure your hypothesis is a specific statement relating to a single experiment.
- A good hypothesis makes a readable and meaningful framework for reporting the findings and conclusions of the study.

Certain criteria for evaluating a usable hypothesis

1. **Representing explanatory power:** A hypothesis must contain a possible explanation of what it is trying to explain. Suppose you attempt to use your laptop and nothing happens. The hypothesis such as "the laptop doesn't operate because the credit card is lost" is not a possible hypothesis. A hypothesis stating that "the laptop is out of charge" is possible and has explanatory power.

2. **Stating the expected relationship between variables**: A hypothesis should make the relationship between two or more variables. "The laptop doesn't operate and it has a charging part" is unprofitable. An effective hypothesis would be: "The laptop doesn't operate because of lack of charge."

3. **Being testable:** A testable hypothesis is verifiable. Variables must be tested and measured operationally based on the related hypothesis. "The laptop's failure is a punishment for my sins" is untestable.

4. **Being consistent with the existing body of knowledge:** The hypothesis should be consistent with previously well-established hypotheses, theories, and laws. "My laptop doesn't operate because the charge in the battery has changed to nuclear energy" is contrary to what is known about the nature of laptops.

5. **Being stated as simply and concisely as possible:** A hypothesis must propose a simple, clear, and comprehensive manner to report the

conclusion of the study. It is necessary to break a general hypothesis into several specific ones to allow for clarity and testability. For example, if you want to investigate the relationship between "teacher evaluation, student motivation, and anxiety", you should state two hypotheses:

- Standardized evaluation on the part of the teacher positively with student achievement.
- Standardized evaluation on the part of the teacher positively with student anxiety.

Testing the research hypothesis

Testing a hypothesis can be based on the following steps:

- State the relationships that are necessary to be observed, in operational terms, if the hypothesis is true.
- State the null hypothesis.
- Choose an effective method to observe and experiment the existing relationships.
- Gather the empirical data and analyze data to make conclusions.
- Assure whether the data is sufficient to confirm or disconfirm the null hypothesis.

Pilot studies

The term "pilot studies" indicates small versions of a complete study (also called 'feasibility' studies), as well as the specific pre-testing of a special research instrument such as a questionnaire or interview schedule. Pilot studies are an important element of a good study design. Conducting a pilot study does not guarantee success in the main study, but it does improve the possibility of success. Pilot studies reach a range of important functions and can make valuable insights for other researchers.

Definition of a variable

A variable is an attribute that changes from one condition to another condition, from one person to another person (like language learning, height, size, weight, temperature), from time to time, object to object. For example height and size are variables that change from person to person and object to object respectively. The opposite of variable is **constant**, *which is a fixed value within a study*.

Specification of meaning

All variables serve within some kind of theoretical framework. That is, variables have theories behind themselves. Following any theory would give different definitions for the variable under examination. Theoretical definitions can be mentioned in the literature and you have access to them by the researchers who previously worked on the area.

You can define your variables in a way to give their general meaning. This type of variable definition is called **constitutive definition**. Variables also can be defined in terms of operations by which they will be measured or manipulated in a particular study. This type of definition is known as an **operational definition**.

1. Constitutive definition

A constitutive definition is the *dictionary type* of definition. It can be considered as a formal definition in which a concept can be defined with other concepts and constructs. For example, motivation may be defined as the act or process of giving someone a reason for doing something. This type of definition helps express the general meaning of a variable but it is not enough for research purposes.

2. Operational definition

An operational definition is the variable in terms of its measurable characteristics. That is when the way it can be measured is clarified. It's the definition which comes from the context which you are doing your research. An operational definition serves as a contextual definition. So, we have to define what kind of variables we are dealing with. It is important to mention that operationalizing is a matter of degree. No operational definition is completely operational because there are an infinite number of physical characteristics that might be considered. If a researcher cannot provide operational definitions of variables, the definitions still exist since the researcher has to go through physical steps to conduct the research. That is, the definitions exist but may be unstated. When they are unstated, it is difficult, if not impossible, to replicate the research. Thus, providing operational definitions is an important activity when conducting research. For example, if you want to have an operational definition of anxiety you should provide "score on an anxiety scale".

An operational definition gives meaning to a variable by specifying operations that researchers must conduct to measure or manipulate the variable. Operational definitions have two types: **measured and experimental**.

1. A **measured operational** definition describes the operations by which investigators measure a variable. For example, motivation may be defined operationally as scores on the Likert-style.
2. An **experimental operational** definition describes the steps a researcher takes to produce certain experimental conditions.

Different types of variables

1. **Concrete variables** can be **measured objectively** like size, age, weight.
2. **Abstract variables** cannot be directly and objectively measured like the degree of language that you already have internalized, the size of your

voice knowledge, the degree that you are motivated.

But how can I get evidence about abstract variables like happiness, intelligence, motivation? Through psychological tests, or through questionnaires? Through these devices we cannot directly access our desirable answer but we just indirectly get evidence to answer the question.

3. **Discrete variables** are of all-or-nothing nature (either exist or do not exist). They are fixed in the sense that you cannot easily change them, like nationality, left-handedness, sex, etc. A variable is said to be discrete if it cannot be divided into parts.

4. **Continuous/interval variables** can range from a minimum point up to a maximum point. For example, height can range from one centimeter up to thousand centimeters.

5. **Categorical/nominal variables** classify subjects by sorting them into groups. The attribute on which they base the classification is termed a categorical variable. Native language, country of residence and the kind of major are examples of categorical variables.

6. **Dichotomous/binary variables** are the simplest type of categorical variable having two mutually exclusive classes and each category is called a dichotomous variable. Male-female, dead-alive and pass-fail are dichotomous variables.

7. **Extraneous variables** are *undesirable* variables that influence the relationship between the variables. They are variables that influence the results of an experiment. A main goal in research design is to reduce and control the influence of extraneous variables as much as possible. For example, pre-knowledge of reading topic influence receiving higher scores in an experimental research on reading comprehension test in a control or experimental group. It would be better, of course, if all students came in with the exact same pre-knowledge.

The importance of variables

When the variables of your research change, a new situation is made and that needs a new type of experimentation. What is very important in doing research is to show that you have already managed to control these variables. You are controlling the variables to trace the change in a particular variable to show if that specific variable can bring a change or not in the language learning process that other variables have to stay constant or neutral. So if a change is made then you attribute that change to the variable that is changing.

What researchers do in research is that they try to control these variables and let a minimum number of variables change in the process. The more the variables are involved the more complex the research would be.

The process of narrowing down the variable depends on the number and nature of variables.

Functions of variables

Variables are considered as attributes of people or objects. They have certain functions in different research projects. What follows is description of the different functions of variables.

1. **Dependent variable (DV)**:   The observed and measured variable is called the dependent variable. It is the most important variable in our research. The dependent variable is the variable which you observe and measure to represent the effect of the independent variable (Hatch & Farhady, 1981). For example, we teach writing composition to two groups of students based on two different methods and we evaluate our students at the end of the course. The students' scores in writing composition would be the dependent variable because those scores are dependent on the independent variable of teaching methods. Independent variables are known to influence the dependent variable, which is the outcome. In experimental studies the treatment is the independent variable and the outcome is the dependent variable.

2. **Independent variable (IDV / IV)**: The manipulated variable is called the experimental treatment or the independent variable. It's the variable that the researcher wishes to see its effect (it doesn't change). It is the variable which is selected, manipulated and measured by researchers. The values of such a variable are independent of the change in the values of other variables. For example, if you want to investigate the effect of feedback on pre- university students' speaking skill then feedback is the independent variable.

3. **Moderator variable (MV)**: It is a kind of variable that might affect the relationship between dependent and independent variable. It might change the **general outcome of research**. The moderator variable (i.e., sex, age) is chosen to investigate whether the outcomes of research are modified because of this variable or not. The researcher can manipulate the independent variable but not the moderate variable.

4. **Control variable:** It is a variable which is held constant to neutralize the potential effect it might have on behavior. For example, we might select all our subjects from intermediate level students in a good language center. In this way we control the language proficiency factor.

5. **Intervening variable:** An intervening variable is defined as in-the-head variable which cannot be seen, heard or felt. It is inferred from behavior. "Motivation" is inferred from increase in test scores. "Anxiety" is inferred from heart-beat, test scores and so on. So, learning, intelligence, anxiety, etc. are among the intervening variables which are neither observable nor measurable. In other words, we are not able to measure or manipulate them directly.

Examples of variables in research

There is no significant relationship between teaching reading comprehension [IDV] and students' achievement in language proficiency [DV]. *Moderator* a variable like sex can always threaten the result of your research and it's very important to control such a variable by selecting your sample population equally (50% male, 50% female). For controlling age, in your research, you should mention the range of age which you were dealing with. For example, this study is done within the age of 20.

Qualitative and quantitative variables

Some variables such as length, weight, etc. are measured and easily quantified. However, some variables like beauty and justice can only be observed, not measured. These variables are called qualitative variables.

Different scales in research

Researchers have to measure their variables in quantitative research. Particular scales are needed to measure variables. Variables can be measured on different scales based on nature of research and function of variable in research. Here, we refer to scales of measurement or levels of measurement of a variable.

Features of different scales

Nominal scales: Nominal scale means placing objects into categories that are qualitatively rather than quantitatively different. The only relationship between categories is that they are different from each other. There is no mathematical value. Numbers do not indicate quantitative superiority they have. The numbers on the shirt of basketball players can be considered as nominal scales. This kind of assignment of names is simply to identify the groups to make difference between them. Nominal variable can make us able to distinguish one variable from another variable. They have just the feature of distinctiveness.

What is your gender?
1. Male
2. Female

A Sample Nominal Scale

Ordinal scales: Numbers define the degree of existence of one variable in ordinal scale. In fact, the extent of the existence of a variable is rank ordered. In ordinal scales the categories can be ranked from high to low or low to high without precise or mathematically calculable distances among the ranks. Some variables are difficult to measure precisely. We have to measure them by degree like anxiety, attitude, etc.

Rank	Score
1	18
2	16
3	15
4	13

A Sample Ordinal Scale

Interval scales: The most objective scales in research are interval scales. Interval scaling is similar to ordinal scaling in that it determines how much of an attribute exists. It is different from having mathematical values. The units of intervals are equal and constant from one class to another. They let us talk about intervals. Interval scale is the most important in the area of social sciences. You cannot talk about absolute precision in social sciences, because you are dealing with human nature and human nature is not easily accessible. Here, absolute zero does not exist. It exists only in natural sciences.

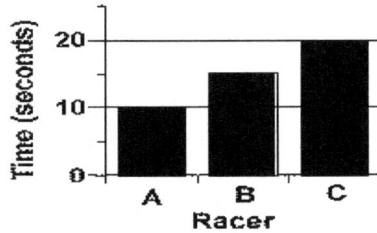

A Sample Interval Scale

Ratio scales: They are similar to interval scales. They also determine how much of a quality exist, the intervals are equal, too. The difference is that a ratio scale has a true zero. Through a ratio scale one can show the negative values as well. They are used in natural sciences. Ratio scales allow us to talk about attributes above zero and attributes below zero.

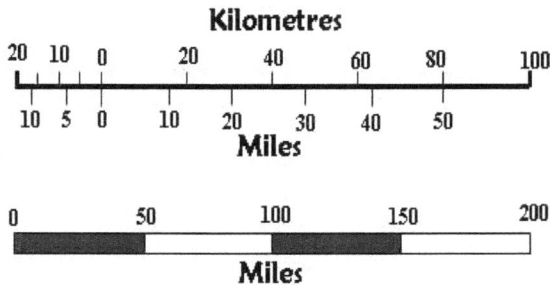

78

A Sample Ratio Scale

Note: As shown in Table 3.1., convertibility of scales usually operates from ratio to interval to ordinal or nominal scales but not the reverse.

■ **Table 3.1.** *Different Measurements and Scales and Their Features* (Adapted from Bachman, 1990, p. 30)

	Distinctiveness	Rank order	Equal interval	Zero value
Nominal scale	+	-	-	-
Ordinal scale	+	+	-	-
Interval scale	+	+	+	-
Ratio scale	+	+	+	+

Natural and social sciences

In natural sciences an ideal condition can be created. You can evaluate the properties of particular objects (test the property of objects). Social science is concerned with society and the relationships among individuals within a society. It is not easy to evaluate the characteristics of a person in an ideal condition.

2. Literature review

The *Literature Review* is a *critical look* at the current research that is important to the work that you are conducting. Obviously, at this point you are not likely to have read everything related to your research questions, but you ought to still be able to identify the key texts with which you will be in conversation as you write your study. Literature reviews often contain both the theoretical approaches to your topic and research (empirical or analytical) on your topic.

The literature review provides the opportunity to understand
- *how* other researchers have written about your topic, in addition to *what* they have written.
- the range of theories researchers use to examine their principal materials or data
- how other researchers connect their specific research topics to larger issues, questions, or practices in the field.

While writing the literature review, keep in mind some major functions or rhetorical goals of the literature review
- It indicates the existing study within a wider disciplinary conversation.

- It situates the specialty, significance of and need for your particular project by making clear how your research questions and approach are distinct from those of other researchers.
- It represents methodological choices.
- It signifies your awareness of the topic and appropriate approaches to conduct it.
- It conveys brief description of the background of the study.
- It critically evaluates important research trends or areas of interest relevant to the study.
- It identifies potential gaps in knowledge.
- It establishes a need for current and/or future research projects.

Essential tips on preparing your literature review

- The literature review should be categorized into recognizable topic clusters and each part should begin with a sub-heading. Search among trends and themes and then synthesize related information. You want to examine the various positions that are relevant to your project, build on findings that lead to your project, or show the places where the literature is lacking, whether because of a methodology you think is incomplete or flawed.
- It is not good to present "Brown says X, Ary says Y" literature reviews. You should be tying the literature you review to specific aspects of your problem, not to review for the sake of reviewing.
- It is not suggested to include all the studies on the subject or a great deal of scholarship that brought you to the subject. The literature review is not the place for such a demonstration. Focus on those pieces of the literature directly relevant to your narrowed subject (question or statement of a problem).
- The use of negative opinion, praise, and blame should be avoided since they are distracting. You should not strongly express your opinions about the previous literature. Your task is to justify your project given the known scholarship.

Note: After evaluating the literature in your field, you should be capable of answering the following questions:
- Why should we study more about this research topic/problem?
- What contributions will my study make to the current literature?

General components of literature review
- Pertinent literature review
- Particular topics directly relating to the subject being investigated
- Significance of the study based on previous research

- The gap in the research that the study will occupy

One part of literature is reviewing. When you have decided on your topic and studied the existing literature, you have to assure that it has not been done by other researchers and it's an area worth investigating. Through literature review you locate your own research within the previous research trying to find a place in the existing literature.

Literature review is the defining feature of research articles. It represents how the current literature links to your study. You build up the existing literature and you present your own study. Some inexperienced researchers might have the feeling that if they do a lot of quotes or reports, this would be considered as plagiarism or replicating other studies and they have nothing to introduce. This is a wrong conception. In fact, through referring to the works of others, you show the value of your study and you are doing your study in the light of the previous study. Your study is not a **replication**. It is a step ahead of the current literature. So, your study becomes valuable because you're going to add to the current study rather than repeating the existing material.

This represents that when you're quoting others' works you increase the **authenticity** of your own research rather than reducing the value of your own research. So, you narrow down the works of others to show to what extent this area has developed as well as to show the gap in the present literature; because a number of articles might have been written, a number of textbooks might have been designed, a number of conferences have been held, and the topic has been investigated from different perspectives. Still when you investigate all these areas you will see a gap. So, in the literature review you try to take a critical attitude toward this study and show that still, there is something which is lacking (something which is not included in the literature) and you link the gap to your own study showing that your study is going to be valuable because it addresses a particular question which has not been investigated by others and was overlooked in other studies.

By referring to the works of others you place your own research within the existing literature. So, if you quote or report from the works of others it's not understating your own work. On the other hand, you are going to take authority to support your study.

In your literature, you might make a number of claims. Your claim has to be supported especially if you're inexperienced in the field you are practicing and you may not be known to the famous members of the discourse community. If you claim and your claims are unsupported, one would believe in what you say unless you are a member of that community, or you take authority to support your claim or use statements of the experts and use those quotes as full proof or as support for the claims you're making; otherwise, you are living in the air. So, to back our claims you need the statements of others.

How and where can relevant literature be accessed?

Articles (experimental, theoretical, and review articles): Articles might be published in journals, and textbooks, as collections of articles. They might be high/less scholarly articles; they might be national or international. They might be conference articles that have not been published yet. Some electronic sites which are authentic and reliable are good, too.

Theses and dissertations: they contain detailed and in depth information.

Encyclopedias: they contain general information.

Abstracts: they contain compact and abridged information.

Almanacs: they are books published every year giving information on various subjects, e.g. sport, the theatre, etc.

Journals: the most authentic sources of literature are the **journals** specially those which are published in scholarly quarterly / yearly journals.

A literature review is not gathering the ideas of others. It's the critical review of the ideas of others in relation to the topic that you have chosen. So, the point of departure in your literature review is the paragraph that you put forward.

The first paragraph usually starts with your own sentence. You should not make any reference to the works of others, because in the first paragraph you have to initiate the situation, introduce the problem, and show that a lot of studies have been done and you're aware of them. So, the first paragraph can set the scene, prepare the background, and direct the mind of the readers to the topic you're going to elaborate on.

You can begin making claims and using the statements of others to support yourself from the second paragraph onward. If your study is experimental (a study of the effect of the systematic manipulation of one variable on another variable) your literature review will have at least two sections.

1. **Theoretical section:** This section focuses on some **key terms** you may have. You refer to the works of others and rely on the definitions and authorities in that field.

2. **Experimental section:** The experimental works which have been done in relation to the study that you are taking up have to be cited. So you might start with different references. The significant point is that you should give reference that has the problem of that particular study, the methodology that the others adopted to conduct and the kind of statistical analyses that they used and the conclusion that they made as a result of the data that they received. So, you have to make reference to question, methodology, result and conclusion.

You have to include all the necessary information in your literature review. It should not occupy one or two pages. It should be one paragraph including *seven* to *ten* lines, not more.

Literature review is not simply a collection of works of others. Whatever study you are referring to should have some connection to the study that you are going to take up. So, you use those studies to establish your place and to show that there is a reason why you are using this study.

All the studies should support your study. Sometimes you take a critical attitude towards one of the studies. You should mention how the studies were done and then raise a number of questions to show there are some shortcomings attached to the study. It might be those shortcomings that lead you to do the study again. So you also have to make reference to all those studies.

Questions that literature review should answer are as follows:

1.   **What is already known about the immediate context of the concern?** You should know what has happened in the field that you are studying. You know the studies that have been done. So, you are not doing a replication. You are doing something as a continuation.

1.   **What are the features of the key terms and concepts?** You have to focus on the key concepts and describe them in detail by relying on the statements that you are borrowing from other people.

2.   **What are the relationships between variables or factors?** If you want to focus on pre-task in relation to reading comprehension, a number of variables might be considered, for example sex, age, etc. Someone else might have been studying pre-task focusing on the age of the language learners and find interesting results about the influence of age on the performance of pre task. So you should consider this in your research. You also have to focus on the variable that you are going to control or manipulate.

3.   **What are the shortcomings?** You want to expand the area that has been investigated. What are the shortcomings? You found a gap, and you want to occupy that gap through your study. So you are going to show in relation to the questions you are going to take up the existing literature is suffering from some flaws.

4.   **What areas need to be further tested?** A literature review should identify a need for further research.

5.   **Why do you study the problem? What is your rational?** You have to show the value of your research and this is shown through depicting the gap in a logical way.

6.   **What contributions is your current study going to make?** What is the importance of this study? This is very important to explain your introduction in your research. In your study, you should say who the consumer of this study is. Who is going to benefit from your study? You're going to show the significance of the study itself. You may carry out a study overlooking the fact that this study has been done. So it's not going to have any significance. If the current studies are convincing enough and general enough to cover the context into

what you're going to do, it neutralizes your study. Your study should have something new to propose and should add something to the literature.

7. **What research design or methodology is satisfactory?** After investigating the territories around the research (topic) you can predict what kind of research seems satisfactory.

If your literature review answers the above questions, then it is an accepted literature, otherwise it's not a good one. If your research is simply the shopping list of the existing materials, researchers will ignore it, no matter how your study has been strictly conducted. How will you arrange the related works in your literature review? Chronologically, alphabetically, etc.?

Unless chronological order will have some significance this is not a right approach. We do not arrange studies alphabetically nor do we arrange them chronologically, because if we arrange them chronologically it would not be related to your study, reflecting on the existing literature without any connection to your study.

Experts arrange studies based on the research, not researchers or time. We have to make literature review on the basis of their connection to the research itself.

When you're moving from site to site on the Internet or browsing the library bookshelves, you may see hundreds of materials related to your study; what should you do?

Until you have identified your problem, you'll find a lot of related materials to your study. On the other hand, you can't define the problem unless you have a literature. So you face dilemma.

As you define your problem, you use the materials and as you use the materials, you'll see some of the materials are more related to your problem and some are less related. When you define the problem you'll try to find the boundary of the problem. Finding the problem should take place simultaneously. As you define the problem you're also narrowing down the materials you're referring.

Keep away from duplication or replication. It's really unsatisfactory to see a researcher plagiarizing. It contradicts the spirit of research. You have to be loyal and faithful to the works of others.

Quoting or reporting the works of others is a support. It proves your claims rather than disproving them or undermining your research. Your literature review is going to occupy the gap of your research. One of the important points you have to decide on in documenting your research is tense. It's a very controversial part in your research. Researchers always complain about the trouble they have in writing tense.

Literature is very poor in relation to the suggestion it has on what tense should be used in studies.

What tense should we use? Choosing the suitable tense partly depends on the writing style. MLA style is used in literature and APA style is used in applied linguistics.

Note: Academic study of non-native speaker of English in the US divides the verb citation as follows:
1. If a single study in the past is referred to, you should use past tense.
2. If an area of enquiry is referred to, use present perfect.
3. If the current status of knowledge is referred to, use present simple.

The first two refer to researchers but the third one refers to the research itself and focuses on the topic. Present simple is also used when you're referring to the statements of significant authorities in the field, for example, works by Richards, Dörnyei, Swales, etc. or when you're referring to a very highly important work like the Quran.

CHAPTER FOUR
Methodology

Introduction

The major variations in research articles are in the *Methodology Section*, because it is in method section which you should mention your **participants**, your **instruments**, the **material** you use as well as, the **procedure** which you use in your study.

In humanities discipline, the method section might not appear at all, because the papers are mostly theoretical in nature. The method section is a part of the empirical studies in any discipline. In the method section, we like to know how the study was conducted; under what circumstances it was conducted.

Your methodology is made of the various methods and materials that you are going to use to get and analyze the information necessary to answer your research question. Not only you have to describe your methodology but also you have to justify it. This means explaining why a special choice of methodology will enable you to do a project that will produce results that are new or unique.

- How will you do your project?
- What qualitative or quantitative research methods will you use? Why? Are you going to take a special approach such as action research, or case studies?
- What material will you use? Surveys? Interviews? Archival or traditional library research? Books? Analytical tools? Why?
- How do special methodologies allow you to answer different questions?
- Does your method have a clear connection with your research questions and/or hypotheses?
- Are the proposed tests, or methods, or scientific procedures suited to the stated objective?
- Will you use statistical analysis? Will you use specific theoretical perspectives to help you analyze a text or explain observed behaviors?
- Will you provide background and rationale for methodologies that are unfamiliar for your readers? (Typically, the social sciences and humanities require more explanation/rationale of methods than the hard sciences.)
- Will you provide a rationale for subject selection (particularly if you have not already provided one)? For instance, if you propose to conduct interviews and use questionnaires, how do you intend to select the sample population? If you are analyzing literary texts, which texts have you chosen, and why?

- Are there any practical limitations that could affect your data collection? How will you attempt to control for potential confounding variables and errors?
- What are the strengths and weakness of your methods and materials?

Key points of preparing your methodology section

- Break down your methodology into subsections. In the physical sciences, these sections include subjects, design, apparatus, instrumentation, process, analysis, etc. In the social sciences, these sections include selection of participants, interview process, profiles, interpretive and analytic framework, methods of qualitative analysis, etc. In the humanities, these sections include scholarly research, archival research, theoretical orientation, etc.
- Remember that your methods section may also require supporting literature.
- Anticipate the audience's methodological concerns. If the audience may have a problem with an aspect of the methodology, accept this difficulty and justify your approach. If your methodology may lead to problems you can anticipate (including timeframe problems), state this openly and show why continuing the methodology is more important than the risk of these problems.

Note: If you have revealed that you have considered even the downside of your methods, their advantages will seem more carefully developed.

Overview of chapters

Some proposals also include a brief explanation of relevant chapters. Consult with your advisor to see if this is necessary for your proposal.

Plan of work/timeline

Many proposals also have a schedule with anticipated completion dates for particular parts of the study. This timeline helps your committee determine if your project is realistic, given available methods and institutional requirements (such as deadlines for submission, etc.). Setting a schedule can also help you manage your time more effectively by setting specific goals for yourself.

Some suggestions to keep in mind while preparing a timeline:

- Consult your advisor as you make your plan of work.
- Do not be overly ambitious; most stages seem to take longer than originally planned.
- Remember that this is a proposed timeline. What is perhaps most important is that you show your awareness of the various elements of the study (design, testing, and length of experiments; negotiation of

entry into the study site; purchase of necessary equipment; drafting; redrafting; etc.).

Components of conceptual framework or methodology

Participants: It is very important to show that the selection of the participants is an objective process." Who are the subjects? How many subjects were involved? Why was this number selected? How were the subjects selected?" **Demographic information** of participants like age, sex, economic background, education social status, affiliations should be included. "Were the participants members of a particular center? Were they selected from universities?" Based on ethics you have to respect the rights of these participants. Other information concerning participants should be included; mention if some subjects left your experiment in the middle of your research. If it is so, it has to be included for whatever reason. In research, it's called **experimental mortality**. For whatever reason you lost your subject, you have to mention that reason.

Materials: What were the materials used in this study? What was the rational for the selection of these materials? Whatever you do in method section should be rational, because it's in the method section that you are making decisions.

Instruments: They are used to gather information from the participants. There are some instruments which can be used such as Test, Questionnaire, Observation, and Interview. Choosing the right instrument for the selection of data is again very crucial because it can affect the whole process of data collection and your judgment in the discussion section. We need to mention the rational for the selection of these instruments. Why were these instruments used? You should persuade your readers that the chosen instruments are reliable and valid.

Procedures: This important component of your methodology section defines the processes and procedures you used throughout conducting your study. It will make your own direction and activity as a researcher. It will also provide your readers with an unambiguous understanding of the specific research actions you undertook. Your description of processes and procedures also provides a basis for readers eventually to evaluate the nature, integrity, and veracity of your findings. For quantitative studies, it is also necessary that your description of procedures be specific enough for other investigators to replicate them if necessary or desired. For qualitative studies, your procedures should be clear enough for other researchers to learn from them how to conduct similar, related, or follow up studies.

- How were your participants divided into groups?
- Was some rationale used (or you just did it haphazardly)?

- How did you employ the instruction?
- What kind of instruction did they receive?
- How long did the instruction continue?
- How was the instruction given to the participants?

If the **control group** needs some **placebo** (false treatment) you should persuade the readers that false treatment did not improve language learners' ability concerning the ability that you are testing.

Generally the method section should answer these two questions:

- How did you collect the data?
- How did you analyze the data?

Consider the following linguistic characteristics of the method section

- The use of **volitional verbs,** e.g. decide.
- **Past passive tense** makes your study more consistent. Generally, verbs in method section would be in the past.
- **Anaphoric** references should be considered.
- **Lexical repetition** brings **cohesion** to method of analysis. It should be described in procedure section. But if it is not mentioned there at the beginning of your data analysis section you have to include it.

Some suggestions for drafting methodology

- Regularly ask yourself who the audience is?
- What does the audience like to know?
- Necessary information should be included. Avoid redundancy.
- Assure yourself that there are no overlaps in different parts. Stay away from the repetition of information in the procedure section.
- Do not use expressions like "I", "we", etc. Use past passive instead to lower the degree of dependency of experiment on the researcher.
- Active and passive verbs should be used based on the situation. The researcher cannot voluntarily decide on active or passive verbs. When you have to show that somebody did something, then you have to use active. It depends on the significance of the point.
- Have a good reason for switching from one tense to another tense.
- Don't shift from active to passive haphazardly.
- Use lexical repetition and anaphoric expressions to achieve coherence in your study,

Data collection

Through the data collection the necessary data on the behaviors of your participants are obtained. There are different models of data collection. You need to select the best method for collecting your data. The best way is to look into the question you have designed.

Tools used for data collection

Data collection tools are helpful because they provide a "picture" of your work. The goal for using tools is to help the researcher define information, process knowledge, and identify opportunities for continuous improvement. You need a **systematic** way of collecting multiple sources of data about your objects of study (people, objects, and phenomena), the time to reflect upon what you are discovering, and the settings in which they take place. If data are collected haphazardly, answering your research questions in a convincingly way will be difficult.

Data are required to quantify information and can be collected in a variety of ways. Triangulation requires the collection of data from a variety of sources, in a variety of ways, with a variety of perspectives.

Different techniques for data collection

Within each general research approach; one or many data collection techniques may be used. Typically, a researcher will decide for one (or multiple) data collection techniques while considering its overall appropriateness to the research, along with other practical factors, such as: expected quality of the collected data, estimated costs, predicted nonresponse rates, expected level of measure errors, and length of the data collection period. It is of course possible that a given research question may not be satisfactorily studied because specific data collection techniques do not exist to collect the data needed to answer such a question. The most popular data collection techniques include: employing available information, **observing, interviewing, and preparing written questionnaires.**

Employing available information

There is usually a great deal of already collected data, although the data might not necessarily have been analyzed or published by those who collected them. Placing these sources and reclaiming the information is a good starting point in any data collection method. **For example,** analysis of the information routinely collected by the board of education regarding English teaching can be very useful for identifying problems the teachers and language learners have.

Using **main informants** is another important technique to get available information. Main informants could be erudite English teachers managing the educational group in the board of education or teaching directors of the EFL institutes. They can be involved in different steps of the research, from the statement of the problem to analysis of the data and development of recommendations. Other sources of available data are **newspapers** and published and unpublished theses and dissertations.

The benefit of using available data is the affordability factor because data are already there and permits examination of trends over the past. Sometimes, it is difficult to be provided with the required records or reports, and the data can be considered as incomplete or disorganized tool.

Observation

Observation is the active gaining of information from a primary source. In living beings, senses are used for observation. In science, the recording of data is through using instruments. Observation is systematically watching and recording behavior and characteristics of living beings, objects or phenomena. Observations can give more accurate information on behavior of people than interviews or questionnaires. There are five important preliminary steps to take in preparing for quantitative direct observation (Ary, Jacob, Sorenson & Razavieh, 2010, 216-217):

1. Select the aspect of behavior to be observed.
2. Clearly define the behaviors falling within a chosen category.
3. Develop a system for quantifying observations.
4. Develop specific procedures for recording the behavior.
5. Train the people who will carry out the observations.

Direct observation requires careful programming and a checklist. It is very objective because researchers are present there. In direct observation, a researcher watches and records while the action is happening. Successful direct observers remain hidden and do not allow their presence to affect the behavior of the subjects they are studying. If language learners become aware of observation process then they may not show natural behavior.

Indirect observation is not as systematic as the direct observation. An indirect observation is when the researcher must use reported observations that include direct observations of others. In some cases, the observations of others may not be true, which may provide the researcher's with incorrect findings. Of course, when the observation is indirect and unknown, the obtained data are quite natural. However, ethical principles of research do not allow the invasion of people's privacy.

A much-used data collection technique is **observation of human behavior**. It can form part of any type of study, but as they are time consuming, they are most often used in small-scale studies. Here, are some ways to deal with observation of human behavior:

- **Participant observation:** The observer participates in ongoing activities and records observations. The technique is used in many studies in Anthropology and Sociology. Often the researcher actually takes on the role being studied; for example, a researcher observes an English class and takes part in the class procedures and activities.
- **Non-participant observation:** Non-participant observation is a

research technique whereby the researcher watches the situation and subjects of his or her study but without taking an active part in the situation under examination. Many theorists criticize this method of research because the subjects may behave differently with the awareness of being watched.

Devices for recording direct observations

Researchers can use checklists, rating scales, and coding sheets to record the data in direct observation.

1. Checklists

A checklist is the simplest instrument, which identifies a list of the behaviors that are to be observed. The observer checks whether each behavior is present or absent through using a checklist. A checklist is different from a scale in that the answers do not show points on a continuum but, rather, nominal categories. The behaviors in a checklist should be operationally defined and readily observable.

Please update the student's performance below. Use the letter codes:
E=Excellent, VG=Very Good, S=Satisfactory, LS=Less than Satisfactory

	Advisor	Student
Attendance/Punctuality:		
Is consistent in attendance	-----------	-----------
Reports to community site on time	-----------	-----------
Attitude:		
Accepts responsibility	-----------	-----------
Is enthusiastic and interested	-----------	-----------
Displays appropriate appearance and dress	-----------	-----------
Is courteous and cooperative	-----------	-----------
Displays emotional maturity	-----------	-----------
Exercises good judgment	-----------	-----------
Is sincere	-----------	-----------
Relates well to a variety of people	-----------	-----------

A Sample Checklist

2. Rating scales

They are often used by observers to show their evaluation of an observed behavior or activity. Generally, rating scales have three to five categories. For example, an observer studying students' preparation for presentation in a classroom may use a scale with the following points:

- *Extremely well prepared*
- *Well prepared*
- *Prepared*
- *Not well prepared*
- *Totally unprepared.*

A 3-point scale might include

- *Very well prepared*
- *Prepared*
- *Not well prepared*

Scales with more than five rating categories are not suggested because it is too difficult to appropriately discriminate among the categories.

3. Coding systems

They are used in observational studies to make categorizing easy and counting of predetermined behaviors as they occur. The researcher does not just represent whether a behavior occurred as with a checklist but, rather, uses agreed-on codes to record what actually occurred. While rating scales can be completed after an observation period, coding is completed at the time the observer views the behavior. Two kinds of coding systems are usually used by researchers:

- **Sign coding** uses a set of behavior categories. Each time, when one of the behaviors occurs the observer codes the happening in the suitable category. If a coding sheet is used in class observational research listed "summarizing" as a teacher behavior, the observer would code a happening every time a teacher summarized material.
- **Time coding** can be used when the observer identifies and records all predetermined behavior categories that occur during a given time period. The time period might be 10 seconds, 5 minutes, or some other period of time.

Interview

An **interview** is a direct face-to-face attempt to gain reliable and valid measures in the form of verbal answers from one or more respondents. The interviewer should be clear on the areas on which the questions should be prepared. He/she should plan to elicit information in as short time as possible. Answers to the questions can be recorded by writing them down either during the interview itself or immediately after the interview or by tape-recording the answers, or by a combination of both.

Different types of interview

Structured interview: The questions are made in advance and you meet each respondent separately. You as a researcher should document the answers. It is possible to have a questionnaire which measures the interviewee on the basis of his/her response. You may also check the interviewee' accuracy or fluency but everything should be the same for everybody.

Unstructured interview: The questions are not pre-determined. Questions are made on the spot. There is a lot of bias. You may ask someone a simple question and the other a difficult question. The interviewer must be very experienced in terms of raising questions. You have to be professional in asking questions between structured and unstructured interviews.

Semi- structure interview: It stands somewhere in between. You may have fixed questions to give to interviewees and some other questions to challenge their creativity.

Different levels of flexibility in interviews

Interviews with high level of flexibility: A flexible interview is used if a researcher has little knowledge of the problem or situation he is carrying out, or if the topic is sensitive. It is often used in exploratory studies. The instrument which is used for this kind of interview may be called an **interview guide** or **interview schedule.**

Interviews with low level of flexibility: Less flexible interviews are used when the researcher is almost aware of expected answers or when the number of interviewees is nearly large. Then, questionnaires can be used with a fixed number of questions in a standard order.

Questionnaires

A questionnaire is a research instrument with a number of questions used for the purpose of gathering information from respondents. Although they are often designed for statistical analysis of the responses, this is not always the case. A written questionnaire (or self-administered questionnaire) can be either open-ended or closed with pre-categorized   answers. A written questionnaire can be used in different ways. It can be sent by mail to respondents with clear instructions on how to answer the questions and asking for mailed responses, given to all or part of the respondents in one place at one time giving oral or written instructions and allowing the respondents to fill out the questionnaires, and hand-delivered to respondents to be collected later.

The term questionnaire is partly inaccurate because many questionnaires do not have any real questions that end with a question mark. In fact, questionnaires are also often referred to under different names, such as inventories, forms, opinionnaires, tests, batteries, checklists, scales, surveys, etc.

Questionnaire in surveys

Survey studies deal with explaining the characteristics of a population by examining a sample of that group. Although survey data can be collected through structured interviews, the basic data collection method in surveys is the use of questionnaires. The results of a questionnaire survey are usually quantitative, although the instrument may also contain some open-ended questions that will require a qualitative analysis. The main methodological issues about surveys are

- how to sample the participants
- how to administer the research tool

The essence of scientific research is trying to find answers to questions in a systematic and disciplined manner and that is why the questionnaire has become one of the most popular research instruments used in the social sciences. Questionnaires are popular because they are almost easy to construct, extremely flexible and especially able to collect a great deal of information quickly in a readily proccessible form. In fact, the frequency of the use of self-completed questionnaires as a research tool in applied linguistics is surpassed only by that of language proficiency tests. Yet, despite the wide use of questionnaires in applied linguistics, there is no enough awareness of the theory of questionnaire design and processing. The usual perception is that anybody with a bit of common sense and good word processing software can make a good questionnaire. Unfortunately, this perception is not true. Like in our everyday life, where not every question elicits the right answer, it is common in scientific research to come across questionnaires that fail. In fact, it is believed that most questionnaires used in applied linguistic research are somewhat unplanned instruments, and questionnaires that represent scores with sufficient reliability and validity are not easy to make in our field.

Different kinds of questions in questionnaires

Factual questions are used to discover certain facts about the respondents, such as demographic characteristics (for example, age, gender, and race), residential location, marital and socio-economic status, level of education, occupation, language learning history, amount of time spent in an L2 environment, etc.

Behavioral questions which are used to find out what the respondents are doing or have done in the past, focusing on actions, life-styles, habits, and personal history.

Attitudinal questions which are used to find out what people think, covering attitudes, opinions, beliefs, interests, and values.

Although questionnaires are often very similar to written tests, there is a fundamental difference between the two instrument types. A test takes a sample of the respondents' behavior or knowledge for the purpose of evaluating the individuals more general underlying competence, abilities, or skills (for example, reading comprehension); so, a test measures how well someone can do something (reading comprehension). In contrast, questionnaire items do not have good or bad answers; they elicit information about the respondents in a non-evaluative manner, without measuring their performance against a set of criteria so, although some commercially available questionnaires are actually called tests, these are not tested in the same sense as proficiency or knowledge tests.

Similarly production questionnaires are not proper questionnaires either. They are commonly used in inter-language pragmatics research, require the informant to produce some sort of authentic language data as a response to situational prompts; so, they are structured language elicitation instruments and, they sample the respondents' competence in performing certain tasks, which makes them similar to language tests.

Steps to preparing questionnaires
Step one: Considering required background

The purpose, research questions, and hypothesis of the proposed research should be examined. The audience, their background especially their educational levels, access, and the process used to select the respondents (sample vs. population) should be determined. A complete understanding of the problem through literature search and readings is a must. Good preparation and understanding of this step provides the foundation for beginning step two.

Step two: Defining the questionnaire conceptualization

After providing a comprehensive understanding of the research, the next step is to create statements/questions for the questionnaire. Here, content from literature/theoretical framework is converted into statements/questions. What's more, a link among the purposes of the study and their translation into content is made. For example, the researcher must indicate what the questionnaire is measuring, that is, attitudes, perceptions, opinions, behavior change, etc. Major variables (independent, dependent, and moderator variables) are identified and defined in this step.

Step three: Selecting an appropriate procedure

The focus here is on writing statements/questions, choice of appropriate scales of measurement, questionnaire format, question ordering, font size, front and back cover, and proposed data analysis. Scales are used to quantify a subject's answer on a particular variable. Considering the relationship between the level of measurement and the suitability of data analysis is essential. For example, if ANOVA (analysis of variance) is a mode of data analysis, the independent variable must be measured on a nominal scale with two or more levels (yes, no, not sure), and the dependent variable must be measured on an interval/ratio scale (strongly agree to strongly disagree).

Step four: Establishing validity

Which type of validity (content, construct, criterion, and face) to use depends on the purposes of the study. The following questions should be answered in step four:

1. Is the questionnaire measuring what it intended to measure?
2. Does it represent the content?
3. Is it appropriate for the sample/population?
4. Is the questionnaire thorough enough to collect all the information needed to cover the purpose and goals of the study?
5. Does the instrument look like a questionnaire?

Step five: Establishing reliability

Reliability of the questionnaire is reached through using a *pilot test*. The pilot test indicates whether the questionnaire consistently measures whatever it measures.

The use of reliability types depends on the nature of data (nominal, ordinal, interval, and ratio). For example, to assess reliability of questions measured on an interval/ratio scale, internal consistency is appropriate to use. To assess reliability of knowledge questions, test-retest or split-half is appropriate.

In a pilot test, data should be collected from subjects not included in the sample. Data can be analyzed through SPSS (Statistical Package for Social Sciences) or software.

Qualitative Questionnaire

(Two Open – ended Questions about Using or Not Using Communicative Approach or Communicative Language Teaching for Teaching English in Iran)

Dear respondents,

I would be very thankful if you would answer the two following questions about using or not using CA /CLT (your reasons and explanation) in Iran. Thank you for your cooperation in advance.

Thanks & Regards

M.Nasseri (MA student)

What is Communicative Language Teaching? (CLT)

Definition of CLT: "An approach to foreign or second language which emphasizes that the goal of language learning is communicative competence."

(Longman dictionary of language teaching and applied linguistics)

Motivation Increase: CLT provides the students with authentic and meaningful interaction.
This increases their motivation and attitude to learn the target language.

Fluency and Accuracy: CLT gives equal importance to both the spoken language and the accuracy of the production.
In CLT "Fluency" sometimes is more important.

Real-life contexts: Students have to produce and receive language in different real-life contexts.
CLT provides them with skills they really need in their real life.

Students' Sense of Autonomy: In this student=centered class the focus is on the interests of the students.
Students will have the opportunity to learn about their learning styles.

CLT is a method of teaching involving developing real situation in the classroom and practicing the basic patterns according to / based on creating situations.

In conclusion :
 CLT should be fun for both teacher and students.
Enabling students to communicate successfully is also very rewarding.

Please answer the given question according to these five aspects as Doukas has mentioned
    1. Group / pair work
    2. Quality and quantity of error correction
    3. The role and contribution of learners in the learning process
    4. The role of the teacher in the classroom
    5. Place / importance of grammar

Now please answer the following questions about CLT.
    1. Is CLT practical for teaching English in classrooms in Iran? Yes or No? If no, why? Please explain the reasons. You can write your answer in English or Persian.
    2. Which principles (aspects) of CLT are more important for you in your classes? Why do you focus on them?

A Qualitative Questionnaire Sample

Dear respondent, the main aim of this study is to investigate teachers' attitudes towards communicative approach in the foreign language classrooms in Iran. Please be assured that the information you provide will be kept confidential. You are not required to write your name. Please answer the questions honestly and sincerely, as it is important for the output of this research.

Thank you very much for taking the time to read and answer this short questionnaire!

Demographic Information

Name (Optional) :

Age: ☐ 20-24   ☐ 25-33   ☐ 35-44   ☐ 45-60   ☐ More than 60

Gender: ☐ Male ☐ Female

Level of Education (Degree): ☐BA in English ☐MA in English ☐PhD in English Teaching **Experience (Year):**

Items	Strongly Agree (5)	Agree (4)	Uncertain (3)	Disagree (2)	Strongly Disagree (1)
1. Group work activities are essential in providing opportunities for cooperative relationships to emerge and in promoting genuine interaction among students.					
2. Group work allows students to explore problems for themselves and thus have some measure of control over their own learning. It is therefore an invaluable means of organizing classroom experiences.					
3. Group work activities take too long to organize and waste a lot of valuable teaching time.					
4. Students do their best when taught as a whole class by the teacher. Small group work may occasionally be useful to vary the routine, but it can never replace sound formal instruction by a competent teacher.					
5. Grammatical correctness is the most important criterion by which language performance should be judged.					
6. For students to become effective communicators in the foreign language, the teachers' feedback must be focused on the appropriateness and not the linguistic form of the students' responses.					
7. The teacher should correct all the grammatical errors students make. If errors are ignored, this will result in imperfect learning.					
8. Since errors are a normal part of learning , much correction is wasteful of time.					
9. Since the learner comes to the language classroom with little or no knowledge of the language, he/she is in no position to suggest what the content of the lesson should be or what					

activities are useful for him / her.					
10. Training learners to take responsibility for their own learning is futile since learners are not used to such an approach.					
11. The learner-centered approach to language teaching encourages responsibility and self-discipline and allows each student to develop his/her full potential.					
12. Knowledge of the rules of a language does not guarantee ability to use the language.					
13. The communicative approach to language teaching produces fluent but inaccurate learners.					
14. For most students language is acquired most effectively when it is used as a vehicle for doing something else and not when it is studied in a direct or explicit way.					
15. The teacher as 'authority' and 'instructor' is no longer adequate to describe the teacher's role in the language classroom.					
16. The teacher as transmitter of knowledge is only one of the many different roles he/she must perform during the course of a lesson.					
17. The role of the teacher in the language classroom is to impart knowledge through activities such as explanation, writing, and example.					
18. Group work activities have little use since it is very difficult for the teacher to monitor the students' performance and prevent them from using their mother tongue.					
19. Grammar should be taught only as a means to an end and not as an end in itself.					
20. It is impossible in a large class of students to organize your teaching so as to suit the needs of all.					
21. By mastering the rules of grammar, students become fully capable of communicating with a native speaker.					
22. Tasks and activities should be negotiated and adapted to suit the students' needs rather than imposed on them.					
23. Direct instruction in the rules and terminology of grammar is essential if students are to learn to communicate effectively.					
24. A textbook alone is not able to cater for all the needs and interests of the students. The teacher must supplement the textbook with other materials and tasks so as to satisfy the widely differing needs of the students.					

A Quantitative Questionnaire Sample

Tests

Tests, whether paper and pencil or performance, are one or the most popular tools of collecting data in research. There are different kinds of paper and pencil tests. Some tests are made by researchers and some by professionals. A major advantage of these tests is that they are objective and provide reliable information.

Functions of tests

Tests serve two main functions (the purpose for which a test is designed):
Prognostic tests: they are predictive tests that identify learning difficulties or problem. They show learners' strengths and weaknesses to ascertain what learning still needs to take place. They are not related to learners' educational background.

1. **Selection tests:** They provide information about examinees' acceptance or non-acceptance into a particular program. The criterion for pass or fail is made by the authorities. There should not be any limitation for examinees who obtain the score. If the number of applicants passing a test is more than the capacity of the educational programs the selection test becomes a competition test like the Entrance Examination for universities in Iran.

2. **Placement tests:** They are placing new students in the appropriate classes. Typically they are used to assign students to classes at different levels. There is no pass or fail in placement tests. The purpose of placement tests is to measure the capabilities of an examinee in following a particular path of language learning.

3. **Aptitude tests:** They contribute to making decisions on the future career of the examinees. They are designed to measure general ability to learn a foreign language before taking a course.

Evaluation of attainment tests: In contrast to prognostic tests, these tests are based on the extent to which examinees have learned the materials they have been taught.

1. **Achievement tests:** They are designed to measure students' language progress. They contain *final achievement tests* administered at the end of a course of study and *progress achievement tests* measuring the progress that students are making during the course.

2. **Proficiency tests:** They are designed to measure people' language knowledge and ability regardless of any training courses that candidates may have previously taken.

3. **Knowledge tests:** They are designed to be used in situations where the medium of instruction is a language other than the examinees' mother tongue to measure knowledge in areas other than the language itself.

Discrete point versus integrative testing

Discrete-point testing: It evaluates each item of language separately at a time. *Gap fills* such as single sentence, cloze, multiple choices, using given words, sentence transformation, sentence construction, and reconstruction and *two-option answers* such as true or false, and correct or incorrect items are considered as discrete-item testing.

Integrative testing: It measures the actual aspects of activities in using language simultaneously. It combines many language elements to complete a task. It involves writing a composition or taking a dictation. Some common integrative tests are cloze, dictation, and composition writing.

Direct versus indirect testing

Direct testing: It refers to test formats which duplicate the setting and performing of the real life situations. Writing samples and oral interviews are referred to as direct tests.

Indirect testing: It is measuring the abilities that underlie the skills in which the researcher is interested. It does not require the test takers' language in use. An inference can be made from learners' performances on more artificial tasks.

Computer adaptive testing: It provides all candidates with an item of average difficulty. Those who can answer well are presented with a more difficult item; those who respond incorrectly are given an easier item.

Communicative language testing: It is believed that in order to make a special language test useful, test performance must correspond to language use in non-test situations. Communicative language teaching makes use of real-life situations that need communication. The researcher sets up a situation that learners encounter in real life. The real-life simulations should change from day to day. Learners' motivation to learn comes from their interest to communicate in meaningful ways about meaningful topics.

Types of assessment

Formative assessment: It promotes effective learning by students (assessment for learning). It evaluates students in the process of learning competences and skills in order to help them to continue the growth of the process. All kinds of informal assessment are formative.

Summative assessment: It identifies what a student has learned at the end of a course or unit of instruction (assessment of learning). Final exams are examples of summative assessment.

Norm-referenced assessment: It shows each student's performance in relation to the performance of others. It does not directly tell us what the student is capable of doing in the language.

Criterion-referenced assessment: It refers to grading of each student's performance in terms of whether a particular description of performance has been met. The purpose is to clarify students based on whether or not they are able to perform tasks satisfactorily. The tasks are set, and those students who perform well **"pass"**; those who do not **"fail"**.

Internal assessment: The assessment activities are made by the class teachers. Internal assessment is an integral part of the course. It enables students to represent the application of their skills and knowledge, and to follow their personal interests, without the time limitations and other constraints that are related to written examinations. The internal assessment should be woven into normal classroom teaching and not be a separate activity set after a course has been taught.

External assessment: External assessments are made, chosen, and controlled by another person or group such as commercial publishers, national administrators, or policymakers. Typical examples of external assessments contain standardized and commercial reading tests. External assessments are administered less frequently than internal assessments, but they usually have greater importance.

Authentic assessment: Simply assessing an isolated skill or a retained fact does not effectively measure a student's capabilities. To accurately evaluate what a student has learned, an assessment method must examine his or her *collective abilities*. The term **authentic assessment** describes the multiple forms of assessment that reflect students' learning, achievement, motivation, and attitudes on instructionally relevant classroom activities. Authentic assessment links between the real language use and test tasks. All content and skills under test should mirror as exactly as possible the factor of authenticity. E.g. in a reading comprehension test, the test maker should choose passages that match topics the test-taker may read outside of the testing situation.

Performance assessments

They are techniques in which researchers directly observe and assesse individuals' performance of a certain task and judge the finished product of that performance. The test taker is asked to conduct a *process* such as a written essay. The performance or product is judged against established **criteria**. In order to conduct a performance test, follow these three basic steps:

1. You should begin with an obvious statement of the objectives, the conditions, and what is going to be asked. A set of test specifications with the critical dimensions to be assessed will lead to a more thorough coverage of the domain. Whether there will be time limits or not should be stated.

2. You should provide an exercise that gives students an opportunity to perform—either a simulation or an actual task. All individuals must be asked to perform the same task.

3. You should make an instrument such as a checklist, a rating scale, or something similar to list the relevant criteria in order to use in evaluating the performance. The same criteria should be used for each individual's performance. Performance tests are useful for measuring abilities and skills that cannot be measured by paper-and-pencil tests. However, they are time intensive and thus more expensive to administer and score.

Key terms in standardized tests
Characteristics of an individual item

Item facility

Item facility (IF) refers to easiness of an item. It is one of the most important characteristics of an item. To calculate item facility all correct responses should be divided by the total number of responses. An item facility should be between *0* to *1*. Too easy or too difficult items are not recommended since they do not provide useful information about the test-takers' knowledge. Item facility *below 0.37 is too difficult* and *more than 0.63 is too easy*.

$$IF = \frac{\Sigma C}{N} = \frac{\text{sum of the correct responses}}{\text{total number of responses}}$$

Item discrimination

Item discrimination (ID) refers to the extent to which an item discriminates more knowledgeable examinees from less knowledgeable ones. It discriminates between weak and strong test-takers. There is a relationship between IF and ID. An item with too high or too low IF has less discrimination power. To calculate ID

- rank total scores from highest to lowest.
- divide test-takers into two equal groups.
- compute the ID through the following formula

$$ID = \frac{CH - CL}{1/2N}$$

CH: test-takers' number of correct answers to a particular item in the high group
CL: test-takers' number of correct answers to a particular item in the low group
N: total number of answers

Choice distribution

Choice distribution refers to the effectiveness of the frequency of the choices. If from 20 items in a multiple-choice test, as an example, 18 test-takers choose the correct answer which is item B, nobody chooses item A, nobody chooses item C, and 2 test-takers choose item D, the distractors should be modified because they are distributed poorly.

Reliability

A reliable test yields similar results if it is given to the same students or matched students on two different occasions. It is the quality of test scores. It deals with true score that is due to an individual's level of ability not error score that is due to other factors. It is possible to measure the reliability of a test through **reliability coefficient** which makes it possible to compare the reliability of different tests. The test **reliability** coefficient can be found between one to zero.

There are some key terms in statistics, which involve collecting numerical information, analyzing information, and making meaningful decisions based on the results of the analyses. These definitions are used in testing and should be learned before estimating reliability as well. As a student, you may like to know how you and the others performed on a test. The measures of the following terms will help gain useful information before measuring reliability.

1. **The mode** refers to the most frequent score in a set of scores.
2. **The median** (MD) refers to the score that divides the set of scores into equal parts.
3. **The mean** ($\bar{x}$) refers to the average of the scores.
   a. $\bar{x} = \dfrac{\Sigma X}{N} = \bar{x} = \dfrac{sum\ of\ scores}{number\ of\ scores}$
4. **Range** refers to the difference between the largest number in a set of scores and the smallest one.
5. **Variance** refers to the extent the scores differ from the mean. It can be calculated through the use of the following formula:
$$V = \frac{\Sigma(X - \bar{x})^2}{N - 1}$$

1. **Standard deviation** refers to the square of the variance. The root of the whole formula for variance is the SD.

$$S = \frac{\sqrt{\Sigma(X - \bar{x})^2}}{N - 1}$$

Reliability estimation

Reliability can be considered as the consistency of scores made by a given test. The degree of the error measurement can cause unreliability. There are different methods to estimate reliability:

- **Test-retest method** is giving a group of test-takers the same test twice. The gap between two administrations should not be too long or too soon. Therefore, around two weeks can be acceptable.
- **Alternative forms method** is using two different forms of the same test to a group of test-takers just one time.
- **Split half method** is splitting or dividing a homogeneous test into two equal halves given to a group of test-takers once.
- **KR-21 method** is the easiest way to estimate reliability.

$$(KR\text{-}21) \ r = \frac{K}{K-1} \cdot \frac{\bar{X}(K-\bar{X})}{KV}$$

K = the number of the items in a test
x̄ = the mean score
V = the variance

Factors contributing to reliability

- **Reliability related to learners:** Learners' anxiety, fatigue, and illness and other physical, psychological issues may cause error scores that are deviant from true scores.
- **Reliability related to raters:** Lacking scoring criteria and inexperienced raters may cause subjectivity and bias to enter into the scoring process.
- **Reliability related to test administration:** Poor conditions of desks, photocopying variations, and the amount of light cause unreliability.
- **Reliability related to test construction:** Too long or too short tests cause unreliability. Subjective tests such as speaking assessment or writing composition have less reliability than a well-organized multiple-choice test. A test with 75 items can be acceptable to have satisfactory reliability.

Validity

A valid test measures exactly what it proposes to measure without irrelevant variables. It offers useful, meaningful information about test-takers' ability. It must be supported by a theoretical rationale. There are different kinds of validity:

- **Content validity:** A test has content validity if its content makes a representative sample of the language skills, structures, etc.
- **Criterion-related validity:** It relates to the extent to which test results agree with those received by some independent and extremely dependable assessment of the learner' ability.
- **Construct validity:** It refers to the underlying ability which is hypothesized in a theory of language ability.

- **Face validity:** A test has face validity if it shows what it is supposed to measure.
- **Consequential validity:** This kind of validity can be emerged from concerns related to societal aspects of assessments. It measures the degree to which all the accumulated evidence supports the interpretation of test scores for the proposed purpose. For example: High-stakes testing may negatively affect present and future educational program.

Relationship between reliability and validity

If a test is valid, it must be reliable. If students receive very different scores on a test every time they take it, the test is not likely to predict anything. However, if a test is reliable, that does **not** mean that it is valid. Reliability is a necessary, but not sufficient, condition for validity.

Projective personality assessment

A projective test is a personality test made to allow a person to respond to ambiguous stimuli. It reveals hidden emotion and internal conflicts. It can be contrasted with a so-called "objective test" in which responses are analyzed based on a universal standard (for example, a true-false exam). The responses to projective tests are content analyzed for meaning rather than being according to presuppositions about meaning, as is the case with objective tests. Projective tests have their origins in psychoanalytic psychology, which claims that humans have conscious and unconscious attitudes and motivations that are beyond or hidden from conscious awareness.

Scales

They are used to measure attitudes, opinions, and other characteristics that cannot be easily measured by tests or other measuring instruments. They are a set of categories or numeric values given to individuals, objects, or behaviors to measure variables. Scales are different from tests in that the results of these instruments, unlike those of tests, do not represent success or failure, strength or weakness. They measure the degree to which an individual shows the characteristic of interest. For example, a researcher may use a scale to measure the attitude of college students toward feedback or any other topic.

Attitude scales

They use multiple responses, usually responses to statements, and combine the responses into a single scale score. An attitude may be explained as a positive or negative affect toward a special group, concept, or social object. The measurement of attitudes evaluates the ability to locate individuals along a continuum of favorableness–unfavorableness toward the object. If researchers cannot place an existing attitude scale on their topic of interest, they must make their own scales for measuring attitudes.

Likert scales: Method of summated ratings

It measures attitudes toward a topic by providing a set of statements about the topic and asking individuals to indicate for each whether they strongly agree, agree are undecided, disagree, or strongly disagree. The different agree– disagree responses have a numeric value, and the total scale score is made by summing the numeric responses given to each item. This total score measures the individual's attitude toward the topic.

For pilot testing all the statements with five response categories put on an agreement–disagreement continuum, are given to a group of subjects. This group should be chosen from a population that is similar to the one in which the scale will be used. The statements should be ordered randomly to avoid any response set on the part of the subjects. The subjects are asked to select the response category that best represents their reaction to each statement: *strongly agree* (SA), *agree* (A), *undecided* (U), *disagree* (D), or *strongly disagree* (SD). Most experts in the field recommend that the researcher can put a neutral or undecided choice because some respondents actually feel that way and do not want to be forced into agreeing or disagreeing.

Express your feelings about what you did in the interview by honestly choosing the best choice that describes your feelings. Thank you for your time.

	Sentence	1	2	3	4	5
		Strongly disagree	Disagree	Undecided (Uncertain)	Agree	Strongly agree
1						
2						
3						

A Likert Scale Template Sample

	Sentence	1	2	3	4	5
		Strongly Agree(5)	Disagree	Uncertain (Undecided)	Agree	Strongly agree
1	Picture description is an interesting activity.					
2	The activity is not up to my level.					
3	The activity is easy.					
4	The activity is short.					
5	I feel it is my teacher's duty to correct my errors					

	all the time.				
6	I feel frustrated when the teacher corrects me.				
7	I feel discouraged when I repeat the same errors.				
8	I feel nervous about speaking after the teacher has corrected my errors.				
9	I feel better when the teacher gives me the rules.				
10	I feel it is better for me to know the corrections of my errors.				
11	I feel that I am not used to being corrected when I do grammatical mistakes.				
12	I feel that this way of correction is new for me.				
13	I am benefitting from my teacher's corrections.				
14	Having my errors corrected is the best way to learn English.				
15	I feel most comfortable with my teacher's direct corrections.				
16	The corrections my teacher has been providing are not important.				
17	I think the most helpful way is correcting my errors directly.				
18	I prefer providing me with rules and information.				
19	I need a lot of time to think about my mistakes.				
20	I need to finish the activities fast so I can attend my other classes.				
21	What you are doing does not improve my English.				

A Likert Scale Sample

Scoring Likert scales

For favorable or positively stated items, you can use the following choices:

- **Strongly agree** is scored 5
- **Agree** is scored 4
- **Undecided** is scored 3
- **Disagree** is scored 2
- **Strongly disagree** is scored 1

For unfavorable or negatively stated items, you can use the following choices:

- **Strongly agree** is scored 1.
- **Strongly disagree** is scored 5.

The score values should not appear on the attitude scale given to respondents. The sum of the weights of all the items checked by the respondent is the individual's total score. The highest possible scale score means $5 \times N$ (the number of items); the lowest possible score means $1 \times N$. Then, divide the total score by the number of items to arrive at a mean attitude score.

Note: In order to make an appropriate attitude scale, the researcher should consider validity and reliability.

Bipolar adjective scales

They show a list of adjectives that have bipolar or opposite meanings. Respondents are asked to put a check mark at one of the seven points in the scale between the two opposite adjectives to represent the degree to which the adjective presents their attitude toward an object, group, or concept.

The weights on each item would then be summed and averaged. This kind of scale is a very flexible approach to measuring attitudes. A researcher can use it to examine attitudes toward any concept, person, or activity in any situation. It is easier and less time-consuming to make than a Likert(/ˈlɪkərt/) scale. Instead of having approximately 20 statements, you need only choose four to eight adjective pairs. It needs very little reading time by participants. The main hardship is the choice of the adjectives to use.

Good	1_ 2_ 3_ 0_3 _2 _ 1_ ✓ Bad
Fast	1_ 2_ ✓ 3_ 0_ 3_ 2_ 1_ Slow

A Bipolar Scale Sample

Rating scales

They show a number of statements about a behavior, an activity, or a concept with a scale of categories. Respondents are asked to show their evaluation or judgment about the behavior or activity on the rating scale. A numeric value may be attached to the categories so that an overall score could be obtained. One of the most widely used rating scales is the **graphic scale,** in which the respondent shows the rating by putting a check at the appropriate point on a horizontal line that goes from one extreme of the behavior in question to the other one.

	Low	Medium	High
Personal appearance	---		
Social acceptability	---		
Speaking skills	---		

A Graphic Scale Sample (Leadership of a Student)

Category scales

They have a number of categories that are made in an ordered series. Five to seven categories are most frequently used. The rater chooses the one that best shows the behavior of the person being rated.

> How creative is this person? (check one)
> Exceptionally creative ----------------------
> Very creative ----------------------------------
> Not creative ------------------------------------
> Not at all creative ----------------------------

A Category Scale Sample (A Teacher's Creativity)

Comparative rating scales

In the graphic and category scales, raters make their judgments without directly comparing the person being rated to other individuals or groups. In **comparative rating scales** raters are instructed to make their judgment with direct reference to the positions of others with whom the individual might be compared. The positions on the rating scale are defined based on a given population with known characteristics.

Area of Competency (to be rated)	Unusually low	Poorer than most students	About average among students	Better than most	Really superior	Not able to judge
1. Does this person show evidence of clear-cut and worthy professional goals?						
2. Does this person attack problems in a constructive manner?						
3. Does he or she take well-meant criticism and use it constructively?						

A Comparative Rating Scale Sample

Inventories

They are tools to obtain information on one or more aspects of an individual's behavior rather than to measure those aspects. Through inventories, the researcher tries to evaluate some aspects of an individual's behavior to describe the individual's likes and dislikes toward a particular phenomenon.

As shown in Table 4.1. data collection techniques and tools are different. Data can be collected through observation, interview, and questionnaires.

Table 4.1. *Data Collection Techniques and Tools*

Data collection Techniques	Data collection tools
Available information	Preparing checklist and forms
Observation	Eyes and senses, pen or paper, Scales, watch, microscope, etc.
Interview	Interview criteria, checklist, question tape recorder, laptop, tablet
Written questionnaire	Questionnaire

Focus group discussion

A focus group discussion lets a group of 8-12 informants freely discuss a certain subject with the guidance of a facilitator or reporter. Based on the type of the research your data collection may vary, if your study is experimental then you may collect your data by observing language learners' performance or you interview the language learners or running a test. Your study may be descriptive in nature, so you're focusing on text and the descriptive characteristics of texts. so you have to access to the type of texts which you wish to work on and you describe them whatever instrument you use, it should be the most practical instrument.

Two important issues in relation to data collection:

1- Sampling
2- Ethics

Sampling

Whether you are collecting your data qualitatively or quantitatively, it is important to define from whom the data should be collected, to what extent, and who should participate in the study.

Some researchers often face an extremely large number of subjects from whom collecting the data became quite difficult. So, in order to simplify the process of data collection **population** certain steps should be taken. The units that constitute the population can be people, objects or events. Population should not be large.

You can't have all **universe or population** in your study. You have to make a selection. And your selection is sometimes **systematic** and sometimes **nonsystematic**. This limited number of subjects or cases is called a **sample**. Since selecting a sample plays a crucial role in data collection and data analysis, different types of samples are established to meet the representative criterion. **The representativeness criterion** requires the true sample reflection of the characteristics of the population. If your sampling is not representative, the results of the study are not generalizable to other potential population which could be included in your study. The sample should have all those features that the population may have.

We do sampling because of providing accessibility, economy, and simplification in research.

Types of samples
Non-probability (non-random) samples

These samples focus on volunteers, **easily available units**, or those that just happen to be present when the research is done. Non-probability samples are useful for quick and cheap studies, for case studies, for qualitative research, for pilot studies, and for developing hypotheses for future research.

Convenience sampling: Also called an **"accidental sampling"**, **"man-in-the-street sampling"**, and **"availability sampling"**. The researcher selects units that are convenient, close at hand, easy to reach, etc. In convenience sampling, the researcher can choose whoever is available and willing to participate in the study. Sometimes it is not possible to do systematic sampling because you don't have access to all the population. This method of sampling might not be as valid as purposive sampling. But on the other hand, there is no other way. You only have to select your sample in that way. Many descriptive studies are conducted through availability and data are collected through availability like studies on genre analysis. This method of selection is non-random sampling on the basis of the notion of accessibility or availability. This is also called nonrandom judgment sampling.

Purposive sampling: The researcher selects the units with some purpose in mind, for example, students who live in dorms to find a certain type of members with predetermined characteristics. Sometimes you are going to limit your sample to only one. So you may wish to choose only one language learner, among all language learners there is a purpose because you are going to do some *case study*. In purposive sampling, the member is very limited, but in availability you don't have access to all population because the number is very large. In experimental studies they say that the limit is *30*. Less than 30 would be unreliable. If you have chosen your participants systematically not non-systematically, experiments have shown that 30 would be the magic number. Of course, it is clear that the greater the number, the more valid the results would be. But if you are doing a surrey research, which you gather your data through questionnaires more than 30 is needed.

Quota sampling: This kind of sampling is considered as the nonprobability equivalent of stratified sampling. The researcher constructs quotas for different types of units. For example, to interview a fixed number of students, half of whom are girls and half of whom are boys. This is different from stratified sampling, where the quota is determined by random sampling. Other samples that are usually constructed with non-probability methods include library research, participant observation, marketing research, consulting with experts, and comparing organizations, nations, or governments.

Snowball sampling: It is a special nonprobability method used when the desired sample characteristic is scarce. It may be too difficult or expensive to locate respondents in these situations. With this approach, you initially contact a few potential respondents and then ask them whether they know of anybody with the same characteristics that you are looking for in your research.

Self-selection: As the name talks, self-selection is self-explanatory. Participants themselves show their willingness to take part in the survey.

Probability-based (random) samples

These samples are based on probability theory. Every unit of the desired population must be identified, and all units must have a known, **non-zero chance** of being included in the sample.

Simple random sampling: The selection of each unit is independent of the selection of every other unit. Selection of one unit does not affect the chances of any other unit. For example, to select a sample of 35 students who live in your college dorm, make a list of all the 350 people who live in the dorm. Give each person a unique number, between 1 and 350. Then refer to a table of random numbers to pull the names from the list that correspond to the 35 numbers you found. These 35 people are your sample. This is also called the **table of random numbers method**. Another way to select this simple random sample is to take 350 small balls and number them from 1 to 350. Put them into a large box and mix them up, and then take 35 balls. Those are the 35 people in your sample. This can be called the lottery method.

Systematic random sampling: This method is useful for selecting **large samples** (one hundred or more). It is less inconvenient than a simple random sample. For example, if a random sample from the population of a school is to be selected putting all the names in a hat would not be practical. In such cases, a list provided by the registrar's office would probably be useful. The researcher, then, can select every 5th, 10th, or 15th student on the list. This type of selection where the researcher selects every nth subject is called systematic random sampling. In systematic sampling, the first sample is random. There is no reason why you choose every 5th or every 10th, but the rest of the sampling is reliable because you systematically select your sample and every member of the population has the chance to be included in the sample. However, you must consider the problems that emerge from systematic random sampling. If the selection interval matches some pattern in the list (e.g., each 5th dorm room is a single unit, where all the others are doubles) you will introduce systematic bias into your sample. This kind of sampling is used with large population; however, the process might be time consuming. Decision on the members of the sample is quite systematic, reliable, and objective.

Stratified (Proportional) random sampling: This kind of sampling is used when the researcher knows that the population has sub-groups (strata) that are of interest. To make sure that you get some students from each group, you can divide the students into groups, and then select the same percentage of students from each group using a simple random sampling method. Stratified sampling is advantageous over simple random sampling in that it takes the proportion of the subject in the population into account and leads to a more representative sample than simple random sampling does. For example, if the researcher wants to be sure that a sample of 8 students from a group of 60 contains both bilingual and monolingual students in the same proportions as in the full population i.e. the group of 60; he/she should divide the population into bilingual and monolingual students. In this case, there are 21 bilingual students and 330 monolingual students. To work out the number of bilingual and monolingual students in the sample,
No. of bilingual in sample = $(8 / 60) \times 21 = 2.7$
No. of monolingual in sample = $(8 / 60) \times 33 = 4.3$
The researcher cannot interview .7 and .3 of a person, so he/she has to "round" the numbers. Therefore the researcher selects **three** bilingual and **five** monolingual students.

Cluster sampling: It is a sampling technique where the whole population is divided into groups, or clusters and a random sample of these clusters is selected. Cluster sampling is typically used when the researcher cannot get a complete list of the members of a population they wish to study but can get a complete list of groups or "clusters" of the population. It is also used when a random sample would produce a list of subjects so widely scattered that surveying them would prove to be far too expensive. For example, to obtain information about the fast reading habits of all high school students in a major city, you could obtain a list of all the school districts in the city and select a simple random sample of school districts. Then, within each selected school district, list all the high schools and select a simple random sample of high schools. Within each selected high school, list all high school classes, and select a simple random sample of classes. Then, use the high school students in those classes as your sample. This sampling technique may well be more practical and/or economical than simple random sampling or stratified sampling. The differences between probability and non-probability are shown in Table 4.2.

Table 4.2. The *Differences Between Probability (Random) Sampling and Non-Probability (Non-Random) Sampling*

Probability (Random) Sampling	Non-Probability (Non-Random) Sampling
uses statistics, and tests hypotheses.	uses exploratory research and generates hypotheses.
estimates population parameters.	need not cover population parameters.
eliminates bias.	doses not indicate the adequacy of the sample.
has random selection of units.	is cheaper, easier, and quicker to conduct.

Sample size

Sample size depends on the type of research method being used (qualitative or quantitative), the desired level of confidence in the results, the amount of accuracy wanted, and the characteristics of the population of interest. Qualitative research is a highly subjective research to gain an understanding of the subjects' feelings, impressions and viewpoints. Gaining such insight is best acquired through the use of smaller, highly targeted samples. Quantitative research will often provide data that's projectable to a larger population because it is so deeply rooted in numbers and statistics.

When researchers ask the question, "How large should the sample be?" they really mean "How small a sample can I get away with?" As a general answer, researchers believe that the larger the sample size, the better representative it would be. Unfortunately, there is no hard and fast rule in making the best sample size. The final answer depends on considering several broad guidelines (Dörnyei, 2011):

A thumbnail: Sample size in the *survey research* literature can range from *one percent to ten percent* of the population, with a minimum of about 100 participants. The more scientific the sampling procedures, the smaller the sample size can be which is why opinion polls can make exact predictions from samples as small as *0.1 percent* of the population. The estimated sample sizes for specific quantitative *correlation research at least 30 participants; comparative and experimental procedures at least 15 have been agreed on by several scholars.*

Statistical consideration: The major requirement in quantitative research is that the sample should include a normal distribution (Hatch and Lazaretto, 1991). In order to do sampling 30 or more people should be included. However, Hatch and Lazaretto also emphasize that smaller sample sizes can be made up for by using special statistical procedures.

Sample composition: If there are any distinct subgroups within the sample that may be expected to behave differently from the others should be identified in advance. For example, in most L2 settings girls have been found to perform differently from boys, we should make the sample size so that the minimum size belongs to the smallest subgroup in the sample.

Safety margin: When you set the final sample size, it is suggested that you leave a decent margin to provide for unforeseen circumstances. For example, some participants may drop out of at least some phases of the project; some questionnaires may be disqualified for one reason or another; and we may also anticipate unexpected subgroups that need to be treated separately.

Reverse approach: Since statistical importance depends on the sample size, our main concern should be to sample enough learners for the expected outcomes to be capable of reaching statistical significance. The researchers can take a reverse approach.
- They approximate the expected magnitude of the expected results.
- Then, they determine the sample size that is necessary to anticipate this effect if it actually exists in the population.

For example, at a $p < .05$ significance level an expected correlation of .40 requires at least 25 participants (refer to chapter seven). These figures can be looked up in correlation tables available in most statistical texts.

General rules for determining sample size
- For populations under 1,000, sample 30%.
- For populations around 10,000 sample 10%.
- For populations over 100,000, sample 1.5%.
- For populations over 1,000,000, sample .2%.
- For populations over 10,000,000 sample .025%.

Large populations require smaller sampling ratios, not smaller samples. Samples of 2500 have been shown to be adequate for even the largest of populations.

Ethics
Ethics refers to the reservation that should be observed by researcher during the data collection. It means these participants as the subjects of the study are human beings and they have their very own rights that you cannot overlook. They have different personalities; they have different attitudes towards language learning. They have different beliefs and you cannot judge or blame them because of their beliefs.

They may be of different sexes (males or females), different nationality or cultural background. You cannot show bias because you're a male or female. They should not be downgraded because of their answers. They might not provide the answer that the researcher expects. Still the researcher has to be satisfied with the answers.

These are some ethical rights which should be considered in any study. For example, the researcher should not reveal their names.

1. **Considering the right of remaining anonymous.** Participants have the right to remain anonymous and the researcher should not reveal their identities if they desire so. So you codify these people, give them codes, each person is characterized by a number, or you can give them some false names.

2. **Considering the right to privacy.** Sometimes the nature of research involves asking certain questions from the respondents which address their private lives such as questions about marriage, divorce, and personal relations. In such cases, the respondents should be given complete freedom not to answer the question if they do not desire so. We should not disclose their private matters.

3. **Considering the right to confidentiality.** Some respondents don't want the information they provide to be publicized. They have the right to ask the researcher to keep the information quite confidential. In such cases, the researcher is not allowed to show curiosity to find out the reason for such an attitude.

Needless to say, Names are not important in our studies, what is important is the behavior of these particular samples in a study. If you want to address individuals in your study, you have to address them with codes.

Data analysis

After collecting data (e.g. student's composition) you have to analyze these data. If you want to analyze student's composition subjectively, the second researcher might rate this composition differently, making different results. This is not because of the differences in language learners but because of the different ways of scoring the composition. As a researcher, you have to show that the method which they use to analyze the data is consistent.

The selection of instruments is so important that it might affect the whole data analysis and discussion. By the end of the procedures, the researcher has to describe his/her method of analysis.

In order to analyze data, researchers should consult a statistician to get practical advice. In data analysis, the number and kind of variables are very important. Researchers should familiarize with pragmatic and non-pragmatic tests.

Two kinds of data in our data analysis

1. **Measurement (parametric) data:** Your measurement data are usually **quantifiable** like scores you obtain on a test.

2. **Categorical (non-parametric) data:** For example, the number of hedging devices in articles or the frequency of free direct and free indirect reported speech in articles. Here, we talk about "frequency"/ "noun

count", etc.

In quantitative measurement, we usually have a number of parameters. These parameters (variables) have been controlled. You have controlled some of the variables in relation to a parameter and at the same time you are manipulating one or more variables in relation to that parameter. So, this type of data is called parametric data.

This is important to determine the type of data we are going to work through. If you're working through categorical data then the statistics which you should employ is related to frequency counting. If you're going to work on the data which is quantifiable or parametric you have to go through other statistics.

Choosing the right statistic is very difficult because there are three very important sources on deciding what statistic we should use:

1. **Size of the sample** that it is very large or not.
2. **Scales** that are involved in the study.
3. **Type of questions**
- **Correlational questions** that calculate co- relation.
- **Mean** and **standard deviation** that indicate the differences and similarities needed to be calculated.

Statistical data analysis

1. **Parametric statistical procedures** rely on assumptions about the shape of the distribution (i.e., assume a normal distribution) in the underlying population and about the form or parameters (i.e., means and standard deviations) of the assumed distribution.
2. **Non-parametric statistical procedures** rely on no or few assumptions about the shape or parameters of the population distribution from which the sample was drawn.

How would you analyze your data?

What kind of statistical measures would you employ for your study? Why did you run ANOVA or T- test?

You should have a reason for running these statistics measures. In doing your study, sometimes you encounter some problems. Sometimes there are **predetermined problems** and sometimes there are **problems that would be manifested during studies**. If you have predicted your problems then you have to describe problems that you anticipated and minimize their effects. You have to show that those problems did not have significant impact on your study. But if you encountered problems in course of doing your study, you have to mention these problems and the strategies you used to minimize the impact of the problems you encountered. For instance, sometimes there would be a problem and you modify this problem by conducting the study. This has to be included again in the procedure section of methodology.

Cronbach's alpha (coefficient alpha)

It is the most common form of reliability coefficient. By convention, alpha should be .70 or higher to retain an item in a scale. Cronbach's alpha is used when measures have items that are not scored simply as right or wrong, such as attitude scales or essay tests (Ary et al., 2010).

$$\alpha = \frac{k}{k-12a} \left(1 - \frac{\sum S^2 i}{S^2 x}\right)$$

K $\quad$ = the number of items on the test
$\sum S^2 i$ = the sum of the variances of the different parts of the test
$S^2 x$ $\quad$ = the variance of the test scores

t-test

t-test is a quantitative procedure to determine the statistical significance difference between means of two sets of scores. It helps to answer the following questions:

- Do the two groups come from the same population?
- Do the two groups only appear different because of chance errors?
- Is there some significant difference between these two groups that show that they are really from two completely different populations?

There are some basic factors to determine the difference between two groups is a true difference or just an error due to chance:

- When the sample is large, it is less likely that the difference is because of sampling errors or chance.
- If the difference between the two means is large, it is less likely that the difference is because of sampling errors.
- If the variance among the participants is small, it is less likely that the difference was created in sampling errors.

The difference between two types of "t-test" depends on your groups or samples. If your two groups are independent and not related in any way, you select the **independent samples t-test**. For example, if you used a random sampling technique to select 25 girls and 25 boys into your study, and these 50 children are not related in any way, you would use independent samples. If you selected 25 boys and then asked their 25 sisters to be in the study, those samples are related, so you would use the **dependent samples test.**

Different types of t-test

- **Independent groups t-test** is the one you use when you want to compare two independent groups of participants on a certain variable which is measured only once.
- **Repeated measures t-test** is also called **matched t-test** or **paired t-test**. It is used when the same participants are being tested on two

occasions (so your dependent variable is measured twice) and you want to know whether the scores on the two occasions were different.

If you have two groups and you are interested in showing the differences of these two groups as a particular variable, then *t*-test would tell you whether there are differences or not, whether your instruction has been effective or not.

If you have a number of pretest scores from the students and the post-test scores, you might be interested in the student's performance in one group. You like to see whether students have made any improvement after the treatment. So you want to compare the students' scores on the pretest with their performance on the post-test.

Matched *t*-tests are set to be a horizontal relation. So, you have two matched *t*-tests, one for your control and one for experimental group. You might as well be interested in group differences, inter-group differences rather than intra-group differences. So, you compare the students' performance on the final test to see if the treatment on this group and treatment on that group would make any difference. In this case *t*- test would be appropriate. So, you calculate *t*-test and you have a particular score. For example, a teacher wants to know whether feedback affects students' speaking performance. Computation of the t-value is shown in Table 4. 3. The first step is assigning the students in a course randomly to two groups. Because of assigning the members of two groups randomly, the mean performances of the two groups in speaking ability should not significantly differ prior to the treatment. After the treatment the mean performances of the two groups should differ significantly if feedback is actually related to speaking performance. The following table represents post-treatment speaking scores (X), deviation scores (x), and squared deviation scores (X^2) of the members of the two groups, one of which worked under feedback conditions and the other under non-feedback conditions. The mean performance score of the students in the non-feedback group is 10 and mean performance score of feedback group is 14.

■ **Table 4.3.** *Computation of the t-Value for Two Sample Means*

Group one Feedback condition			Group two non-feedback condition		
X1	X1	$X^2 1$	X2	X2	$X^2 2$
18	+4	16	13	+3	9
17	+3	9	12	+2	4
16	+2	4	12	+1	4

16	+2	4	11	+1	1
16	+2	4	11	+1	1
15	+1	1	11	+1	1
15	+1	1	10	0	0
15	+1	1	10	0	0
14	0	0	10	0	0
14	0	0	10	0	0
13	-1	1	9	-1	1
12	-2	4	9	-1	1
11	-3	9	8	-2	4
10	-4	16	7	-3	9
8	-6	36	7	-3	9

$$\frac{\sum X1}{n1} = \frac{210}{15} \qquad X^21 = 106 \qquad \frac{\sum X2}{n2} = \frac{150}{15} \qquad X^22 = 44$$
$$\bar{x}1 = 14 \qquad\qquad\qquad\qquad \bar{x}2 = 10$$

Obviously, there is a difference. You now need to show whether this difference is because of chance. To do this you should estimate the amount of difference between two groups would be anticipated through chance alone under a true "Null hypothesis". You can calculate the standard error of the difference between two means (S $\bar{x}1$- $\bar{x}2$).

$$S\ \bar{x}1\text{-}\ \bar{x}2 = \sqrt{\frac{\sum X^21 + \sum X^22}{n1 + n2 - 2} \left(\frac{1}{n1} + \frac{1}{n2}\right)}$$

S $\bar{x}1$- $\bar{x}2$ = the standard error of the difference between two groups
$\sum X^21$ = the sum of squared deviation scores in group one
$\sum X^22$ = the sum of squared deviation scores in group two
n1   = the number of students in group one
n2   = the number of students in group one
Error term for the *t*-test is the standard error of the difference between two means.

$$S\ \bar{x}1\text{-}\ \bar{x}2 = \sqrt{\frac{106 + 44}{15 + 15 - 2} \left(\frac{1}{15} + \frac{1}{15}\right)} = \sqrt{\frac{150}{28} \left(\frac{2}{15}\right)} = \sqrt{0.714} = 0.84$$

The value 0.84 is the expected difference between the mean speaking scores for the two, randomly drawn from the population, groups and was not because of different treatments. Here we expect an average difference of 0.84 through chance under a null hypothesis.

How is that score defined? This score is called **t-score** or **observed score** (t_o: t- observed). How would you indicate that this t_o is significant or not significant? (There is a table of T- scores at the back of all statistics books). There is a list of scores there. These scores are called **critical scores** or **critical t (t_c)**. By critical t, we mean those scores in the table for critical t.

You have some horizontal rows. You have to set your level of significance for **one- tailed test** or for **two-tailed test** (see chapter seven).

If you set your level of significance for one tailed test you've got to check a particular column, if you set it for two-tailed tests, then you have to go for other columns to check. But what is the level of significance? Level of significance has to do with **degree of freedom (df)**.

With Degree of freedom we have a sample of language learners and we have divided this sample into two (groups G1 and G2 representing a population of language learners). How do I know that my sample would be representative of my population? It may be claimed that you have chosen them systematically, but this is not enough. Statisticians in this case would talk about particular criteria called *degree of freedom*. DF is calculated in this way.

$$DF = (N_E - 1) + (N_c - 1), E = \text{experimental and } C = \text{control group.}$$

Then, the results could be considered as they represent the population. DF in the table is shown on the left side of table, it begins with one and it's infinite. *As df gets smaller, tc increases and as a gets smaller, tc increases. There is an inverse relationship between df and tc.*

Probability level (α decision)

You have obtained the t-score. How could you make sure that t-score is a reliable score? because there is always at least a great deal of possibility that you would make mistakes; especially, in humanities you cannot claim that the probability of making mistakes is zero, that I am making mistakes because we're dealing with human being we are not dealing with stones.

$\alpha = .01$ means 99% there is the probability that the results that I have obtained are true and its just 1% of the probability that my result are at fault. In applied linguistics we set this probability level either at .01 or .05 indicating that there is the probability of up to 1% or 5% that the result might be false and we show it this way.

[$\alpha \leq .01 \leq .05$]

We have to leave some space for mistakes which might be made. Levels of significance or probability levels appear on two rows, one-tailed test or two- tailed test, and we usually set or level of significance for two tailed test because the relationship is non-directional. You do not know whether your treatment would be effective or not? There is always the probability that control group might perform better, and then α decision level is set to .01 or. 05.

That's when you have two groups. When you have more than two groups, for example three groups, two groups have received a particular instruction and one group has received no instruction: (control group).

G1 →T1 (task1)
G2 →T2 (task 2)

G3 —→(control)

By the end of the term, you have calculated the students' performance through a proficiency test and you wish to compare the scores of the students. So, you calculate the mean as well as the SD and there are some noticeable differences between the means. But this superficial observation is not enough.

ANOVA (Analysis of Variance)

An **ANOVA** can be called an **F test**. It is related to the *t*-test. The main difference is that the *t*- **test** measures the difference between the **means** of two groups, but an ANOVA tests the difference between the means of **three or more groups**. A one-way ANOVA (single factor ANOVA) tests differences between groups that are only classified on one independent variable. You can also use multiple independent variables and test for interactions using factorial ANOVA. *The advantage of using ANOVA rather than multiple t-tests is that it reduces the probability of a type-I error. Making multiple comparisons increases the likelihood of finding something by chance.* One potential drawback to an ANOVA is that you lose specificity. All an **F- test** tells you is that there is a significant difference between groups, not which groups are significantly different from each other. To test for this, you use a **post-hoc comparison** to find out where the differences are, which groups are significantly different from each other, and which are not. Some commonly used **post-hoc comparisons** are **Scheffe's** and **Tukey's**. If you have two variables you have to use two-way ANOVA, if you have three variable then you use three- way ANOVA and if you have four variables you have to use four -way ANOVA so depending on the number of variables we calculate N-way -ANOVA.

ANOVA would do the same way as *t*- test. So, you get your scores and you should go to the table for calculation; we do not have a table for ANOVA. We have to use f- ratio (F-score). You will check it in F- score and you would see that it's significant, but there is a problem and the problem is that here you have three groups and two groups have received treatment you do not know whether the difference has to do with your first group or second group or third group. In case of two groups it would be easy but here it's difficult.

ANOVA just tells whether the differences are significant or not. It would not tell us where the differences lie. So, in order to find out if the difference lies in G1 or G2 you've got to go through other tests like Duncans, tuckey or scheffe'.

It's very important to indicate your dependent as well as independent variables, because until you don't exactly know what the independent variable and what dependent variable is, you cannot apply right statistics.

Correlation coefficient

The quantity r, called the *linear correlation coefficient*, measures the strength rather than the direction of a linear relationship between two variables. The linear correlation coefficient is sometimes referred to as the *Pearson product moment coefficient* in honor of its developer Karl Pearson.

$$r = \frac{n\sum xy - \left(\sum x\right)\left(\sum y\right)}{\sqrt{n\left(\sum x^2\right) - \left(\sum x\right)^2}\sqrt{n\left(\sum y^2\right) - \left(\sum y\right)^2}}$$

n is the number of pairs of data.

The value r is such that $-1 \leq r \leq +1$. The + and − signs are used for positive linear correlations and negative linear correlations, respectively. If x and y have a strong positive linear correlation, r is close to +1. An r value of exactly +1 indicates a perfect positive fit. Positive values indicate a relationship between x and y variables such that as values for x increase, values for y also increase. If x and y have a strong negative linear correlation, r is close to -1. An r value of exactly -1 indicates a perfect negative fit. Negative values indicate a relationship between x and y such that as values for x increase, value for y decrease. If there is no linear correlation or a weak linear correlation, r is close to 0. A value near zero means that there is a random, nonlinear relationship between the two variables. r is a dimensionless quantity; that is, it does not depend on the units employed. A perfect correlation of $\pm$ 1 occurs only when the data points all lie exactly on a straight line. If r = +1, the slope of this line is positive. If r = -1, the slope of this line is negative. A correlation greater than 0.8 is generally described as *strong*, whereas a correlation less than 0.5 is generally described as *weak*. These values can vary based upon the "type" of data being examined. A study utilizing scientific data may require a strong correlation than a study using social science data.

Chi square

In relation to **categorical data**, the first thing is to go through frequencies/percentages. You calculate the frequency of accuracy of elements and compare the frequency of accuracy of this element with the frequency of accuracy of that element. **To compare the frequencies,** we use **chi square formula**.

The chi square (/kaI skwer/) is used to determine whether there is a relationship between two nominal variables. Nominal data cannot be averaged meaningfully because the numbers are meaningless by themselves. In return, they tell us the number of participants in each category. The chi square tests the hypothesis by essentially calculating whether the difference between the observed and expected frequencies in each category could have occurred because of chance sampling errors or because the treatment (or experimental condition) had an effect on the outcome.

For example: Suppose we have the data in Table 4.4 that display the number of students who elect different majors, and we want to know whether those numbers differ from chance. In other words, are some majors selected more often than others, or is the selection pattern essentially random?

■ **Table 4.4.** *Number of Students Selecting Different Majors*

Literature	Computer	Art	Music	History	Math
50	85	25	60	80	300

The null hypothesis here, of course, is that there is no difference between this distribution of major selections from what would be expected by chance. So what chi square does is compare these numbers (the observed frequencies) with those that would be expected by chance (the expected frequencies). The formula for chi square is:

$$X^2 = \sum \frac{(O-E)^2}{E}$$

Where:

X^2 is the value for chi square.

$\sum$ is the sum.

O is the observed frequency

E is the expected frequency.

The first question is, how do we get the expected frequencies? That's easy. If we are testing the observed frequencies against what we would expect by chance, since we have five categories of majors, we would expect one-fifth of the individuals to fall in each of the categories. One-fifth (20%) of 300 is 60. So, if the selection of majors is largely a chance pattern, we would expect to find 60 people in each category.

Table 4.5. displays the observed and expected frequencies for each major, computes the difference between them (O–E), squares O–E ((O–E)²), divides the squares by the expected frequencies ((O–E)²/E), and sums those quantities to give us our X^2, which is 39.17.

■ **Table 4.5.** *Observed and Expected Frequencies for Each Major*

Major	O(observed frequency)	E(expected frequency)	O–E	(O–E)²	(O–E)²/E
Literature	50	60	-10	100	1.67
Computer	85	60	25	625	10.42
Art	25	60	-35	12.25	20.42
Music	60	60	0	0	0.00
History	80	60	20	400	6.67
Math	300	300			39.17

Now you should determine if we can reject the null hypothesis. We do it the same way we did for the *t*-test and the correlation. We enter the chi square significance table (at the end of a statistics book) with our chi square value (39.17) and the appropriate degrees of freedom. For chi square, the degrees of freedom are equal to the number of rows minus one (R–1). In our case, we have five rows, so df = 4.

Entering the chi square table with our result of 39.17 and df = 4, we find that we need a chi square value of 13.28 to reject the null hypothesis at the .01 level of confidence. We clearly have that, so we can say that the distribution of major selections is not simply a chance pattern; or $X^2 = 39.7$ p <.01, df = 4.

Chi-square enables us to pass judgment concerning whether the differences between the frequencies are statistically significant.

MANOVA (Multivariate Analysis Of Variance)

IDV = 1   DV >1

It is a statistical test procedure for comparing multivariate means of several groups. When you want to compare means of more than two groups but here you have one independent variable and more than one dependent variable. MANOVA can be considered a valid alternative to the **repeated measures** ANOVA when sphericity is failed.

Pair wise comparison

It is used when you have one group, and more than one independent variable.

Kruskal-Wallis test

The Kruskal–Wallis one-way analysis of variance by ranks is a non-parametric method to test whether samples come from the same distribution. It is used to compare more than two samples that are independent, or not related.

Factor analysis

Factor analysis can be considered as a "data reduction" technique that decreases the number of variables studied to a more restricted number of underlying "factors." Factor analysis is based on a model that conveys that correlations between pairs of measured variables can be explained by the connections of the measured variables to a small number of non-measurable (latent), but meaningful variables, which are termed factors.

The aims of factor analysis are to:

- identify the number of factors
- define the factors as functions of the measured variables

- study the factors which have been defined

Multiple regression analysis

Regression analysis is a statistical process for estimating the relationships among variables. When correlation is used, one variable is not predicted from the other one. In the **linear regression** model, the **dependent variable** is assumed to be a linear function of one or more independent **variables** plus an error introduced to account for all other factors. Like other forms of regression analysis, **logistic regression** makes use of one or more predictor **variables** that may be either continuous or categorical data.

Triangulation

As the name implies, triangulation is a strategy that controls bias and helps to make valid conclusions because it uses *at least three* (thus, the "tri-" prefix) different types of methods or tools to collect data from which conclusions are drawn. Many researchers claim that triangulation strengthens a study by combining methods. It means using several kinds of methods or data, including using both *quantitative* and *qualitative* approaches. Through using at least three different methods, the researcher is about to obtain multiple, diverse perceptions of a single concept.

CHAPTER FIVE
Results, Discussion, Conclusion, and Implications

Results

In the *Results Section*, you should write what is not written in tables and stated in figures. Repeating the same thing which is there in the table is a common fault to make, because you are giving only redundant and unnecessary information. The results section must be comprehensible and it should indicate the trends. In this section, you should solve two problems as far as research is concerned:

1. **You have to document your result.**
2. **You have to use statistical measures.**

Depending on how you have defined your problem and how you have raised the question (whether your questions are cause-effect, or question of frequency types) you should select appropriate statistical measures for your analysis. Nowadays, researchers have the inclination for software programs like SPSS to do statistics to avoid degree of errors (See Chapter Six).

Applying statistics is one thing, documenting your research is another thing. The serious mistake that many inexperienced researchers make in the way of documenting the result is that they restate all those information which is stated in the table.

What is included in result section?

There are a number of moves (social functions that are served through language).

- **Justifying the methodology:** you should begin by giving the readers a kind of assurance concerning the methodology, the experiment that you selected to conduct your study and give them kind of assurance concerning statistics that you employ. This is very important to give readers certainty that whatever you have done is objective.

- **Interpreting the results:** say whatever is not said in figures. Make comparisons and contrasts instead of talking about those figures. But it's not enough, you should also talk about why this group acted better, why that group scored higher than this group, offer possible reasons or why this group acted like that.

- **Citing agreement with previous studies:** Here still you are making a comparison but the comparison is between your own study and the study of the past. You have to make references to the studies of others which have been done in line with your study, nationally as well as internationally and find out to what degree your work conforms to the results of those studies. So, if you have worked on task-based instruction, then you have to compare your study with those of TB study done recently, not studies done in 1980s. You have to rely on the recent studies (2000 onwards)

- **Evaluative commenting on the data:** once you have found agreement with the previous studies, now you have to make an evaluation of the scores that you have obtained.

- **Admitting difficulty in interpretation:** sometimes you come up with some data which are very difficult to interpret in the sense that you look at it from one way and it got one interpretation and you look at it another way and it can have a different interpretation. Sometimes your data is not expressive enough and it's vague; you have not come up with explicit results. Your result can be interpreted in multiple ways, in two ways, three ways, or more ways depending on how you look at it or you might find yourself at loss, because your data is not logical at all.

- **Discrepancies** can be defined as the differences between the results of your study and the studies of others. Sometimes what you have done in your study and what others have done in their studies is close. Despite this similarity of the context, your results are different. You have to interpret this. Sometimes you have made references to the same studies and now you see that your results are different; when you look deep into other studies, you see that the context was different from the study done on the other circumstances and you did not mentioned them. You have to mention that this discrepancy is because of this difference in context / or treatment or… (All of these are obligatory moves/ none of them is optional).

The results section in detail

The *Results* section should be structured around the Research Questions and/or Research. However, if you are writing a thesis, then the demographics of the participants might be included in an introductory section to Chapter Four.

Start the Results section by reviewing the purpose of the study. The purpose of the study was described clearly back in the Introduction. Since then, the reader has read the Literature Review and Methods sections, so it is quite probable that they have forgotten the purpose of the study. A brief refresher of the general purpose of the study is helpful.

The rest of the Results section will answer each Research Question and/or Research Hypothesis one by one, in the order that they were listed in Chapter One. See the guidelines below for presenting the results of the Research Questions and Research Hypotheses.

1. **Write the Research Question/Hypothesis.** It is important that the reader is reminded of the Research Question/Hypothesis before the statistics are described. The reader should not have to flip back to the introduction to understand what variables are being analyzed.

2. **Explain the statistics used to answer the Research Question/Hypothesis.** The appropriate statistic was already selected in Method of Data Analysis. Describe the rationale for selecting that particular statistic, and which variables were entered into the statistic.

3. **Explain the measurement of each variable.** Analyzing the data requires that each variable be translated into numbers or labels. However, how those numbers or labels were arrived at in the data analysis is often not apparent. Therefore, explain how each variable was translated into numbers or labels. If the variable is academic achievement and students completed an exam, explain how the final score for each student on the exam was calculated. If the variable is intrinsic motivation, explain that the scores on the five intrinsic motivation items on the questionnaire were averaged to get a total motivation score. If responses to an open-ended interview question were coded into themes, explain how the themes were determined and how the interview responses were coded. The reader should have a clear understanding of all of the numbers that will be presented in the statistics and how the numbers were calculated based on the data collected

4. **Present the statistics.** Most likely, the statistics will be presented in a Table or Figure.

5. **Interpret the statistics.** What are the key statistics that are important for answering the research question? If analyzing a Research Hypothesis, explain the finding: was the statistic significant? However, you cannot just say the finding was significant; it is vital to also explain the meaning of the significant result. If comparing different groups, which group had the highest mean score? If

examining the effect of one variable on the other, explain what that effect is. If a significant relationship is found, explain the nature of that significant relationship.

One of the most common errors in reporting the Results is a lack of clear reporting. Numbers are reported in a table, but it is unclear how the numbers were calculated based on the items from the questionnaire. The reader should know how each statistic was calculated based on the questionnaire items.

A second error is that the statistics are not thoroughly explained. Research hypotheses particularly need a detailed explanation to interpret the key findings. However, an opposite mistake is to repeat all statistics from the Table or Figure in the body of the text. Not all statistics from the table or figure need to be repeated; only those key statistics that are necessary for interpreting the key findings. If all of the statistics are reported in the body of the text, there would be no need for the Table or Figure.

Below are three sample reports of the results. Notice how all statistics are clearly explained. Each step presented above is noted by its number in the examples.

Discussion, Conclusion, and Implications

The second to last step in conducting a research study is to interpret the findings in the *Discussion* section, draw *Conclusions*, and make *Recommendations*. It is important that everything in this last section is based on the results of the data analysis. In an empirical research study, the conclusions and recommendations must be directly related to the data that was collected and analyzed. Simply put, look at the key topics in the conclusion and recommendations. If that topic was not precisely assessed by the questionnaire, then you cannot draw a conclusion or make a recommendation about that topic. A paper can only make valid conclusions and recommendations on those variables that the study has empirical data to support.

Discussion

In this section, you should interpret the results and draw inference. Open the discussion part by highlighting the research questions and original hypotheses. Clarify the similarities and differences between your results and the works of others. Show:

- What you have contributed to the bulk of research
- How the original problem has been solved.
- Finally, see what implication you can draw from your study.

The conclusion should have a variety of moves such as the following:

- A summary of the major findings of the study (like an abstract)
- A call for further research
- A statement of the limitations of the study
- Pedagogical implications
- A statement of overall significance of the topic addressed in the study.

Steps to writing an effective discussion section

The purpose of the Discussion is to state your interpretations and opinions, explain the implications of your findings, and make suggestions for future research. Its main function is to answer the questions posed in the Introduction, explain how the results support the answers and, how the answers fit in with existing knowledge on the topic. The Discussion is considered the heart of the paper and usually requires several writing attempts.

The organization of the Discussion is important. Before beginning you should try to develop an outline to organize your thoughts in a logical form. You can use a cluster map, an issue tree, numbering, or some other organizational structure. The steps listed below are intended to help you organize your thoughts.

To make your message clear, the discussion should be kept as short as possible while clearly and fully stating, supporting, explaining, and defending your answers and discussing other important and directly relevant issues. Care must be taken to provide a commentary and not a reiteration of the results. Side issues should not be included, as these tend to obscure the message. No paper is perfect; the key is to help the reader determine what can be positively learned and what is more speculative.

Organize the Discussion from the specific to the general: your findings to the literature, to theory, to practice.

- Use the same key terms, the same verb tense (present tense), and the same point of view that you used when posing the questions in the Introduction.
- Begin by re-stating the hypothesis you were testing and answer the questions posed in the introduction.

- Support the answers with the results. Explain how your results relate to expectations and to the literature, clearly state why they are acceptable and how they are consistent or fit in with previously published knowledge on the topic.
- Address all the results relating to the questions, regardless of whether or not the findings were statistically significant.
- Describe the patterns, principles, and relationships shown by each major Finding/Result and put them in perspective. The sequencing of providing this information is important; first state the answer, then the relevant results, then cite the work of others. If necessary, guide the reader to a figure or table to enhance the "story".
- Defend your answers, if necessary, by explaining both why your answer is satisfactory and why others are not. Only by giving both sides to the argument can you make your explanation convincing.
- Discuss and evaluate conflicting explanations of the results. This is the sign of a good discussion.
- Discuss any unexpected findings. When discussing an unexpected finding, begin the paragraph with the finding and then describe it.
- Identify potential limitations and weaknesses and comment on the relative importance of these to your interpretation of the results and how they may affect the validity of the findings. When identifying limitations and weaknesses, avoid using an apologetic tone.
- Summarize concisely the principal implications of the findings, regardless of statistical significance.
- Provide recommendations (no more than two) for further research. Do not offer suggestions which could have been easily addressed within the study, as this shows there has been inadequate examination and interpretation of the data.
- Explain how the results and conclusions of this study are important and how they influence our knowledge or understanding of the problem being examined.

In your writing of the Discussion, discuss everything, but be concise, brief, and specific.

This section might be called Discussion or it might be called Summary of Findings. The purpose of this section is to highlight the major statistical findings from the results section and interpret them. First, restate the overall purpose of the study. Then, explain the main finding as related to the overall purpose of the study. Next, summarize other interesting findings from the results section. Explain how the statistical findings relate to that purpose of the study. One way to do this is to take every research question and hypothesis in turn and explain in plain terms what the statistical results mean. Also describe how the results are related to education in general. All explanations must be supported by the results of the data analysis.

Generally, the Discussion section does not need to include any numbers. No statistics need to be repeated from the results, nor does the discussion need to refer to table numbers. Instead, simply explain the results in language that is easy for a non-researcher to understand.

Also try to integrate the findings into the results of other research studies. An example paragraph from a Discussion section is given below:

This study found that Nigerian teachers have a mix of beliefs regarding early literacy development, some accurate beliefs and other inaccurate beliefs. The teachers sampled in this study were accurate in their agreement about the importance of oral language. Indeed, with the lack of materials often available for early childhood educators in Nigerian classrooms, instruction focused on oral language may be one of the most successful and cost-effective ways of improving early literacy skills. The four instructional strategies previously mentioned - songs, rhymes, and word play; storytelling; circle time; and dramatic play (Roskos et al., 2009) - are relatively easy to implement and require few instructional materials. However, agreeing to the importance of oral language in literacy development is different from having the expertise to effectively teach oral language skills. Additional research needs to be conducted to determine how well early childhood education teachers use instructional strategies that promote oral language in the classroom. Particularly in Africa where high quality reading materials are oftentimes scarce, early childhood teachers need to be well trained in teaching strategies that foster oral language.

Limitations

All studies have limitations in terms of the sample, measurement or manipulation of key variables, and procedure for data collection. This section should report the limitations that resulted from the research methods. How could the research be conducted with a different research design? How may the participants and sampling techniques not be representative of the target population? How might the target population be limited? How were the instruments inadequate? Were there any problems with the treatment? What problems resulted from the study's procedures? What other unexpected problems arose in the data collection?

You frequently read that the study was limited by time, money, or other resources. However, every single research study ever conducted in the history of this world was limited by money, resources, and time. These factors are external to the study and should not be mentioned. A sample Limitations section is given below.

One of the limitations of this research study was the constitution of the sample. First, students were not randomly selected from a larger population to participate in the study. Information about the study was sent home with all of the students at Tonganoxie Elementary School. The parents then had to sign and return an informed consent document. This might have biased the sample. However, the teachers at Tonganoxie Elementary School commented that students from a range of ability levels participated in the study. The sample was also relatively homogeneous with mostly Caucasian middle class students who lived in a relatively rural community. Therefore, the results might not generalize to other student populations, particularly those in an urban community or those with greater diversity in ethnicity and social class.

Since the experimenter in the study also authored the paper, the experimenter might have biased students' responses during the task. However, this conclusion was unlikely since the results for the Number Series task were contrary to the original hypothesis. Regardless, a blind administration of the experiment would have been desirable.
A ceiling effect also most likely influenced performance on the Equivalence task, with most students having nearly perfect scores. This effect might have masked differences in performance between the Pictorial and Numeral conditions, particularly in the high ability and second grade samples.

Conclusion and Implications

The final section of the paper is the Conclusion section. Briefly summarize the overall conclusion of the data analysis based on the purpose of the study. Also explain the importance of the major finding to educational practice. An example conclusion is given below.

After the portrayal of the arguments and results of the research come the conclusions. A conclusion is the last paragraph in your research paper, or the last part in any other type of presentation. Why do it?
A conclusion is like the final chord in a song. It makes the listener feel that the piece is complete and well done. The same is true for your audience. You want them to feel that you supported what you stated in your thesis. You then become a reliable author for them and they are impressed by that and will be more likely to read your work in the future. They may also have learned something and maybe have had their opinion changed by what you have

written or created! How do I do it?

A conclusion is, in some ways, like your introduction. You restate your thesis and summarize your main points of evidence for the reader. You can usually do this in one paragraph. In the following example, the thesis statement is in **bold**. Notice that it is written in 2 sentences. This is a stylistic choice for impact.

Here the questions asked in the problem formulation are explicitly answered. In the case that you posed hypotheses, this is the place to present whether the research results confirm or refute these.

In addition, you may consider answering the following questions:

- How far are the research results generalizable to other cases than those researched?
- How do the research results relate to the findings and conclusions of other authors? Where do results match, where do they differ, and how is this explained?
- What has the research added to the knowledge about the topic at hand?
- What future line of research does your work open?

Depending on the aim of the thesis, it may also be valuable to provide an answer to (one or more) of the following questions:

- What does the research say about the adequacy of the methods followed and the materials chosen? Can any methodological recommendations for future research be derived from this? How could future researchers do a better job?
- Which policy recommendations can be made on the basis of the research?
- Which predictions can be made on the basis of the research?

Literacy is a fundamental human right (UNESCO, 2006). However, learning how to read is a difficult endeavor that requires competent instructors. This study provided evidence that primary school teachers in Nigeria need additional professional development to improve their beliefs about literacy development so they can be more effective literacy instructors. Only competent, well trained teachers will help Nigerian children develop a high level of literacy that is necessary for being effective in today's world.

The "Implications for research" should comment on the need for further research, and the nature of the further research that would be most desirable.

Recommendations

Next, give recommendations based on the results of the study. What practical steps can educators take to implement the key findings of the research study? **Remember, these recommendations must be supported by the statistical findings from the data analysis.** If the statistical results found that a new teaching program improves mathematical exam scores, then the only valid recommendation that can be made is that the new teaching program should be implemented in order to improve exam scores. However, if the data analysis found that the new teaching program does not improve mathematical exam scores, then the researcher cannot conclude that the new teaching program should be implemented, because the program was found to be ineffective in improving exam scores.

Educators can only change their own behavior; they cannot change the government. Therefore, the most beneficial recommendations will be those that educators themselves can implement.

Below is a sample recommendation. Notice how the first sentence provides the empirical support for the recommendation.

This study found that there is considerable variation in the students' judgments of acceptability of ethical study practices, providing evidence that university students are not certain about the right way to study. Thus, teachers need to spend class time educating students about positive, effective study skills. Few students understand and use good study practices without explicit instruction (Weinstein, Meyer, Husman, Van Mater Stone, & McKeachie, 2006). Therefore, direct instruction in study skills is necessary. For example, teachers should instruct their students on how to set goals for their education learning as well as instruction on specific study practices such as effectively reading textbooks and studying notes for the exam. When teachers spend the time necessary for teaching study skills, then students will not be uncertain about ethical study practices and will be more prepared for their exams. As Murdock and Anderman (2006) note, students who are confident in their abilities engage in less cheating behaviors.

After the recommendations have been written, reread each recommendation. Consider which statistical result from the results section supports that recommendation. If there is no statistical result to support the recommendation, then it must be canceled.

Suggestions for Further Research

Every research study provides one or two answers about education, but also opens the door to five to ten additional questions. Based on the Discussion/Summary of Findings and Limitations of the study, what additional research should be conducted? What questions arose because of the major finding of your study? How can other research studies improve over the limitations that were described in the Limitations section? A sample of Suggestions for Further Research section is below.

Educational researchers need to continue conducting empirical research to ascertain the factors that contribute to cheating amongst students. First, researchers should identify the types of malpractices that are most frequent amongst students. Second, researchers should determine what types of factors influence students to engage in examination malpractice. Finally, experimental research should be conducted to test various strategies for preventing examination malpractice to determine which strategies are most effective.

The actual benchmarks against which theses or dissertations are judged

- Problem formulation: clarity and precision, originality, argumentation and delineation; how is the problem formulation operationalized?
- Purpose and relevance of the research: is the purpose of the research clear; does the research have scientific and/or social relevance?
- Build-up of argument: systematic elaboration of the problem formulation, logical consistencies, interrelatedness of separate parts of the thesis, clear line of argumentation, well-founded conclusions.
- Knowledge of the topic of the thesis, partly shown in the way and extent to which the literature is used.
- Scientific insight: how scientific theories and methodologies are used, justification of theoretical assumptions, description and application of theoretical concepts (consistency in use; relating to common understanding of concepts).
- Quality of the research: way of material collection (operationalization of concepts, research techniques, choice of empirical field), accounting for methods used and choices made, analysis of data.
- Policy and/or research recommendations: are the recommendations well formulated and sufficiently sustained?
- *Controllability*: precise references, correct quotation, literature list.
- *Language*: precision, clarity, readability.

- *Style*: layout, spelling, punctuation, clear structure, headings, etc.
- Measure of independence in achieving points mentioned above.
- Measure of creativity in achieving points mentioned above.

Your presentation needs to address the following:
- What is the **problem** you are studying?
- Why is it **important**?
- What **results** have you achieved so far and why do they matter?
- How is this **substantially** different from prior work?
- What do you need to do to complete your work?

Tips for presentation and proposal/thesis defense sessions

Proposal defenses consist of four parts: first, the candidate introduces him/herself, and then presents a summary of the work. Then he/she answers the questions posed by the committee. Finally, the committee meets in private to discuss the presentation and assess the score to be granted.

- Avoid high-level talks: "... they usually fail to convey the intellectual substance, creativity, and ingenuity of the speakers' accomplishments - what takes the work out of the routine. Naturally, these comments apply to all of our speakers who want to impress people with their ability as opposed to the breadth of their knowledge or the size of their project." (Ed Coffman)
- When presenting experimental work, be prepared to defend your methodology. What was your sample size? Confidence intervals?
- Talk to your audience, not to your slides.
- Project; speaking softly conveys the impression that you are unsure of what you are saying.
- Make sure that all your graphs are readable. Check this in the actual presentation environment (using a video projector), not just on your laptop screen. A common problem is that the lines are too thin.
- Avoid using flashy or cheesy animations like PowerPoint word art. You are not going to advertise something. This can distract from the message and make you look unprofessional.
- Keep to the allotted time of no more than allotted minutes.
- Your work plan should be sufficiently detailed so that the committee can judge whether it is realistic or not. You don't have to account for every day between the proposal and your thesis defense, but a roughly

monthly or quarterly granularity is to be expected, depending on how far away your anticipated graduation date is. Specify the experiments you need to run, the software you need to write and the algorithms you want to try out. This should not just be one page that says "I will do miraculous things".

- The committee should be handed a copy of your slides.
- No more than 25 slides, plus "back up" slides with additional material in case of questions. The committee will get anxious once the presentation lasts longer than 35-40 minutes.
- List your contributions early and explicitly. You don't want to create the impression that related work is yours, and vice versa.
- One of the most important concerns during the proposal is to convince the audience that you are aware of all related work. Since some of your work may date back a few years, it is not sufficient to just copy the reference list from your first paper. Check common recent conferences to see whether any recent work applies to your thesis. If applicable, point out your work predates work presented by somebody else done more recently. (Given the duration of most theses, it is not uncommon that others pursue a direction after you have stopped working on it.)
- When presenting your contributions, be sure to use "I" and not "we" so that the committee will know what aspects of the work were yours, and which were group projects.

Plagiarism

To plagiarize means to take the work or an idea of someone else and pass it off as one's own. If you copy, paraphrase or translate materials from websites, books, magazines or any other source in your thesis without giving full and proper credit to the original author(s), you are committing plagiarism. If you do so, you may be facing the possibility of expulsion from your program.

The fair use of evidence from primary and secondary sources is the basis of academic discourse. The abuse of this fairness undermines the very nature of scholarly research.

Plagiarism is a form of theft and fraud and should be avoided at all costs. If you find yourself in doubt about quotation or correct use of a source, it is always a good idea to provide full information. Your supervisor or academic advisor can help you if you have doubts.

CHAPTER SIX
An Overview of Research Methods in Applied Linguistics

Introduction
What is research? Research simply means trying to find answers to questions by looking at what other people have said or by conducting one's empirical investigation. The process of answering questions or discovering causes not only is illuminating but also effective to develop most professions.

In applied linguistics providing new insights into the teaching and learning process is the primary reason of doing research.

Research is **(generative) cyclical**. It never comes to a standstill because each piece of research raises new questions for more research. Either the results lead the investigator onto related questions or the original question with which the research began cannot be answered or confirmed. So, the investigation must begin again but with a gain in knowledge and experience.

Research can be considered as the organized, systematic search for responses to the asked questions in the scientific sense. In short, it is *"disciplined inquiry"* (Dörnyei, 2011, p 15).

This chapter deals with the characteristics of a good researcher, different kinds of research, and classification of research methods. It provides researchers with essential knowledge to consider the significance of research and its different methods.

Research is a cyclical and generative process
Research is a continuous phenomenon that never stops since every part of research makes another question. Figure 6.1. indicates ongoing feature of research.

Figure 6.1. The Research Cycle (Adapted from Seliger & Shohamy, 1989, P. 254)

Characteristics of good researchers

To be a good researcher first requires the intention to be involved in research and immediately thereafter to show a dedicated interest to do the best research possible. From there we must accumulate the knowledge needed to advance the current ideas already existent in the research world.

Good researchers

- have high level of common sense to keep their feet firmly on the ground.
- have strong curiosity about the topic.
- have creative mind to create original ideas.
- need to be disciplined to be able to follow the systematic nature of research.
- should have a sense of social responsibility to the field to generate knowledge and communicate his/her findings with others.

Sources of gathering information for research

- **Sensory experience:** The information through the researcher's senses helps them to find solutions to the problem.

- **Experts:** Experts in a special field have great amount of knowledge to offer.

- **Logic:** It helps to observe the facts and relationships among them by deductive and inductive thinking.

    A. **Deductive reasoning** is the process of reasoning from one or more general statements (premises) to gain a logical conclusion. This approach attributed to Aristotle and the Greeks. This syllogistic reasoning contains a major premise, a minor premise, and a conclusion. The major premise was established by dogma and the minor premise is related to the major premise. For example:

    Major premise: All men are mortal.

    Minor premise: David is a man.

    Conclusion: David is mortal.

    B. **Inductive reasoning** is reasoning which attempts to supply strong evidence for the truth of the conclusion. While the conclusion of a deductive reasoning is supposed to be certain, the truth of an inductive reasoning is supposed to be *probable*, based on the evidence given. This approach was established by Francis Bacon who emphasized on direct observation of phenomenon to arrive at conclusions or generalizations.

- **Scientific methods:** Aristotle's deductive method and Bacon's inductive method were integrated in Charles Darwin's work in the 19th century. Scientific methods are more principled to act as objectively as possible to make formal and systematic research. This deductive–inductive method is known as a model of a scientific approach. The major premise of deductive method was replaced by a hypothesis or an assumption that was tested by logical analysis of collected data.

Characteristics of research

- It should be **systematic** to follow special pre-established rules.
- It should be **logical** to show the accuracy and validity of the premises.

147

- It should be **practical** to allow another researcher to become interested in making the same assumption.
- It should be **replicable** to provide new researchers with detailed, precise, and reliable information.
- It should be **generative** to lead many other new questions.

Educational researches

Educational research is generally classified into two groups:

1. **Quantitative research** uses objective measurement to collect numeric data to answer questions or predetermined hypothesis. It needs a well-controlled setting.
2. **Qualitative research** focuses on understanding social phenomena, and human participants in natural settings. It does not begin with formal hypothesis but may result in a hypothesis.

Classification of quantitative researches

1. Experimental research
2. Non-experimental research

Experimental research

Experimental research: It studies the effect of one variable on another one. The **independent variable** is called experimental treatment. In order to have a good **experiment**, a random process must be used to make an equal and independent chance for each subject. Two groups of subjects are needed: **experimental group** and **control group.**

The experimental group receives a particular treatment while the control group faces no treatment. Sometimes the control group receives unproductive treatment called **placebo** to make the subjects believe they are receiving the real experimental treatment. Sometimes researchers are not able to provide random subjects to experimental treatment instead, they use already assembled groups such as classes. This kind of research is called **quasi-experimental.**

Non-experimental research

Non-experimental research does not manipulate the variables but looks for relationships among them. It contains

- Ex post facto research

- Correlational research
- Survey research

Ex post facto research is similar to an experiment but researchers don't manipulate the independent variable, they simply compare groups differing on preexisting independent variable to determine any relationship to the dependent variable.

Correlational research collects data from all variables to determine if they are related (correlated). Correlation shows how much two variables vary directly (correlated) or inversely (negative correlation). The degree of relationship is shown by a numeric index called **coefficient of correlation**.

Both ex post facto and correlational researches indicate relationships between variables. In ex post facto research participants are grouped into at least two groups on one variable and then are compared on the other variable. In correlational research one group of individuals is measured on at least two continuous variables.

Survey research or descriptive research summarizes the characteristics of different groups to measure their opinions toward some issues by the use of questionnaires and interviews.

Classification of qualitative research

Interpretive study: It means understanding a phenomenon through interviews, observations, and document review to make descriptive perception of the phenomenon.

Case Study: It means focusing on one individual, group, organization, or a program to arrive at a detail description to generate a possible theory.

Content analysis or document analysis: It means analyzing recorded material to learn about human behavior.

Ethnography or field research: It means studying naturally occurring behavior within a culture or social group.

Grounded theory: It means developing a theory of social phenomena based on the field data collected in a study.

Historical research: It means analyzing documents to gain insight into past events.

Narrative inquiry: It means examining the stories people tell about their lives.

Phenomenological studies: It means exploring the subject's thoughts and feelings to elicit an individual's experience.

Main features required for a qualitative research

Required context: This kind of research represents concern for context. It means that human behavior is not far from social, cultural, political, and historical effects. Therefore; a qualitative research is always bounded by a special setting. Thus, it is believed that human behavior is context-bound.

Descriptive data collection: This kind of research needs data that are not in the form of numbers and statistics, but in the form of words. The participants, their experiences, their attitudes, their feelings, and their assumptions can be considered as collected data.

Form of design: In this kind of research, researchers rarely design all parts of a study before they start data collection. In quantitative research researchers define the variables and needed statistical methods to analyze the data right before they start collecting data. In contrast, the design in qualitative research emerges as the study goes on.

Data collection from human instrument: In qualitative research, the human can be considered as the first instrument in data collection and data analysis through applying interviews, document analysis, and non-structured observation. This method of data collection and data analysis is different from quantitative inquiry.

Using inductive analysis: In this kind of research inductive analysis is used. It means the research proceeds from data to hypotheses to theory while in deductive analysis the research proceeds from theory to data, continues with hypotheses and goes to data.

Conducting research in natural settings: In this kind of research real-world behavior is studied once it takes place in natural settings or fields such as in a classroom, in a school, or in an institute. Thus, it is not artificial and behavior is not manipulated.

In general, if we consider the continuum of quantitative and qualitative researches, the following factors are placed as shown in Table 6.1.

■ **Table 6.1.** *The Continuum Quantitative and Qualitative Inquiries*

Quantitative		Qualitative
Elemental (Constituent)	◄ - - - - - - - - - - - - - - - - - - - ►	Integrated (Holistic)
Deductive	◄ - - - - - - - - - - - - - - - - - - - ►	Inductive
More Control	◄ - - - - - - - - - - - - - - - - - - - ►	Less Control

As shown in table 6.2. tools for data collection and the possible advantages and constraints should be considered as the following:

Table 6.2. *Tools for Data Collection*

Technique	Advantages	Possible constrain
available information	It is inexpensive.	Data is sometimes inaccessible. Information may not be precise or complete.
Observation	It provides more precise, detailed, and relevant information. It deals with information facts.	It may cause ethical issues like confidentiality, privacy, and observer bias. The presence of the data observer may influence the situation. Thorough training of observer and his/her assistant is required.
Interview	It is appropriate to interview both literates and illiterates. It deals with clarification of questions. It includes more response than written questionnaires.	The interviewer may influence responses. Reports of events can be less precise than information received from observations.
Interview (flexible small scale)	It provides in-depth information and permits exploration of spontaneous response.	The interviewer may influence the responses. It is difficult to analyse open-ended data.
Interview (Fixed large scale)	It is easy to analyse.	The interviewer may miss important information because spontaneous responses are usually not
Administration of written questionnaires	It is less expensive. It covers anonymity factor. Therefore, it may lead to more honest responses. It does not need research assistants.	It is impossible be used with illiterate people. Questions may be misunderstood. There is usually a low rate of response.

Characteristics of quantitative research vs. qualitative research
Quantitative research

- **Purpose:** Cause-effect, relationships between variables and quest for generalizability and universal laws are considered.
- **Design:** Prior design and categorization are used.
- **Approach:** Deductive approach is used and it starts with test hypothesis.
- **Tools:** Standardized instruments are used.
- **Sample:** Large samples are used.
- **Analysis:** Numeric data and statistical analysis should be used (the most important characteristic).

Qualitative research

- **Purpose:** Understanding of social phenomena is considered.
- **Design:** The design evolves during the research.
- **Approach:** Inductive approach and generating hypothesis are used.
- **Tools:** Face-to-face interaction is used.
- **Sample:** Small samples are used.
- **Analysis:** Interpretation and narrative explanation are used.

Strengths and weakness of quantitative research
Strengths

- It confirms and tests already made theories about how and why phenomena occur.
- It tests hypotheses that are made before the data are collected.
- It can generalize research findings when the data are based on sufficient size random sampling.
- It can generalize a research finding when it has been replicated on various populations and subpopulations.
- It is useful to obtain data that permit quantitative predictions to be made.
- Researchers can make a situation that removes the confounding influence of many variables, letting one establish cause-and-effect relationships.
- Data collection is relatively quick (e.g., telephone interviews.)
- It provides precise, quantitative, and numerical data.

- Data analysis can be relatively less time consuming (using statistical software).
- The research results are relatively independent of the researcher (e.g., statistical significance).
- It may have more credibility with many people in power (e.g., administrators, politicians, people who fund programs).
- It can be useful for studying large numbers of people.

Weaknesses

- Researchers' categories that are used might not reflect local people's understandings.
- Researchers' theories that are used might not reflect local people's understandings.
- Researchers might skip phenomena occurring because of the focus on theory or hypothesis testing rather than on theory or hypothesis generation (called the *confirmation bias*).
- Produced knowledge may be too abstract and general for direct application to specific local situations, contexts, and individuals.

Strengths and weakness of qualitative research

Strengths

- Data are based on the participants' own categories of meaning.
- It is useful for studying a restricted number of participants in detail.
- It is useful for describing complicated phenomena.
- It provides individual case information.
- It can provide comparisons and analysis.
- It provides understanding and description of people's personal experiences of phenomena.
- Researchers almost always identify contextual and setting factors as they relate to the phenomenon of interest.
- Researchers can study dynamic processes.
- Researchers can use the primarily qualitative method of grounded theory to inductively generate a tentative but explanatory theory about a phenomenon.
- It can determine how participants interpret constructs (e.g., self-esteem, IQ).
- Data are usually collected in naturalistic settings.

- It is especially responsive to local situations, conditions, and stakeholders' needs.
- Researches are especially responsive to changes that occur during the conduct of a study.
- Data lend themselves to exploring how and why phenomena occur.
- Researchers can use an important case to demonstrate a phenomenon to the readers of a report.
- It determines idiographic causation (i.e., determination of causes of a particular event).

Weaknesses
- Produced knowledge may not generalize to other people or other settings.
- It is not easy to make quantitative predictions.
- It is difficult to test hypotheses and theories with large participant pools.
- It may have lower credibility with some administrators and commissioners of programs.
- It takes more time to collect the data when compared to quantitative research.
- Data analysis is time consuming.
- The results are more easily influenced by researchers' personal biases and idiosyncrasies

Mixed methods research

A mixed method study is made of the collection or analysis of both qualitative and quantitative data in one study. Researchers collect multiple data using different strategies, approaches, and methods in a way that the result of the research is in complementary strengths and non-overlapping weaknesses.

Purposes of mixed methods research

Combining methods can be because of receiving more understanding of a target phenomenon and confirming a set of findings.
- **Function of complementarity** indicates yielding rich understanding by clarifying and elaborating on certain aspects of research. It covers a fuller portrait of social world.

- **Function of development** deals with using qualitative and quantitative methods sequentially so that the findings of the first method notify the development of the second.

- **Function of initiation** means mixed methods may not always produce complementary results. Researchers intentionally use different methods to make discrepancies, paradoxes, or contradictions to lead to new perspectives.

- **Function of expansion** represents the desire of a researcher to increase the scope of a study through including multiple components.

Strengths and weaknesses of mixed research

Strengths

- It uses words, pictures, and narrative to add meaning to numbers.
- It can provide quantitative and qualitative research strengths.
- Researchers can make and test a grounded theory.
- It can answer a more complete range of research questions because researchers are not confined to a single method or approach.
- Researchers can use the strengths of an additional method to overcome the weaknesses in another method by using both in a research study.
- It can provide stronger evidence for a conclusion through convergence and corroboration of findings.
- It can add insights and understanding that may be missed when only one method is used.
- It can be used to improve the generalizability of the results.
- Both qualitative and quantitative research can be used together to produce more complete knowledge necessary to inform theory and practice.

Weaknesses

- It is not easy for a single researcher to conduct both qualitative and quantitative research, especially if two or more approaches are expected to be done concurrently. It might need a research team.
- Researchers have to learn about multiple methods and approaches and understand how to mix them.
- It is more expensive and time consuming.

Classification of research methods

1. Historical research method
2. Descriptive research method
3. Experimental research method

Historical research method

Historical research method is a good way to understand the current state of a phenomenon. It covers the origin, development, modification of a process. In historical research method, there is no living subject and it seems nonscientific but this is a misunderstanding because it enjoys particular merits. Some contemporary problems can be solved by conducting historical research. Sometimes, it has some suggestions for future state of affairs. It can help researchers to understand causes and effects of interactions in different cultures.

Steps in conducting a historic research

- **Formulating the problem:** Data are used to explain and predict a phenomenon based on documents left from the past.

- **Formulating the hypotheses:** Collected data can be used to compare events in different fields.

- **Collecting sufficient data:** Data can be collected from official records and documents, nonofficial records such as personal records, oral stores, artistic remains, and published materials, facilities, and manuscripts.

- **Criticizing the data:** Because of limited available material authenticity and truthfulness of documents should be carefully examined.

- **Interpreting and explaining the findings:** It is the responsibility of historical researchers to compare the similarities and differences found in the past events, but it is not within their power to predict about future events.

Descriptive research method

Descriptive research method plays an important role in applied linguistics by manipulation of variables, introducing treatments, and establishing control and experimental groups. It includes a variety of techniques and methods to cope with any kind of research question.

Survey: Researchers ask questions directly from participants to collect data to explain the existing state of a phenomenon.

- **School survey** deals with the learning settings, characteristics of educational personnel, nature of learners, and learning process.
- **Community survey** deals with the close relationship between schools and other communities.
- **Public opinion survey** deals with making decisions based on the information collected on the public's attitudes and opinions.

Inter-relational methods: They give deeper insights into the features of a phenomenon through investigating the relationship among factors.

- **Case study** is a descriptive or explanatory analysis of a person, group or event.
- **Field study** is collecting information outside of a laboratory, library or workplace setting.
- **Correlational study** indicates whether a statistical relationship between variables exists, both in direction and in magnitude in a positive or negative way.
- **Causal-comparative study** is a form of study that tries to identify the cause and effects of relationship between two or more groups. It is a common form of design in education research.

Developmental methods: They not only show the existing condition but also describe the development of variables over time. It can be **longitudinal** to study the development of subjects over a long period of time or **cross-sectional** to obtain data within a short period of time.

Experimental research method

Experimental research method is the peak of scientific research to remedy the shortcomings of descriptive and historic methods. It enables researchers to make strong conclusions about the relationship between variables. It can also help researchers to make cause-effect relationships among the variables (Farhady, 2002).

Steps in conducting experimental research

- Making a research question
- Changing the research question to a hypothesis
- Following a systematic approach
- Coming up with an answer

Special features of experimental research

- **Selecting subjects randomly:** Randomization stops bias over subjects to give an equal chance to every member of a population.

- **Employing experimental and control groups:** After randomizing, subjects are divided into two groups. There should not be significant differences among the members of two groups.

- **Pretesting:** It is used to make researchers confident about the equality of the groups before the experiment. Generally, before pretesting, researchers can use a sample of Oxford Placement Test (OPT) to determine the homogeneity of the participants. A Sample model test is available on the internet.
  https://www.oxfordenglishtesting.com

- **Post-testing:** After offering a treatment to the experimental group and a placebo to the control group, researchers expect to observe the predicted changes in the dependable variable through posttest.

- **Delayed Post-testing:** In some cases it is suggested that after performing post-test, researchers make some interval sessions to continue normal instruction, and then at least two weeks after post-test, delay post-test can represent deeper effect of dependable variable in long term.

Differences between pretest and posttest scores

- Experimental group should perform differently from the pretest to the posttest.
- Control group should not perform differently from the pretest to the posttest.
- Because of the existence of treatment, the performance of experimental group should be different from control group.
- If there is no difference between two groups after posttest, the effectiveness of the treatment is under question.

Classification of experimental research

- **True experimental:** If all the special features of experimental research such as randomization, pretest, post-test are met, this method is called true experimental.

- **Pre-experimental:** If one or two of the requirements are not met pre-experimental method includes **one-shot case study** that has no control group and the subjects are given one experimental treatment for a given time. At the end of the program, the subjects are given a test to show the effect of the treatment. **One-group pretest posttest study** is similar to the one-shot case study but a pretest is given before the treatment to the subjects. There are two tests, pretest and posttest. **Intact group study** is used mostly by teachers because it is impossible to select students randomly, they are chosen on the basis of some criterion, e. g. scores, success, or even self-selection. After selecting two groups both groups will receive a posttest, but the experimental group will receive the treatment while the control group will not.

- **Quasi-experimental:** In applied linguistics it is difficult to make true experimental research in case of randomization, defining numerous variables, and evaluating treatment. Because of these limitations, conducting research shouldn't be abandoned. The goal is getting approximate to standards of true experimental method. Quasi-experimental methods are compromises between true experimentation and the nature of the human language behavior. It classifies as **time-series study** which is used when there is no control group. The subjects are given several pre-tests and several posttests. After several pretests researchers will have an idea about possible changes in the behavior of the subjects when there is no treatment. Then, the treatment is introduced and finally a few posttests are administered to provide a learning trend. **Equivalent time-series method** can be used when the treatment is introduced after the first pretest. Then the treatment is followed by a posttest. This procedure is continued for three to five times, and the scores obtained after the experimental treatment are compared with scores obtained after the placebo.

Research validity

1. **Internal validity**
2. **External validity**

Internal validity

Internal validity refers to the extent to which the findings of research are because of the manipulations made by the research not other factors. Researchers must try to control variables to limit the outcome to the independent variable only. There are some threats to the internal validity. **The effect of history** refers to whatever happens to the subjects of the study outside the experimental environment. **The effect of maturation** refers to any systematic changes over time, regardless of specific events. **The effect of testing** refers to giving some awareness to subjects after pretesting and post-testing. **The effect of selection** refers to the manner in which the participants are selected. **The effect of mortality** refers to the loss of subjects during the experiment.

External validity

External validity refers to the extent to which the outcome of the research can be *generalizable* in other similar situations.

Note: In the case of using the findings of the research by others in the field, considering internal and external validity is very important. Thus, researchers ought to pay attention to obtain a logical degree of internal and external validity in conducting their research to provide the generalizability of the research.

What is action research?

"Action research" is related to the link between research-teaching and the researcher-the teacher to gain a better understanding of the educational environment and improve the effectiveness of the teaching setting. The main feature of action research is enhancing practice and introducing change into the social enterprise. There are three reasons that show why action research is not becoming prominent (Dörnyei, 2011): Teachers'

1. lack of time: Teachers often complain about not having sufficient time.
2. lack of incentives: Teachers need official recognition, financial reward, or release time.
3. lack of expertise: The average classroom practitioners might not have the research knowledge and skills to carry out reliable and valid research. They need the support of a trained and professional supervisor.

Generally, action research makes teachers agents rather than recipients of teaching and learning information. Teachers are claimed to build educational theories of practice if they are involved in supportive teaching climate. "Exploratory practice" is similar to action research to offer ways for teachers to be aware of classroom events through using a sequence of reflective pedagogical practices (Allwright, 2005).

The teacher-researcher link should be viable and active. Teachers were passive recipients of researcher knowledge in the past. We should not expect teachers to generate their theories nowadays. It is necessary to find some doable form of teacher-researcher link between these two extremes. The best place to start is in pre-service and in-service teacher training courses to remove an additional burden on teachers' busy daily lives. There is a positive note from Richards (2004) that indicates teachers' integration into the research processes.

Most ESLO [i.e. EFL/ESL] teachers are natural researchers. We are used to working out the needs of our students, evaluating the effects of particular approaches, spotting things that work or don't work and adjusting our teaching accordingly. Very few teachers approach their work mechanically and nearly all of us reflect on what we do in the classroom.

Guidelines for qual. and quan. research proposal writing

Qualitative researchers attempt to gather an in-depth understanding of human behavior and its reasons. They search for the *why* and *how* of decision making, not just *what*, *where*, *when*. They use smaller but focused samples. An outline of recommended components in a qualitative proposal follows (Ary, Jacob, Sorenson & Razavieh, 2010, p. 586):

1. **Introduction**
   a) Purpose of the study
   b) Situating the self
   c) Initial guiding questions
   d) Review of relevant literature/discourse
2. **Research procedure**
   a) Site and selection of the sample
   b) Description of the setting
   c) Role of the researcher
   d) Data collection methods
   e) Ethical issues
3. **Data analysis/presentation**

a) Data analysis strategies
b) Validity and dependability issues

4. **Importance/significance of the study**
5. **Time schedule and budget**
6. **References**
7. **Appendices**

The following outline shows the typical components of a quantitative research proposal which refers to the systematic empirical investigation of social phenomena through statistical, mathematical or numerical data or computational techniques (Ary, Jacob, Sorenson & Razavieh, 2010, pp. 575-6).

1. **Introduction**
   a) Statement of the problem
   b) Review of the literature
   c) Statement of the hypothesis(es)
   d) Significance of the study
2. **Methods**
   a) Participants and methods of selection
   b) Instruments
   c) Procedures
3. **Analysis of data**
   a) Data organization
   b) Statistical procedures
4. **Protection of human participants** (ethical considerations in conducting research on human subjects)
5. **Time schedule and budget**
a. **Time schedule**
b. **Budget**
6. **References**

Although it is not necessary to follow this outline rigidly, this outline provides a useful guide for writing any proposal because all aspects listed here must be considered. You need to be aware, however, that your university department might need a specific format.

CHAPTER SEVEN
Statistics & SPSS in Applied Linguistics

Introduction

Statistics is the science of gathering, analyzing and drawing conclusions from data. It is an especially useful branch of mathematics that is not only studied theoretically but one that is also used by researchers in many fields to organize, analyze, and summarize data. Its methods and analyses are used to convey research findings and to support hypotheses and give credibility to research methodology and conclusions. It is important for researchers to understand statistics so that they can evaluate the credibility and usefulness of information, and make appropriate decisions.

Statistics has several applications. It has been divided into two basic areas called **descriptive statistics** and **inferential statistics** by mathematicians.

Descriptive statistics

Descriptive statistics refers to describing what researchers have found when carrying out a research. It deals with e.g. sample data. This kind of statistics is used to show the results of an experiment in an easy and clear way. It neither explains the cause of the result nor makes any prediction. It summarizes a given data set, which can either be a representation of the entire population or a sample.

Knowledge of some basic statistical procedures is essential for researchers to carry out research. The first step is familiarizing with scales of measurement as shown in Table 7.1. (**nominal scale**, **ordinal scale**, **interval scale**, and **ratio scale**) mentioned in previous chapters.

■ **Table 7.1.** *Determining Scales of Measurement (Adapted from Ary, Jacob, Sorenson & Razavieh, 2010, p.104)*

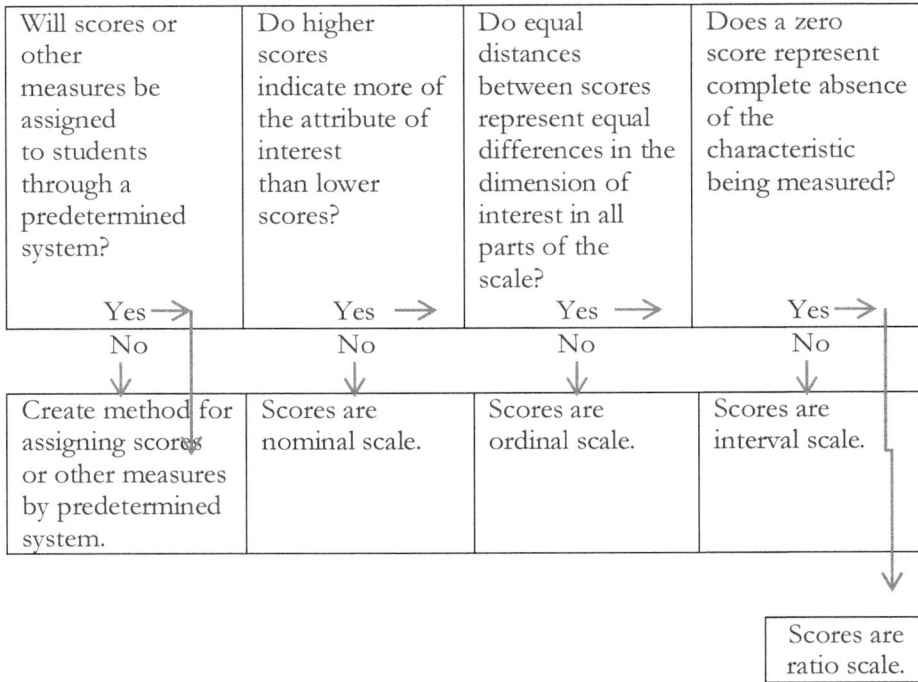

Will scores or other measures be assigned to students through a predetermined system?	Do higher scores indicate more of the attribute of interest than lower scores?	Do equal distances between scores represent equal differences in the dimension of interest in all parts of the scale?	Does a zero score represent complete absence of the characteristic being measured?
Yes →	Yes →	Yes →	Yes →
No ↓	No ↓	No ↓	No ↓
Create method for assigning scores or other measures by predetermined system.	Scores are nominal scale.	Scores are ordinal scale.	Scores are interval scale.

Scores are ratio scale.

Essential concepts in descriptive statistics

Raw score

Raw score refers to the scores that appear in a list. It indicates the number of points a student earned on a test. For example, on a reading test each question is worth 1 point, so if a student correctly answered 30 questions out of 50, his or her raw score would be 30.

Rank order

Rank order refers to putting the values in numerical order and then assigning new values to denote where in the ordered set they fall. We give the smallest value the number 1, the next largest value the number 2, the next largest number 3 etc. The numbers 1,2,3,... that are assigned to the various values are called the ranks. If there are n values in the sample, the largest value will have rank 'n'. Sometimes there are ties in the data. This means that two or more values are the same, so that there is no strictly increasing order. When this happens, we average the ranks for the tied values. For example, to rank the following sample of 14 values:-2 34 -5 -7 25 2 34 34 67 28 -2 0 7 23 Sorting the values into the order of magnitude gives:-7 -5 -2 0 2 2 7 23 25 28 34 34 34 67.

Frequency distribution or f

Frequency distribution or f refers to the arrangement of the values that one or more variables take in a sample. Each entry in the table has the frequency or count of the occurrences of values in a special group or interval, and in this way, the table summarizes the distribution of values in the sample.

Score	Frequency
20	2
18	4
16	5
15	4
14	3
10	3
9	1

A Frequency Distribution Sample

Relative frequency

Relative frequency refers to the frequency of each score divided by the total number of scores. The relative frequencies are usually multiplied by 100 and the result is called **percentage.** It shows **N percent** of the subjects receive a particular score.

Cumulative frequency or F

Cumulative frequency or F refers to showing how many scores are below the given score in a distribution. Researchers should add the frequency of successive intervals in the previous work. It is done from the last two frequencies in the list. It is recorded from the bottom to the top. In order to compute the percentile rank, **F** should be divided by the total number of scores. The result is then multiplied by 100.

Drawing a frequency distribution
Graphs

A graph is useful because it communicates information visually. A is used to compare the amounts or frequency of occurrence of different characteristics of data. This type of display allows us to compare groups of data, and to make generalizations about the data quickly.

The bar graph

The bar graph also called bar chart is a graphical display of data using bars of different heights. The bar graph usually has a vertical and a horizontal axis. It is used with categorical data.

Key points

- Categories are often on the horizontal axis.
- The bars should be separated from each other by a gap.
- Number of people (frequency) is on the vertical axis – this could be presented as a percentage rather than the actual number of people.

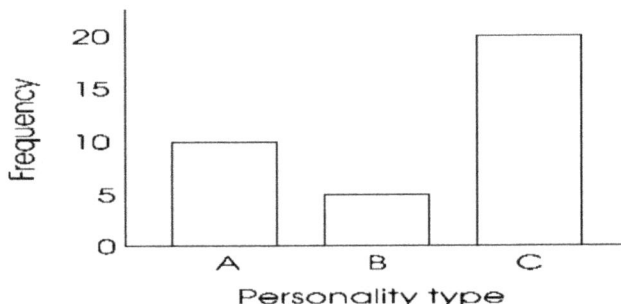

A Bar Graph Sample

The line graph

The line graph is a way of visually showing related data where individual items of data are joined by a line. They are useful for presenting data over time to compare changes to a variable over a set period. Joining up the points gives an instant picture of past trends (increases or decreases) and can be used to infer those trends to make predictions for the future. The variable represented is continuous; i.e. it is something that can be measured. You will be expected to be able to read graphs for specific measurements and trends. A graph is made within two axes: x and y. The vertical one is the y axis and the horizontal one is the x axis. The axes will not always start measuring from 0. If they don't, this is called the suppression of zero, this will affect the appearance of the line(s) on the graph making them steeper than they would be if the scale started at 0 and occupied the same space as the scale would be smaller.

Make sure you

- read the title of the graph to check what it represents.
- check where the axes start.

- check which units are being used on each axis.
- check the scale on each axis.

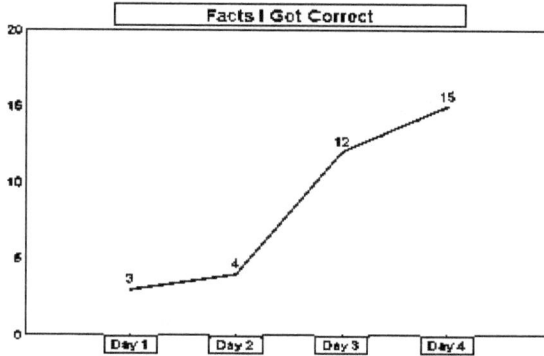

A Line Graph Sample

The pie graph

The pie graph uses "pie slices" to show relative sizes of data. You can use pie charts to show the relative sizes of many things. A pie chart is a way of illustrating information by using a circle as the whole and sections of the circle to represent parts of the whole.

- A pie chart provides the proportions of the data at a glance.
- They are useful for representing categorical data.

Always work out the total/whole.

Remember a proportion is always part of the whole.

Here is how many students got each grade in the recent test:

A	B	C	D
4	12	10	2

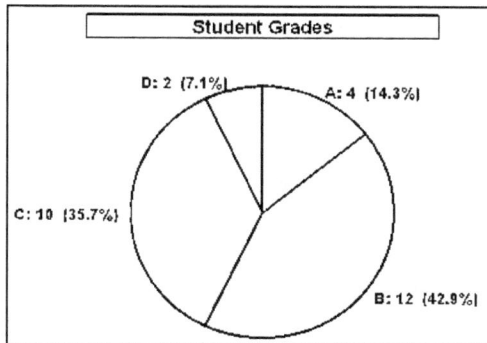

A Pie Graph Sample

169

The histogram

The histogram looks like a bar chart with the bars together. The difference is that the data collected is either discrete or continuous data. It means that the categories of data are related to each other. It contains a set of rectangles with bases along the intervals between class boundaries and with areas proportional to the frequencies in the corresponding classes. The rectangles are all adjacent, since the bases cover the intervals between class boundaries, not class limits. With equal class intervals the heights of rectangles will be proportional to corresponding frequencies, while for unequal classes they will be proportional to corresponding frequency densities.

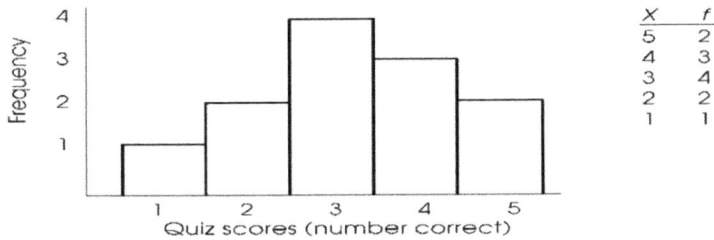

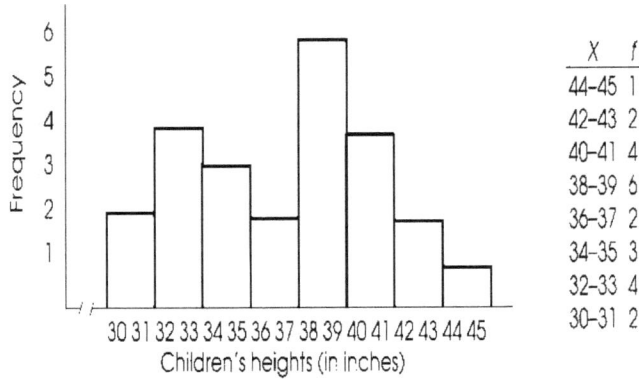

X	f
5	2
4	3
3	4
2	2
1	1

X	f
44–45	1
42–43	2
40–41	4
38–39	6
36–37	2
34–35	3
32–33	4
30–31	2

A Histogram Sample

There are some differences between histogram and bar graph. Table 7.2. represents the differences.

■ **Table 7.2.** *Histogram & Bar Graph in Comparison*

Histogram	Bar Graph
1. It consists of rectangles touching each other.	It consists of rectangles normally separated from each other with equal space.
2. The frequency is represented by the area of each rectangle.	The frequency is represented by height. The width has no significance.
3. It is two dimensional.	It is one dimensional.

The frequency polygon

The frequency polygon is a graphical device for understanding the shapes of distributions. They have the same purpose as histograms, but are especially useful for comparing sets of data. Frequency polygons are also a good choice for displaying *cumulative frequency distributions*.

To make a frequency polygon, start just as for histograms, by selecting a *class interval*. Then, draw an X-axis showing the values of the scores in your data. Mark the middle of each class interval with a tick mark, and label it with the middle value represented by the class. Draw the Y-axis to show the frequency of each class. Place a point in the middle of each class interval at the height corresponding to its frequency. Finally, connect the points. You should include one class interval below the lowest value in your data and one above the highest value. The graph will then touch the X-axis on both sides.

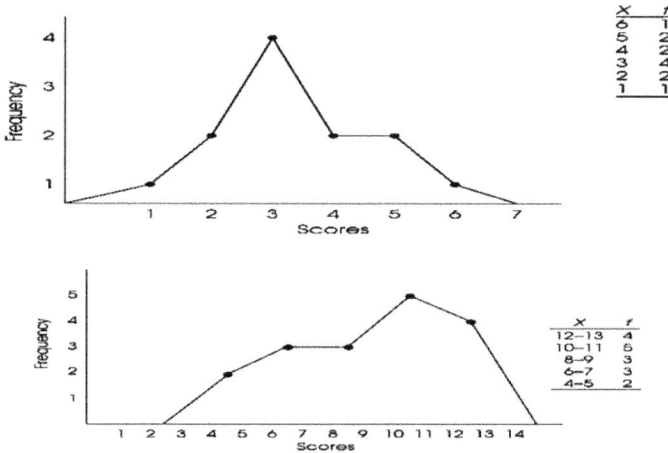

A Polygon Sample

Measures of central tendency

Students not only like to know how they performed on an examination, but also how well the other students performed through measuring **the mode, median, and mean** as mentioned before.

The **mean** is the arithmetic average. For example, 5-7-4-6-8-6 Mean=36÷6=6 Mean contains the whole and the individual values of all scores, but it is difficult to calculate a large number of scores through mean.

The **median** is considered as the middle score of a group of scores. In order to find the median value you can place the scores in order of size and find the middle number. For example, 2-8-7-1-3-9-5

Median=1

For even numbers, find the two middle numbers of the set add them up and then divide them by two. For example, 2-8-6-9-7-1-3-5

Median= 9+7÷2=8

Median is more representative than the mean when we have extreme scores. It is also easier to calculate than the mean, but it extracts less information than the mean because it does not apply exact numerical values of the scores.

The **mode** shows which score occurs most frequently. For example, 2-3-8-9-2-8-2-7-9-2-   Mode=2

If two adjacent scores have equal and greatest frequency, you should take an average of the two values. When two nonadjacent scores have equal highest frequency it is bimodal and we should report both modes.

Bimodal Distribution

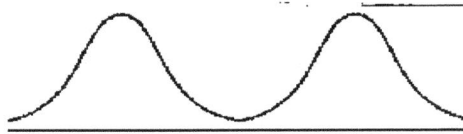

Some score patterns have two (or more) central clusters, rather than one.

A Bimodal Distribution Sample

The mode is very easy to find, but it is very crude if there is no difference in the frequencies of the scores.

A distribution in which the values of mean, median and mode coincide (i.e. mean = median = mode) is known as a symmetrical distribution. Conversely, when values of mean, median and mode are not equal the distribution is known as asymmetrical or skewed distribution. In moderately skewed or asymmetrical distribution a very important relationship exists among these three measures of central tendency.

Measures of dispersion or variance

In many ways, measures of **central tendency** are less useful in statistical analysis than measures of **dispersion** of values around the central tendency.

Measures of dispersion are descriptive statistics that describe how similar a set of scores are to each other. The more similar the scores are to each other, the lower the measure of dispersion will be. The less similar the scores are to each other, the higher the measure of dispersion will be. Generally, the more spread out a distribution is, the larger the measure of dispersion will be.

Which of the distributions of scores has the larger dispersion?

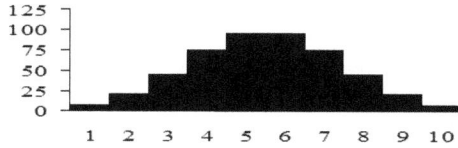

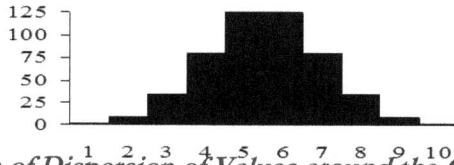

Samples of Dispersion of Values around the Central Tendency

The upper distribution has more dispersion because the scores are more spread out. That is, they are less similar to each other. There are three main measures of dispersion:

- The range
- Variance / standard deviation

The range

The *range* means the difference between the largest score in the set of data and the smallest score in the set of data, $X_L - X_S$

What is the range of the following data:

4 8 1 6 6 2 9 3 6 9

The largest score (X_L) is 9; the smallest score (X_S) is 1; the range is $X_L - X_S = 9 - 1 = 8$

The above range calculation is called the **actual range**. We may have **possible range** which deals with the highest and the lowest possible scores. In the above example, the lowest possible score is zero and the highest possible score is 10 (with the assumption that there were 10 items in the test. Therefore, the possible range can be 10 (10-0=10).

173

When to use the range

The range can be used when you have ordinal data or you are presenting your results to people with little or no knowledge of statistics. The range is rarely used in scientific work as it is fairly insensitive. It depends on only two scores in the set of data, X_L and X_S

Two very different sets of data can have the same range:
1 1 1 1 9 **vs.** 1 3 5 7 9

Variance

Variance measures how far a set of numbers is spread out. (A variance of zero indicates that all the values are identical.) Variance is always non-negative. A small variance shows the data points tend to be very close to the mean (expected value) and to each other, while a high variance indicates that the data points are very spread out from the mean and from each other.

What does the variance formula mean?

It says to subtract the mean from each of the scores. This difference is called a *deviate* or a *deviation score*. The deviate shows us how far a given score is from the typical, or average, score. Therefore, the deviate is a measure of dispersion for a given score. Why can't we simply take the average of the deviates? That is, why isn't variance defined as:

$$V = \frac{\Sigma(X - \bar{x})^2}{N - 1}$$

One of the definitions of the *mean* was that it always made the sum of the scores minus the mean equal to 0. Thus, the average of the deviates must be 0 since the sum of the deviates must equal 0. To avoid this problem, statisticians square the deviate score prior to averaging them. Squaring the deviate score makes all the squared scores positive. Variance is the mean of the squared deviation scores. The larger the variance is, the more the scores deviate, on average, away from the mean. The smaller the variance is, the less the scores deviate, on average, from the mean.

Standard Deviation

When the deviate scores are squared in variance, their unit of measure is squared as well. Since squared units of measure are often awkward to control, the square root of variance is often used instead. The standard deviation is the square root of variance

$$S = \frac{\sqrt{\Sigma(X - \bar{x})^2}}{N - 1}$$

Standard deviation $= \sqrt{Variance}$ Variance = (standard deviation)^2

174

The lowest standard deviation is 0. It indicates that there is no deviation at all. In fact, 68.26 % of all scores lie between +1 and -1 SD from the mean. 95.44% of all scores lie between +2 and -2 SD from the mean. 99.72% of all scores lie between +3 and -3 SD from the mean.

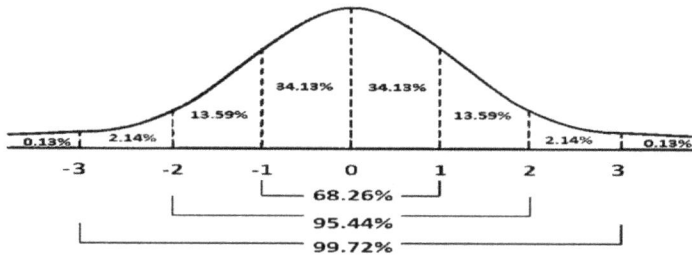

A Normal Curve & SD from Mean Sample

Frequency distribution curves

After collecting data, a researcher should organize and simplify the data so that it is possible to get a general overview of the results. This is the goal of descriptive statistical techniques. One method for simplifying and organizing data is to construct a **frequency distribution**. A **frequency distribution** is an organized tabulation representing exactly how many individuals are located in each category on the scale of measurement. A frequency distribution presents an organized picture of the entire set of scores, and it shows where each individual is located relative to others in the distribution.

Frequency distribution tables

A frequency distribution table is made of at least two columns – one listing categories on the scale of measurement (X) and another for frequency (f). In the X column, values are listed from the highest to lowest, without skipping any. For the frequency column, tallies are determined for each value (how often each X value occurs in the data set). These tallies are the frequencies for each X value. The sum of the frequencies should equal N.

A third column can be used for the proportion (p) for each category: p = f/N. The sum of the p column should equal 1.00. A fourth column can display the percentage of the distribution corresponding to each X value. The percentage is found by multiplying p by 100. The sum of the percentage column is 100%.

Regular frequency distribution

When a frequency distribution table lists all of the individual categories (X values) it is called a **regular frequency distribution**.

Grouped frequency distribution

Sometimes, however, a set of scores covers a wide range of values. In these situations, a list of all the X values would be quite long – too long to be a "simple" presentation of the data. To solve this problem, a **grouped frequency distribution** table is used.

In a grouped table, the X column lists groups of scores, called **class intervals**, rather than individual values. These intervals all have the same width, usually a simple number such as 2, 5, 10, and so on. Each interval starts with a value that is a multiple of the interval width. The interval width is chosen so that the table will have approximately ten intervals.

Relative frequency

Many populations are so large that it is not possible to know the exact number of individuals (frequency) for any specific category. In these situations, population distributions can be represented using **relative frequency** instead of the absolute number of individuals for each category.

Smooth curve

If the scores in the population are measured on an interval or ratio scale, it is usual to present the distribution as a smooth curve rather than a histogram or polygon. The smooth curve represents the fact that the distribution is not showing the exact frequency for each category.

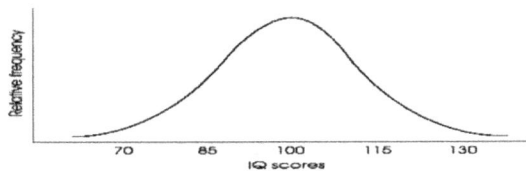

A smooth curve sample

A graph shows the **shape** of the distribution. A distribution can be **symmetrical** if the left side of the graph is (roughly) a mirror image of the right side. One example of a symmetrical distribution is the bell-shaped normal distribution. On the other hand, distributions are **skewed** when scores pile up on one side of the distribution, putting a "tail" of a few extreme values on the other side.

Positively and negatively skewed distributions

In a **positively skewed** distribution, the scores pile up on the left side of the distribution with the tail tapering off to the right. In a **negatively skewed** distribution, the scores tend to pile up on the right side and the tail points to the left.

Symmetrical distributions

Skewed distributions

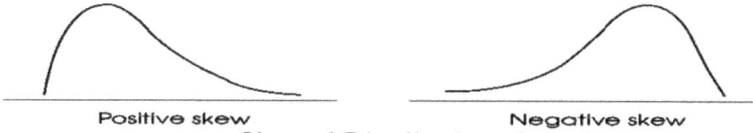

Positive skew   Negative skew

Skewed Distributions Samples

Leptokurtic and platykurtic curves

Distributions also can be different from each other in terms of how large or "fat" their tails are. They are in another form referred to as **kurtosis**. The below samples show two distributions that differ in this respect. The left distribution has relatively more scores in its tails; its shape is called leptokurtic(/ˌleptəˈkərtik/). The right distribution has relatively fewer scores in its tails; its shape is called platykurtic(/ˌplatiˈkərtik/).

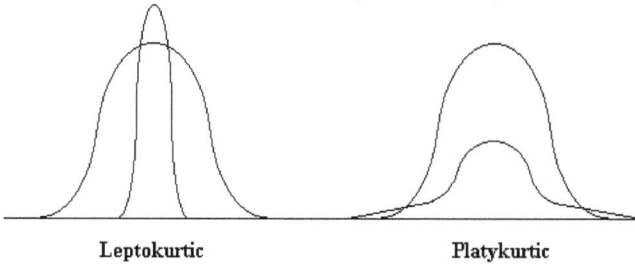

Leptokurtic   Platykurtic

Leptokurtic and platykurtic curves Samples

Percentiles, Percentile Ranks, and Interpolation

The relative location of individual scores in a distribution can be described by percentiles and percentile ranks. The **percentile rank** for a particular X value is the percentage of individuals with scores equal to or less than that X value. When an X value is described by its rank, it is called a **percentile**.

Interpolation

When scores or percentages do not correspond to upper real limits or cumulative percentages, you must use interpolation to show the corresponding ranks and percentiles. **Interpolation** is a mathematical process based on the assumption that the scores and the percentages change in a regular, linear fashion as you move through an interval from one end to the other.

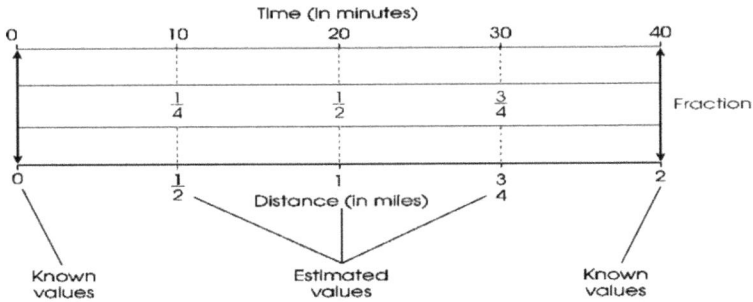

An Interpolation Sample

Stem-and-leaf displays

A stem-and-leaf display provides a very efficient method for obtaining and displaying a frequency distribution. Each score is divided into a **stem** consisting of the first digit or digits, and a **leaf** consisting of the final digit. Finally, you go through the list of scores, one at a time, and write the leaf for each score beside its stem.

The resulting display provides an organized picture of the entire distribution. The number of leafs beside each stem corresponds to the frequency, and the individual leafs identify the individual scores.

TABLE 2.3

A set of $N = 24$ scores presented as raw data and organized in a stem and leaf display.

Data			Stem and Leaf Display	
83	82	63	3	23
62	93	78	4	26
71	68	33	5	6279
76	52	97	6	283
85	42	46	7	1643846
32	57	59	8	3521
56	73	74	9	37
74	81	76		

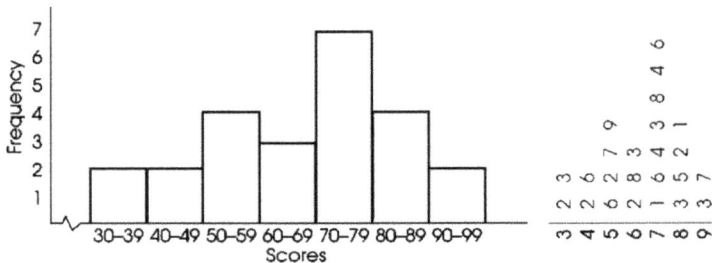

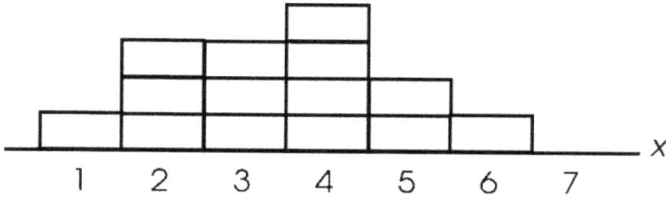

Stem & Display Samples

Standard Scores

The standard score is a very useful statistic because it (a) allows us to calculate the probability of a score occurring within our normal distribution and (b) enables us to compare two scores that are from different normal distributions. To explain what this means in simple terms, let's use an example. A teacher sets English Literature coursework for the 50 students in his class. We make the assumption that when the scores are presented on a histogram, the data is found to be normally distributed. The mean score is 60 out of 100 and the standard deviation (in other words, the variation in the scores) is 15 marks. Having looked at the performance of the teacher's class, one student has asked the teacher if, by scoring 70 out of 100, she has done well. Bearing in mind that the mean score was 60 out of 100 and that she scored 70, then at first sight it may appear that since she has scored 10 marks above the 'average' mark, she has achieved one of the best marks. However, this does not take into consideration the variation in scores amongst the 50 students (in other words, the standard deviation). After all, if the standard deviation is 15, then there is a reasonable amount of variation amongst the scores when compared with the mean. Whilst she has still scored much higher than the mean score, she has not necessarily achieved one of the best marks in her class. The question arises: How well did she perform in her English Literature coursework compared to the other 50 students?

Z-score

If the standard deviation in a given test is clear, it is easy to calculate the Z-score:

$$Z = \frac{X - \bar{x}}{SD}$$

If the score is the same as the mean, the value of z is zero. If the mean is greater than the mean, z is positive and if the score is smaller than the mean, z is negative.

T-score

Another standardized score is T-score. When we have the z-score it is possible to calculate T-score. When the mean is 50 and standard deviation is 10 the T-score is

$$Z=\frac{X-\bar{x}}{SD} = Z=\frac{T-50}{10}$$
$$T=10Z+50$$

Test results in z are below the mean. But if we use T-score the test results will increase.

Stanine

Stanine scores are a method teachers use to evaluate students' scores on standardized tests. "Stanine" is a shortened way of saying "standard nine," because it is a system that divides the standard curve of test results into nine groups. Most test scores fall into groups four through six, while scores in groups one through three are below average and those in groups seven through nine are above average. Each stanine group is placed in relation to the mean score and has a span of 0.5 standard deviations. Since z-scores tell you how many standard deviations a given test score differs from the mean, calculating z-scores is an easy way to determine which of the nine stanine groups each student's test score falls within. There exists a normal distribution with a mean of 0 and a standard deviation of 1.

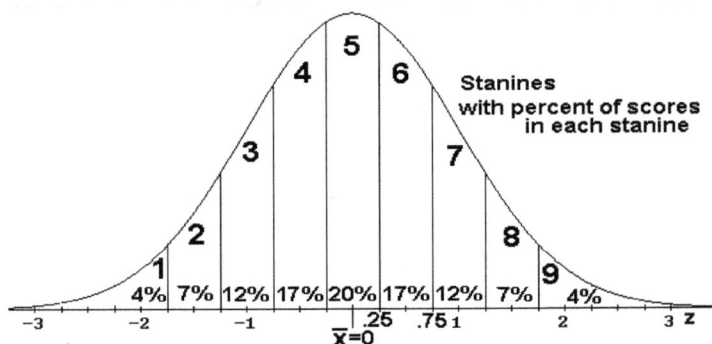

A Standard Normal Distribution with Nine Specific Intervals Sample

When the center interval is within a quarter of a standard deviation of the mean, and each of the other intervals are a half standard deviation wide (exclusive of the tails), the distribution has been marked in stanines (the standard nine intervals).
It is often used to:

- compare two or more distributions of data, particularly test scores.

- estimate or to compute probabilities of events involving normal distributions.
- facilitate using words rather than numbers in presenting statistical data.

The mean difference

The **mean difference** is a measure of statistical dispersion equal to the average absolute difference of two independent values drawn from a probability distribution. A related statistic is the **relative mean difference**, which is the mean difference divided by the arithmetic mean.

Correlation

Correlation determines the existing relationship between two or more variables. There are different kinds of correlations.

The linear correlation

The linear correlation: It is shown by a scatter diagram with one vertical and one horizontal line to show two variables. It can suggest a **linear relationship**, a **curvilinear relationship**, and **no relationship.**

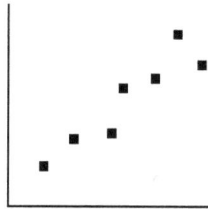

Postive linear relationship   Negative linear relationship

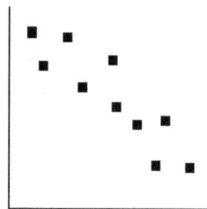

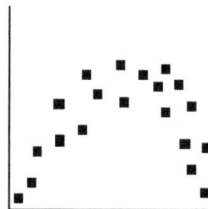

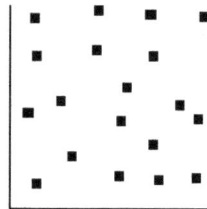

Non-linear relationship   No relationship

Correlational relationships samples

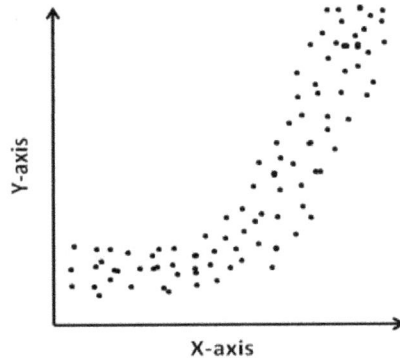

A Curvilinear Correlation Sample

The coefficient of correlation

The coefficient of correlation: After determining the existence of a linear correlation between two variables, the coefficient of correlation shows the strength of the linear relationship. Karl Pearson developed a formula that has the value between +1 and -1. The correlation is high when it is close to +1 or -1 and low when it is close to 0.

The rank order correlation

The rank order correlation: Spearman rank order correlation coefficient rho (p) is used if the data exist only in ranked (ordinal) form or if the number of paired variables is more than 9 or fewer than 30.

The point biserial correlation

The point biserial correlation: (rpb) is used with tests which have different sections or subclasses.

Inferential statistics

We have seen that descriptive statistics provide information about our immediate group of data. For example, we could calculate the mean and standard deviation of the exam marks for the 100 students and this could provide valuable information about this group of 100 students. Any group of data like this, which includes all the data you are interested in, is called a **population**. A population can be small or large, as long as it includes all the data you are interested in. For example, if you were only interested in the exam marks of 100 students, the 100 students would represent your population. Descriptive statistics are applied to populations, and the properties of populations, like the mean or standard deviation, are called **parameters** as they represent the whole population (i.e., everybody you are interested in).

Often, however, you do not have access to the whole population you are interested in investigating, but only a limited number of data instead. For example, you might be interested in the exam marks of all students in the UK. It is not feasible to measure all exam marks of all students in the whole of the UK so you have to measure a smaller **sample** of students (e.g., 100 students), which are used to represent the larger population of all Iranian students. Properties of samples, such as the mean or standard deviation, are not called parameters, but **statistics**. Inferential statistics are techniques that allow us to use these samples to make generalizations about the populations from which the samples were drawn. It is, therefore, important that the sample accurately represents the population. Inferential statistics arise out of the fact that sampling naturally incurs sampling error and thus a sample is not expected to perfectly represent the population. It is believed that inferential statistics deals with the world of probability.

Limitations of inferential statistics

There are two main limitations to the use of inferential statistics. The first and most important limitation, which is present in all inferential statistics, is that you are providing data about a population that you have not fully measured, and therefore, cannot ever be completely sure that the values/statistics you calculate are correct. Remember, inferential statistics are based on the concept of using the values measured in a sample to estimate/infer the values that would be measured in a population; there will always be a degree of uncertainty in doing this. The second limitation is connected with the first limitation. Some, but not all, inferential tests require the user (i.e., you) to make educated guesses (based on theory) to run the inferential tests. Again, there will be some uncertainty in this process, which will have repercussions on the certainty of the results of some inferential statistics. In order to make generalization from sample to population, hypothesis testing is needed. There are two main methods used in inferential statistics:

- estimation
- hypothesis testing.

In estimation, the sample is used to estimate a parameter and a confidence interval about the estimate is constructed.

In the most common use of hypothesis testing, a null hypothesis is put forward and it is determined whether the data are strong enough to reject it.

Inferential statistics and Probability

Probability: Formally considering, the probability of an event is the proportion of desired events to possible outcomes.

Probability of an event (p) $= \dfrac{number\ of\ desired\ events}{number\ of\ possible\ outcomes}$

Probability is used to make predictions about scores in a distribution.

The probability of a certain score belonging to a certain group: In order to quantitatively show the probability of a score belonging to a group, the raw score should be changed into a Z score. Then, the Z score should be interpreted based on the probability distribution. The Z for the mean in any distribution is zero. It is in the middle of the distribution and in the center of the normal curve. A vertical line which is drawn at right angles with the X axis at this center divides the normal curve into two parts; 50 % to the right and 50% to the left. If we go 1SD to the right and draw a line, 34.13%
of the area between the curve and the X axis is between this line and the line which is drawn from the mean. The area between -1SD and +1SD is 68.26%. If a member is selected randomly from this normal distribution, and this person is predicted to belong to the area between -1.96 % and +1.96, the probability of this prediction to be correct is 95%. There is 5% possibility of error. 95% confidence interval is used for making predictions. We try to accept p < .05 or less than 1% (p <.01).

The probability of a certain mean score belonging to a certain population: When we choose a large number of groups from the population, the mean of the means of the groups would be considered the same as the mean of the population. In addition the standard deviation of these group means would be equal to the standard deviation of the population adjusted for the sample size.

Hypothesis testing

Hypothesis testing: A hypothesis should be tested to be supported or rejected.

Levels of significance

Levels of significance: Levels of significance can be used as predetermined value used as a criterion to determine whether a given data set differs significantly from what would be expected. The level of significance of p <.05 can indicate that the results of the study is acceptable
if we are at least 95% sure.

Critical values of Z

Critical values of Z: Instead of dealing with percent of error in levels of significance, you can indicate whether a value belongs to the distribution of not by computing the Z value.

Critical values of the t distribution

The probability density function of the t-distribution
The t-distribution is a symmetric distribution and its shape depends on the degrees of freedom (df). The t-distribution has thicker tails than the normal distribution but, as the df increases, the t-distribution approximates the normal distribution. The area under the pdf to the right of t is equal to $\alpha/2$.

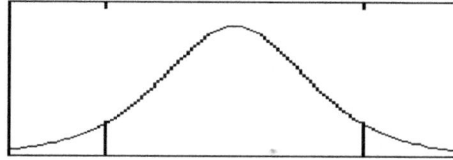

A t-discrimination sample

P-value

In statistical significance testing, the ***p*-value** is the probability of getting a test statistic result at least as extreme as the one that was actually observed, thinking that the null hypothesis is true. A researcher will often "reject the null hypothesis" when the *p*-value turns out to be less than a certain significance level, often 0.05 or 0.01. Such a result indicates that the observed result would be highly unlikely under the null hypothesis. Many common statistical tests, such as chi-squared tests or Student's *t*-test, produce test statistics which can be interpreted using *p*-values.

Testing directional and non-directional hypothesis

In directional hypothesis, it is claimed that there is a direction (+ or -) between the two variables. In a non-directional or a null hypothesis no particular direction is predicted. In other words, directional hypothesis works with one side of the distribution which is called **one-tailed** test of the hypothesis while non-directional hypothesis with two sides of distribution is called **two-tailed.** At the p <.05 level of significant we accept results when the probability of error is less than 5%. When we want to show this 5% we can either put the 55% at one end or into two and compile each half on each end of the curve.

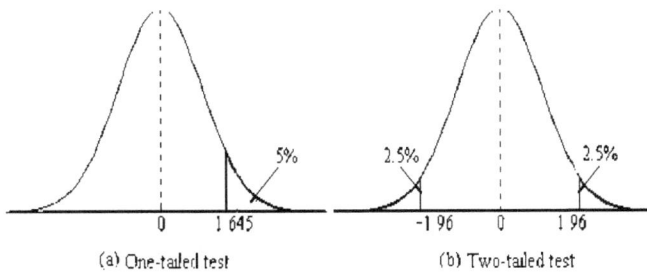

5%	2.5% 2.5%
0 1.645	-1.96 0 1.96
(a) One-tailed test	(b) Two-tailed test

A One-tailed Test & Two-tailed Test Sample

Confidence interval

Generally speaking, psychologists have made a convention about certainty by agreeing that 95% confidence is an "acceptable" level of certainty. To obtain it, multiply the standard error of the mean (SEM) by 1.96 and then add it to and subtract it from the mean CI= M ± (1.96) (SEM). SEM is the proportion of standard deviation(s) to the root of number in sample (n).

Null hypothesis H0

A type of hypothesis used in statistics that proposes that no statistical significance exists in a set of given observations. The null hypothesis attempts to show that no variation exists between variables, or that a single variable is no different than zero. It is presumed to be true until statistical evidence nullifies it for an alternative hypothesis. The null hypothesis assumes that any kind of difference or significance you see in a set of data is due to chance.

Alternative hypothesis

The alternative or experimental hypothesis reflects that there will be an observed effect for our experiment. In a mathematical formulation of the alternative hypothesis there will typically be an inequality, or not equal to symbol. This hypothesis is denoted by either H_a or by H_1. The alternative hypothesis is what we are attempting to demonstrate in an indirect way by the use of our hypothesis test. If the null hypothesis is rejected, then we accept the alternative hypothesis. If the null hypothesis is not rejected, then we do not accept the alternative hypothesis. Going back to the above example of mean human body temperature, the alternative hypothesis is "The average adult human body temperature is not 98.6 degrees Fahrenheit." If we are studying a new treatment, then the alternative hypothesis is that our treatment does in fact change our subjects in a meaningful and measureable way.

Type I error (Alpha error)

The first kind of error that is possible involves the rejection of a null hypothesis that is actually true. This kind of error is called a type I error, and is sometimes called an error of the first kind. Type I errors are equivalent to false positives.

It occurs when the null hypothesis is rejected when, in fact, the null hypothesis should be retained. Type I errors can be controlled. The value of alpha, which is related to the level of significance that we selected has a direct bearing on type I errors. Alpha is the maximum probability that we have a type I error. For a 95% confidence level, the value of alpha is 0.05. This means that there is a 5% probability that we will reject a true null hypothesis. In the long run, one out of every twenty hypothesis tests that we perform at this level will result in a type I error.

Type II error (Beta error)

The other kind of error that is possible occurs when we do not reject a null hypothesis that is false. This sort of error is called a type II error, and is also referred to as an error of the second kind. Type II errors are equivalent to false negatives.

How to avoid errors

Type I and type II errors are part of the process of hypothesis testing. Although the errors cannot be completely eliminated, we can minimize one type of error. Typically when we try to decrease the probability one type of error, the probability for the other type increases. We could decrease the value of alpha from 0.05 to 0.01, corresponding to a 99% level of confidence. However, if everything else remains the same, then the probability of a type II error will nearly always increase. Many times the real world application of our hypothesis test will determine if we are more accepting of type I or type II errors. This will then be used when we design our statistical experiment.

Population, sample, parameter, and statistic

An important idea when starting statistics is to understand the difference between *populations* and *samples*. **Populations** consist of everything or everybody you want to measure. Since it is usually impossible to deal with all members of a population in the research, researchers choose a limited number of members. Based on the research conducted on a **sample**, we can obtain some numerical values. The data convey the features of the sample. These obtained values are called **statistics**, while the corresponding values in the population can be called **parameters**. As Table 7.3 shows, descriptive statistics deal with sampling and statistics, while inferential statistics deal with populations and parameters.

■ **Table 7.3.** *The Relationship between Descriptive and Inferential Statistics*

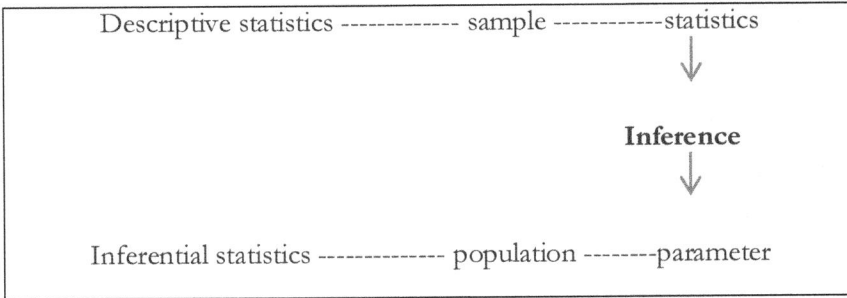

Descriptive statistics ------------ sample ------------statistics

$\downarrow$

Inference

$\downarrow$

Inferential statistics -------------- population --------parameter

Table 7.4. classifies different statistical methods. It also represents two sub-categories of inferential statistics.

■ **Table 7.4.** *Statistical Methods*

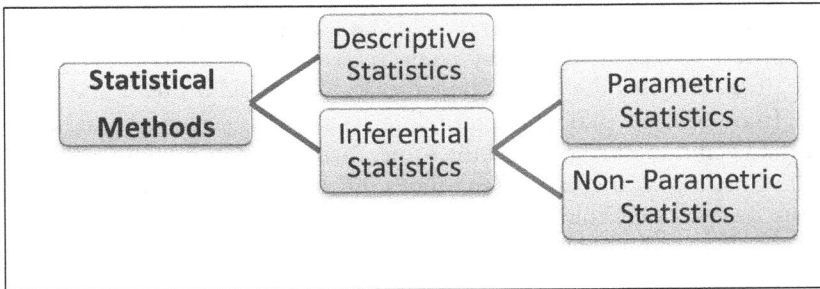

Statistical Package for the Social Sciences (SPSS)

SPSS Statistics is a *software package* used for *statistical analysis*. The current versions (2014) are officially named **IBM SPSS Statistics.**

For many students, using statistics in their research is very stressful. This chapter provides a simple guide using IBM SPSS to analyze the collected data.

The data you enter must come from responses to a questionnaire, information collected from interviews, coded observations of actual behavior, or objective measurements of output or performance.

As a guide to IBM SPSS, you must know how to use the Windows menus, the left and right buttons on the mouse, and the click and drag techniques to highlight text. You should be able to minimize/maximize windows, start/exit programs, move between simultaneously running programs, open, save, rename, move, and close files. It is also necessary to know how to use Windows Explorer to copy files from a memory stick to the hard drive, and back again.

Preparing a codebook

Before entering the information into IBM SPSS, you should make a "codebook" to define and label variables and assign numbers to each of the possible responses. Each item or question in the questionnaire should an especial variable name. Variable names should not be long, they should begin with a letter not a number, full stops, spaces or symbols should not be used. Each response must be given a numerical code before it can be entered into IBM SPSS. When you have made your codebook, you are ready to enter the data.

Variable	SPSS variable name	Coding instructions
Identification number	ID	Number assigned to each survey
Sex	Sex	1= Males 2= Females

A Codebook Sample

Starting IBM SPSS

You can put your cursor on the icon SPSS on your desktop and double click. You can also click on **Start,** go to **All Programs.** Click on **File** from the menu across the top of the screen, choose **Open,** slide to **Data.** The **Open File** will allow you to search to find where your data file is stored. To save a file, go to the **File** menu (top left-hand corner) and choose **Save.**

If working on a data file is finished and you want to open another file, click on **File**, choose **Open**, slide to **Data**, find the directory where the second file is stored, click on the desired file, and click the **open** button. To start a new data file, click on **File**, from the drop-down menu, click on **New** and then click on **Data**.

Windows

There are different types of windows in IBM SPSS Statistics:

Data editor window: It displays the contents of the data file. You can open, close, save, create, and enter your data.

Viewer: Statistical results, tables, and charts are displayed in the Viewer. You can edit the output and save it for later use. A Viewer window opens automatically the first time you run a procedure that generates output.

Pivot table editor: Output that is displayed in pivot tables can be modified in many ways with the Pivot Table Editor. You can edit text, swap data in rows and columns, add color, create multidimensional tables, and selectively hide and show results.

Chart editor: You can modify high-resolution charts and plots in chart windows. You can change the colors, select different type fonts or sizes, switch the horizontal and vertical axes, rotate 3-D scatterplots, and even change the chart type.

Text output editor: Text output that is not displayed in pivot tables can be modified with the Text Output Editor. You can edit the output and change font characteristics (type, style, color, size).

Syntax editor: You can paste your dialog box choices into a syntax window, where your selections appear in the form of command syntax. You can then edit the command syntax to use special features that are not available through dialog boxes. You can save these commands in a file for use in subsequent sessions.

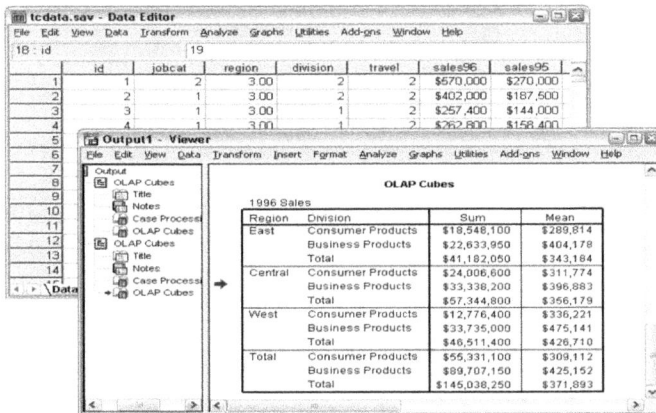

A Data Editor Window & Viewer Sample

A Syntax Editor Sample

Menus

Dialogue boxes: When you choose a menu option in drop-down menus across the top of the screen, you are asked for more information. Dialogue box comes when you want to use the **Frequencies**. Click on **Analyze**, **Descriptive Statistics**, **Frequencies**.

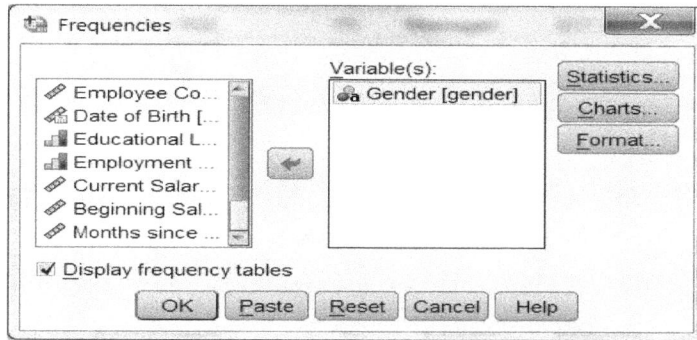

A Frequencies Dialogue Box Sample

On the left is a variable selection list with all of the variables in your data set. If your variables consist of variable labels select the variables you want to analyze by clicking on them, click the arrow button to the right of the selection list, and the variables are moved to the analysis list on the right. On the far right of the dialog are several buttons that lead to further dialog boxes with options for the frequencies command. At the bottom of the dialog box, click **OK** to issue your command to SPSS, or **Paste** to have the command written to a **Syntax Editor**.

Closing IBM SPSS

Click on the **File** menu at the top left of the screen, click on **Exit**. Save your output and data file regularly throughout your work.

Getting help

If you need help, use the in-built **Help** menu. Click on **Help** from the menu bar with a number of choices. For specific topics, work through a **Tutorial**, or consult a **Statistics Coach**. It proves a useful guide.

Changing the IBM SPSS "Options"

The options let you define how your variables, the type of tables, and other aspects of the program will be displayed. To open the **Options** screen, click on **Edit** from the menu at the top of the screen and choose **Options**. Do not click on **OK** until you finish all the changes.

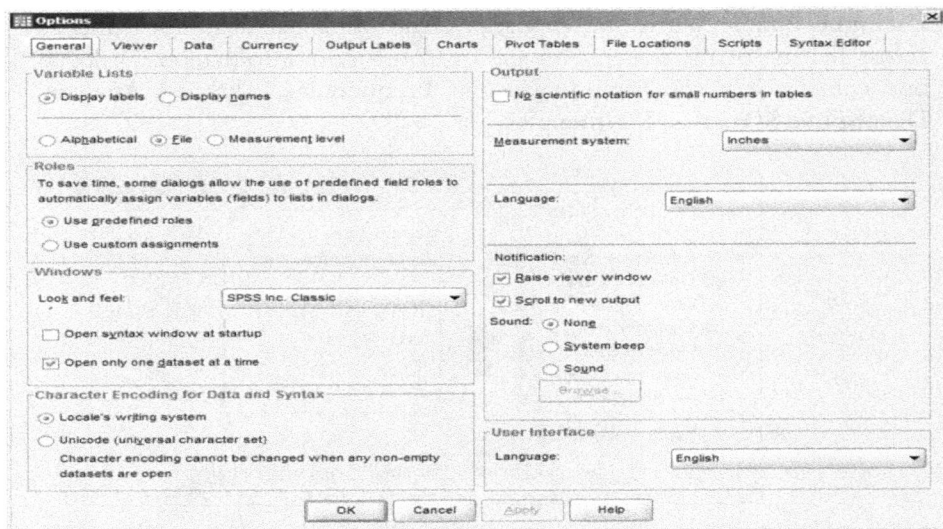

An Options Screen Sample

General tab: To keep the variables in file order, make sure the option **File** in the **Variable Lists** section is chosen. In the **Output** section on the right-hand side, tick **No Scientific notation for small numbers in tables** to stop getting some strange numbers. In the **Notification** section, the options **Raise viewer window** and **Scroll to new output** should be selected.

Data tab: To make changes to the way that your data is displayed click on the **Data**.

Output tab: To customize how you want the variable names and value labels displayed in your output click on **Values** and **Labels** from the drop-down options in this section.

Charts tab: To change the appearance of the charts click on the **Charts** tab.

Pivot Tables tab: To choose the format of tables click on **Pivot Tables**.

Defining the variables

Before entering the data, tell IBM SPSS about the variable names. The **Data Editor** window has two views: **Data View** and **Variable View. In Data View** window each of the columns is labeled **Var.**

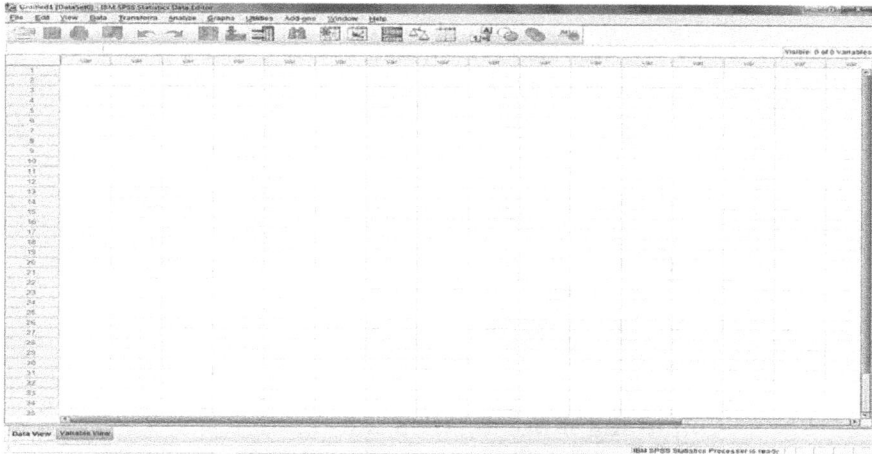

A Data Editor window Sample

Procedure for defining your variables

Click on the **Variable View** tab at the bottom left of your screen to change **Name, Type, Width, Decimals, Label, Values**, and **Missing**.

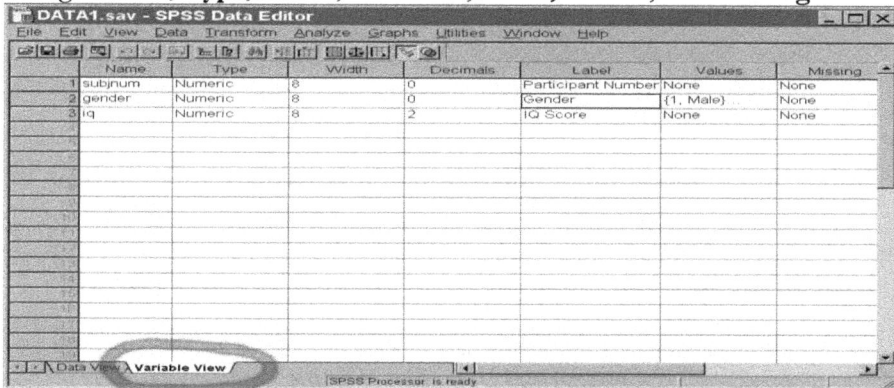

	Name	Type	Width	Decimals	Label	Values	Missing
1	subjnum	Numeric	8	0	Participant Number	None	None
2	gender	Numeric	8	0	Gender	{1, Male}	None
3	iq	Numeric	8	2	IQ Score	None	None

A Variable View Sample

Entering data

- Click on the **Data View** tab at the bottom left-hand side of the screen of the **Data Editor**.
  - Click on the first cell of the data set.
  - Type in the number.
  - Press the right arrow key on the keyboard to move to the second cell.
  - Move across the row to make sure that the values are entered properly.
  - Press the Home Key on the keyboard to move back to the start.

Descriptive statistics

Procedure for obtaining codebook to gain a summary of the cases in your data file

- Click on Analyze, go to Reports and select Codebook.
- Choose the variables you want and move them into the **Codebook Variable** box.
- Click on the **Output** and untick all the **Options** except **Label, Value Labels** and **Missing Values**.
- Click on the **Statistics** tab with ticked options in both sections.
- Click on **OK** or on **Paste** to save **Syntax Editor**.

Obtaining more detailed information

It can be obtained through using **Frequencies, Descriptives** or **Explore** procedures listed under the **Analyze, Descriptive Statistics** drop-down menu.

Categorical variables

- Click on **Analyze**, click on **Descriptive Statistics**, then **Frequencies**.
- Choose your interesting categorical variables. Move them into the **Variable** box.
- Click on **OK.**

	Frequency	percent	Valid Percent	Cumulative Percent
Valid 1Male	185	42.1	42.1	42.1
2 Female	254	57.9	57.9	100.0
Total	439	100.0	100.0	

A Categorical Variables Sample

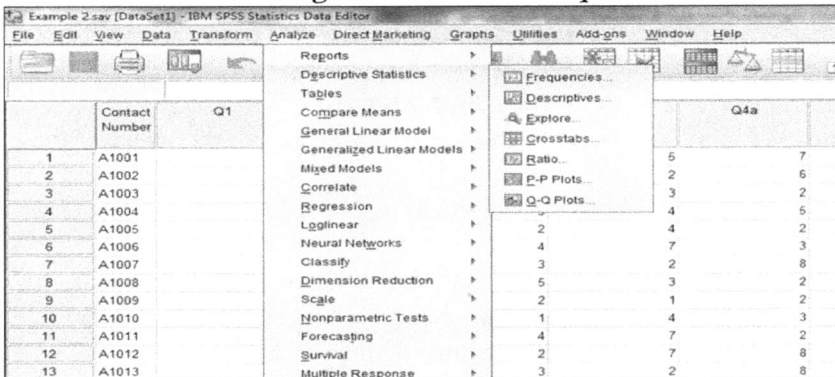

A Descriptive Statistics Sample

Continuous Variables

- Click on **Analyze**; choose **Descriptive Statistics**, then **Descriptives**.
- Click on your favorite continuous variables, and then move them into the **Variables** box.
- Click on the **Options** button. **Mean, standard deviation, minimum, maximum** should ne ticked. Then click on **skewness, kurtosis**.
- Click on **Continue**, and **then OK**.

Missing data

It is important to inspect your data file for missing data. Run **descriptives** to find out what percentage of values is missing for each of your variables. The **options** button offers you some choices to deal with missing data.

Assessing the normality of the distribution of scores

- Click on **Analyze**, select **Descriptive Statistics**, and then **Explore** from the menu at the top of the screen.
- Click on the variable(s) you want. Click on the arrow button to move them into the Dependent List box.
- Put your ID variable in the **Label cases** by: box.
- Make sure that **Both** is chosen in the **Display** section.
- Click on the **statistics, Descriptives, Outliers**, and **Continue**.
- Click on the **Plots** button. Under **Descriptives**, click on **Histogram** to choose it. Click on Stem-and-leaf to unselect it. Click on **Normality plots with tests** and click on **Continue**.
- Click on **Options** button. In the **Missing section**, click on **Exclude cases pairwise**. Click on **Continue** and then **OK**.

Using graphs to describe and explore the data

Histograms: They can be used to show the distribution of a single continuous variable.

- Click on **Graphs**, from the menu. Choose **Legacy Dialogs**. Choose **Histogram**.
- Click on the variable that you want and move it into the **Variable** box.
- Click on **OK**.

Bar Graphs: Basically, we need one categorical and one continuous variable.

- Click on **Graphs**, from the menu. Choose **Legacy Dialogs**. Select **Bar**. Click on **Clustered**.

- Click on **Summaries for groups of cases** in the Data chart are section, click on **Define**.
- Click on **Other statistic** in the **Bars represent** box.
- Click on the first categorical variable. Click on the arrow button to move it into the **Category axis** box.
- Click on another categorical variable and move it into the **Define Clusters by**: box.
- Click on the **Options** button and on **Display error bars** to display error bars.
- Click on **Continue** and then **OK**.

Line graphs: With a bar graph you can inspect the mean scores of a continuous variable across a number of different values of a categorical variable. It can be used for exploring the results of a one-or two-way analysis of variance.

- Choose **Graphs**, then **Legacy Dialogs**, then **Line** from the menu at the top of the screen.
- Click on **Multiple**. In the Data in Chart Are section, click on **Summaries for groups of cases**. Click on **Define**.
- In the **Lines represent** box, click on **Other statistics**. Click on the variable that you want. Click on the arrow button. The variable should appear in the box listed as **Mean**.
- Click on another categorical variable and move it into the **Define Lines by**: box.
- Click on the **Options** button if you want to add error bars to the graph. Click on the **Display error bars** box.
- Click on **OK**.

Scatterplots: They are usually used to find the relationship between two continuous variables.

- Click on **Graphs**, then **Legacy Dialogs** and the on **Scatter/Dot** from the menu at the top of the screen.
- Click on **Simple Scatter** and then **Define**.
- Click on the first variable, usually the independent one.
- Click on the arrow to move it into the box **Y axis**.
- Move to the other variable into the box **X axis**.
- Move the ID variable in the **Label Cases by**: box
- Click on **OK**.

Editing a chart or graph

In order to edit a chart or a graph, you should open the **Chart Editor** window. In order to do this, you should place your cursor on the graph that you want to modify. Double-click and a new window opens. There is a smaller **Properties** window pop up. If it does not appear, click on the **Edit** menu and choose **Properties**.

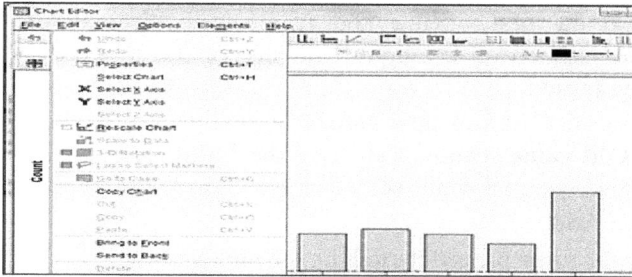

A Chart Editor Menu Bar Sample

Manipulating the data

When you have entered the data appropriately, you should manipulate the raw data into a suitable form to conduct analyses and test your hypotheses.

Using Syntax to record procedures

Syntax Editor window can be used to record the commands generated using the Windows menus for each procedure.

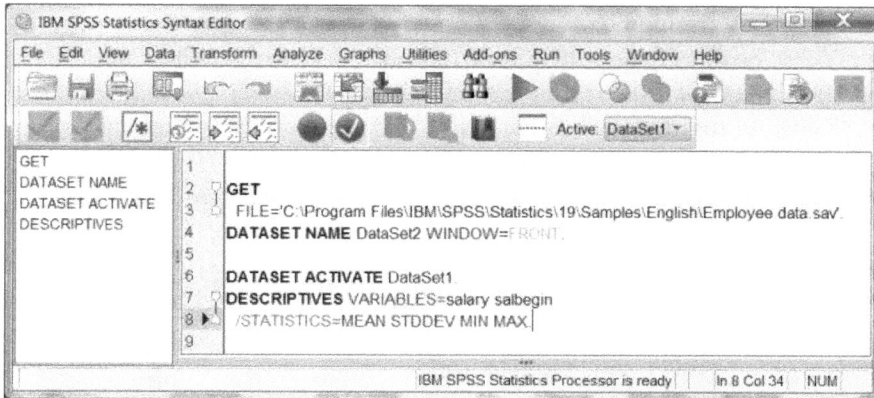

A Syntax Editor window Sample

Calculating total scale scores

Before performing statistical analyses, you should calculate total scale scores for any scales which are used in the study involving two steps:

Step one: You should reverse any negatively worded items.

- Click on **Transform** from the menu at the top of the screen. Click on **Recode Into Different Variables.**

- Choose the items you intend to reverse (op2, op4, op6). Move them into the **Input Variable-Output Variable** box.
- Click on the first variable and type a new name in the **Output Variable** section on the right-hand side of the screen. Click on the **Change** button.
- Click on the **Old and new values** button. Type 1 in the **Value** box in the **Old value** section. Type 5 in the **Value** box (It will change all scores that were originally scored as 1 to 5) in the **New value** section.
- Click on **Add**.
- Repeat the same procedure for the remaining scores.
- Click on **Continue** and then **OK**.

The new variables with reversed scores can be found at the end of the data file. You can check it in the **Data Editor** window. You should choose the **Variable View** tab and go down to the bottom of the list of variables.

Step two: You should add together scores from all the items that make up the subscale or scale. You should do this if you have a complete data file as IBM SPSS does not update this command when you add extra data.

- Click on **Transform** from the menu at the top of the screen. Click on **Compute Variable**.
- Type in the new name you want to give to the total scale scores in the **Target Variable** box.
- Click on the **Type and Label** button. Click in the **Label** box and type in a description of the scale. Click on **Continue**.
- Click on the first item in the scale (op1) from the list of variables on the left-hand side.
- Click on the arrow button to move it into the **Numeric Expression** box.
- Click on + on the calculator.
- Repeat all the process until all scale items appear in the box.
- The complete numeric expression should be as op1+op3+op5+Rop2+Rop4+Rop6.
- Double-click that all items are true and + signs in the right places. Click **OK**.

Checking the reliability of a scale

Before you start, you should check that all negatively worded items in the scale have been reversed.

- Click on **Analyze** from the menu at the top of the screen. Choose **Scale** and then **Reliability Analysis**.
- Click on all the individual items that make up the scale. Move these into the box of **Items**.

- Make sure **Alpha** is chosen in the **Model** section.
- Type in the name of the scale or subscale in the **Scale label** box.
- Click on the **Statistics** button. In the Descriptive for section, choose **Item, Scale,** and **Scale if the item deleted**. In the **Inter-Item** section, click on **Correlations**. In the summaries section, click on **Correlations**.
- Click on **Continue** and then **OK**.

Table7. 4 *Summary Table of the Characteristics of the Main Statistical Technique (taken from Pallant, 2013, pp, 123-124)*

Purpose	Example of question	Parametric statistics	Non-parametric statistics	Independent variable	Dependent variable	Essential features
Exploring relation-ships	What is the relationship between gender and dropout rates from therapy	None	Chi-square	One categorical variable sex: M/F	One categorical variable Dropout/complete therapy: yes/no	The number of cases in each category is considered, not scores.
	Is there a relationship between age and optimism scores?	Pearson product-moment correlation coefficient	Spearman' Rank Order Correlation (rho)	Two continuous variables Age, Optimism scores		One sample with scores on two different measures, or same measure at Time 1 and Time 2
	After controlling for the effects of socially desirable responding bias, is there still a relationship between optimism and life satisfaction?	Partial correlation	None	Two continuous variables and one continuous variable for which you wish to control Optimism, life satisfaction, scores on a social desirability scale		One sample with scores on two different measures, or same measure at Time 1 and Time 2

	How much of the variance in life satisfaction scores can be explained by self-esteem, perceived control and optimism? Which of these variables is the best predictor?	Multiple regression	None	Set of two or more continuous independent variables Self-esteem, perceived control, optimism	One continuous dependent variable Life Satisfaction	One sample with scores on all measures
	What is the underlying structure of the items that make up the Positive and Negative Affect Scale? How many factors are involved?	Factor analysis	None	Set of related continuous variables items of the positive and Negative Affect Scale		One sample, multiple measures
Comparing groups	Are males more likely to drop out of therapy than females?	None	Chi-square	One categorical independent variable Sex	One categorical dependent variable Dropout/complete therapy	You are interested in the number of people in each category, not scores on a scale
	Is there a change in participants' anxiety scores from Time 1 to Time 2?	Paired sample t-test	Wilcoxon signed Rank Test	One categorical independent (two levels) Time 1/Time2	One continuous dependent variable Anxiety score	Same people on two different occasions
	Is there a	One-way	Kruskal-	One	One	Three or

difference in optimism scores for people who are under 35 yrs, 36-49 and 50+ yrs?	between groups ANOVA	Wallis Test	categorical independent (three or more levels)\n\nAge group	continuous dependent variable\n\nAnxiety score	more groups: different people in each group
Is there a change in participants' anxiety scores from Time 1, Time 2 and Time 3?	Two-way repeated ANOVA	Friedman Test	One categorical independent variable (three or more levels)\n\nTime 1/Time2/Time3	One continuous dependent variable\n\nAnxiety score	Three or more groups: Same people on two different occasions
Is there a difference in the optimism scores for males and females, who are under 35 yrs, 36-49 yrs and 50+ yrs?	Two-way between groups ANOVA	None	Two categorical independent variables (two or more levels) Age group, Sex	One continuous dependent variable Optimism score	Two or more groups for each independent variable: different people in each group
Which intervention (maths skills/confidence building) is more effective in reducing participants' fear of statistics, measured across three time periods?	Mixed between-within ANOVA	None	One between-groups independent variable (two or more levels), one within-groups independent variable (two or more levels) Type of intervention, Time	One continuous dependent variable Fear of Statistics Test scores	Two or more groups with different people in each group, each measured on two or more occasions
Is there a difference between males and females, across three	Multivariate\n\nANOVA(MANOVA)	None	One or more categorical independent variables (two or more levels)	Two or more related continuous dependent variables Anxiety,	

different age groups, in terms of their scores on a variety of adjustme nt measures(anxiety, depressio n and perceived stress)?			Age group, Sex	depression, and perceived stress scores
Is there a significan ce difference in the fear of Stats Test scores for participan ts in the maths skills group and the confidenc e building group, while controllin g for their scores on this test at Time 1?	Analysis of covarianc e (ANOCV A)	None	One or more categorical independent variables (two or more levels), one continuous covariate variable Type of intervention, Fear of Stats Test scores at Time 1	One continuous dependent variable Fear of Statas Test scores at Time 2

Correlation
Preliminary analysis for correlation
Generating a scatterplot

- Click on **Graphs** from the menu at the top of the screen. Choose **Legacy Dialogs.**
- Click on **Scatter/Plot** and then Simple Scatter. Click **Define**.
- Click on the first variable. Move it into the **Y-Axis** box. Generally, the dependent variable is placed along Y-axis.
- Click on the second variable which is the independent variable and move in into the **X-axis** box.
- In the **Label Cases by**: box, put your ID variable.

- Click on **OK**.

Using Pearson r or Spearman rho to determine the direction of the relationship between the variables

- Click on **Analyze** from the menu at the top of the screen. Choose **Correlation**, then **Bivariate**.
- Choose your two variables and move them into the box called **Variables**.
- In the **Correlation Coefficients** section, the **Pearson** box is the default choice. Tick the **Spearman** box to request the **Spearman rho**.
- Click on the **Options** button. For Missing Values, click on the **Exclude cases pairwise** box. You can obtain means and standard deviations under **Options**.
- Click on **Continue** and then **OK**.

Obtaining correlation coefficients between one group of variables and another group of variables

- Click on **Analyze** from the menu at the top of the screen. Choose **Correlate**, then **Bivariate**.
- Move the variables that you want into the **Variable** box.
- Click on **Paste** to open the **Syntax Editor** window.
- Put the cursor between the first group of variable and other variables. Type in the word **WITH**.
- Alternatively you can click on **Correlations** on the left-hand side of the screen.
- Click on the green triangle or arrow-shaped icon (>), or click on **Run** from the **Menu**, and then choose **Selection** from the drop-down menu that appears.

Comparing the correlation coefficients for two groups
Step one: Split the sample

- Click on **Data** from the menu at the top of the screen. Choose Split File.
- Click on **Compare Groups**.
- Move the grouping variable into the box labeled **Groups based on**. Click on **OK** or on **Paste** to save to **Syntax Editor**. Click on **Run** in using Syntax.

Step two: Follow the steps to request the correlation between your variables of interest. The results will be reported separately for the two groups.

Partial correlation

Partial correlation let you know to explore the relationship between two variables, while statistically for the effect of another variable that you think may be influencing the relationship.

- Click on **Analyze** from the menu at the top of the screen. Choose **Correlate**, then **Partial**.
- Click on the two continuous variables that you want to correlate. Click on the arrow to move these into the **Variables** box.
- Click on the variable you want to control for. Move into the **Controlling for** box.
- Click on **Options**. In the **Missing Values** section, click on **exclude cases pairwise**. In the **Statistics** section, click on **Zero order correlations**.
- Click on **Continue** and then **OK** or **paste** to save to **Syntax Editor**.

Multiple regression

Multiple regression is not one technique but a group of techniques to explore the relationship between one continuous dependent variable and a number of independent variables (usually continuous). Multiple regression is related to correlation, but allows a more complex exploration of the interrelationship among a set of variables.

Standard multiple regression

- Click on **Analyze** from the menu at the top of the screen. Choose **Regression** and, then **Linear**.
- Click on the continuous dependent variable and move it into the **Dependent** box.
- Click on independent variables and click on the arrow to move them into the **Independent** box.
- Make sure **Enter** is chosen foe **Method**.
- Click on **Statistics** button. Choose **Estimates, Confidence Intervals, Model fit, Descriptives, Part and partial correlations** and **Collinearity diagnostics**. In the **Residuals** section, choose **Casewise diagnostics** and **Outliers outside 3 standard deviations**. Click on **Continue**.
- Click on the **Options** button. Select **Exclude cases pairwise** in the **Missing Values** section. Click on **Continue**.
- Click on the **Plots** button. Click on ***ZRESID** and arrow to move this into the **Y** box. Click on ***ZPRED** and the arrow button to move this into the **X** box. In the section headed **Standardized Residual Plots**, tick the **Normal probability plot** choice. Click on **Continue**.

- Click on the **Save** button. In the section labeled **Distances**, choose **Mahalanobis** box and **Cook's**. Click on **Continue** and the **OK** or **Paste** to save to **Syntax Editor**.

Hierarchical multiple regression

Hierarchical multiple regression also refers to sequential regression. We will enter our variables in steps or blocks in a predetermined order. We do not let computer decide, as would be the case for stepwise regression.

- Click on **Analyze** from the menu at the top of the screen. Choose **Regression**, then **Linear**.
- Select the continuous dependent variable and move it into the **Dependent** box.
- Move the variables you want to control for into the **Independent** box. It will be the first block of variables to be entered.
- Click on the button labeled **Next**. This will give the second independent variables box.
- Select the next block on independent variables.
- Make sure that this is set to the default (**Enter**) in the **Method** box.
- Click on **Statistics** button. Choose **Estimates**, **Model fit**, **R squared change**, **Descriptives**, **Part and partial correlations** and **Collinearity diagnostics**. Click on **Continue**.
- Click on the Options button. Click on **Exclude cases pairwise** in the **Missing Values**. Click on **Continue**.
- Click on the Plots button. Click on ***ZRESID** and the arrow button to move this into the **Y** box. Click on ***ZPRED** and the arrow button to move this into the X box.
- Tick the **Normal probability plot** option, in the section headed **Standardized Residual plots**. Click on **Continue**.
- Click on the Save button. Click on **Mahalanobis** and **Cook's**. Click on **Continue** and the **OK** or on **Paste** to save to **Syntax Editor**.

Logistic regression

Logistic regression lets you test models to predict categorical outcomes with two or more categories. The independent (predictor) variables may be either categorical or continuous, or mix of both in one model. There is a group of logistic regression techniques in IBM SPSS that can allow you to explore he predictive ability of sets or blocks of variables, and to specify the entry of variables.

- Click on **Analyze** from the menu at the top of the screen. Click on **Regression** and then **Binary Logistic**.
- Select the categorical dependent variable and move it into the **Dependent** box.

- Click on the predictor variables and move them into the box labeled **Covariates**.
- Make sure that **Enter** is displayed for **Method**.
- Click on the **Categorical** button if you have any categorical predictors. Highlight each of the categorical variables and move them into the **Categorical covariate** box.
- Highlight each of your categorical variables in turn. Click on the button labeled **First** in the **Change contrast** section. Click on the **Change** button. The word (first) is appeared after the variable name. Repeat for all categorical variables. Click on **Continue**.
- Click on the **Options** button. Choose **Classification plots, Hosmer-Lemeshow goodness of fit, Casewise listing of residuals,** and **CI for EXP (B)**.
- Click on **Continue** and **OK** or **Paste** to save to **Syntax Editor**.

Factor analysis

Factor analysis is not the same as other techniques presented in this chapter. It is not made to test hypotheses or to tell whether one group is different from another. It is considered as "data reduction" technique in IBM SPSS. It takes a large group of variables and searches for a way the data might be "reduced" or summarized using a smaller group of factors or components. Select **Edit** from the menu, choose **Options**, tick in the box **No scientific notation for small numbers in tables**.

- Click on **Analyze** from the menu at the top of the screen. Choose **Dimension Reduction**, and then **Factor**.
- Choose all the required variables. Move them into the **Variables** box.
- Click on the **Descriptives** button.
- Make sure that **Initial Solution** is ticked in the **Statistics**. Choose the options **Coefficients and KMO and Bartlett's test of sphericity** in the section marked **Correlation Matrix**.
- Click on the **Extraction** button. Make sure **Principal components** is shown or choose one of the other factor extraction techniques in the **Method** section. Make sure the **Correlation matrix** option is chosen in the **Analyze** section. Choose **Screeplot** and make sure the **Unrotatated factor solution** option is also chosen in the **Display** section. Choose Based on Eigenvalue in the Extract section. Click on **Fixed number of factors** and type in the number, if you want to force a specific number of factors. Click on **continue.**
- Click on **Rotation** button and select **Direct Oblimin** and press **Continue**.
- Click on the **Options** button. Click on **Exclude cases pairwise** in the **Missing Values** section. Click on **Sorted by size** and **Suppress**

small coefficients in the **Coefficient Display Format**. Type the value pf .3 in the box next to **Absolute value below**.

- Click on **Continue** and then **OK** or on **Paste** to save to **Syntax Editor**.

Non-parametric statistics

Chi-square
Chi-square for goodness of fit

It is often used to compare the proportion of cases from a sample with hypothesized values or those obtained previously from a comparison population.

- Click on **Analyze** from the menu at the top of the screen. Choose **Non-parametric Tests**, then **Legacy Dialogs** and then **Chi-Square**.
- Click on the categorical variable and click on the arrow to move in into the **Test Variable List** box.
- Click on the **Values** option in the **Expected Values** section. In the Values box, you need to type in two values. The first value corresponds with the expected proportion for the first coded value for the variable. Click on **Add**. Type the second value, which is the expected proportion for the second coded value. Click on **Add**. You need to type in as many proportions as appropriate if your variable has more than two possible values.
- Click on **OK** or **paste** to save to **Syntax Editor**.

Chi-square test for independence

It is used if you want to explore the relationship between two categorical variables. Each of these variables can have two or more categories. This test compares the observed frequencies or proportions of cases that take place in each of the categories, with the value that could be expected if there was no association between the two variables being measured. Open the **survey 5ED.sav** data file.

- Click on **Analyze** from the menu at the top of the screen. Click on **Descriptive Statistics**, and then **Crosstabs**.
- Click on one of your variables to be your row variable and click on the arrow to move in into the box marked **Row(s)**.
- Click on the other variable to be your column variable and click on the arrow to move it into the box marked **Column(s)**.
- Click on the **Statistics** button. Tick **Chi-square** and **phi and Cramer's V**. Click on **Continue**.

- Click on the **Cells** button. In the **Counts box**, there should be a tick for **Observed**. Click on the **Row**, **Column** and **Total** boxes in the **Percentage** section.

- Click on **continue** and then **OK** or on **Paste** to save to **Syntax Editor**.

McNEMAR' S test

If you have matched or repeated measures designs (e.g. Pre-test/post-test), Chi-square test is not used. You need to use McNEMAR' S test. You need to have two variables, the first recorded at Time 1 and the second recorded at Time 2. Both variables should be categorical.

- Click on **Analyze** from the menu at the top of the screen. Click on **Descriptive Statistics**, and then **Crosstabs**.

- Click on one of your variables and click on the arrow to move it into the box marked **Row(s)**.

- Click on the other variable and click on the arrow to move it into the box marked **Colum(s)**.

- Click on the Statistics button. Tick **McNemar** and then click on **Continue**.

- Click on the **Cells** button. In the **Counts** box, tick for **Observed**. Click on the **Row**, **Column** boxes in the **Percentage** section.

- Click on **Continue** and then **OK** or **Paste** to save to **Syntax Editor**.

Cochran's Q test

The McNemar's test is suitable when you have only two time options. When there are three or more time points, you need to use Cochran's Q test.

- Click on **Analyze** from the menu at the top of the screen. Click on **Nonparametric Tests**, then on **Legacy Dialogs** and then on **K Related Samples**. Click on the three categorical variables that show the difference time points and then on the arrow to move them into the **Test Variables** box.

- Click on the **Cochran's Q** option in the **Test Type** section. Remove the tick for **Friedman** test by clicking in the box.

- Click on **OK** or on **Paste** to save to Syntax **Editor**.

Kruskal-Wallis test

It is the non-parametric alternative to a one-way between –groups analysis of variance. It lets you compare the scores on some continuous variable for three or more groups.

- Click on **Analyze** from the menu at the top of the screen. Choose **Nonparametric Tests**, then **Legacy Dialogs** and then **K Independent Samples**.

- Click on your continuous, dependent variable and move it into the **Test Variable List** box.
- Click on your categorical, independent variable and move it into the **Grouping Variable** box.
- Click on the **Define Range** button. Type in the first value of your categorical variable in the **Minimum** box. Click on **Continue**.
- Tick the **Kruskal-Wallis H** box in the **Test type**.
- Click on **Continue** and then on **OK** or **Paste** to save to **Syntax Editor**.

t-test

Independent-samples *t*-test

It is used if you want to compare the mean score, on some continuous variables, for two different groups of participants.

- Click on **Analyze** from the menu at the top of the screen. Choose **Compare means** and then **Independent Samples T test**.
- Move the dependent (continuous) variable into the **Test variable** box.
- Move the independent (categorical) variable into the **Grouping variable**.
- Click on **Define groups** and type in the numbers used in the data set to code each group. If you are not able to remember the codes choose **Variable Information** from the pop-up box that appears.
- Click on **Continue** and then **OK** or on **paste** to save to **Syntax Editor**.

Calculating effect size for independent –samples *t*-test

Effect size statistics can make an indication of the magnitude of the difference between your groups. It is not just about whether the difference would have taken place by chance. There are many different effect size statistics. The most common ones are eta squared and Cohen's d. Eta squared ranges from 0 to 1 and shows the proportion of variance in the dependent variable which is explained by the independent variable. Cohen's d represents the difference between groups in terms of standard deviation units.

IBM SPSS does not have effect size statistics for t-test in the output. There are many different websites that let you calculate an effect size statistics.

It is possible to calculate Eta squared by hand using the information provided in the output.

$$\text{Eta squared} = \frac{t^2}{t^2 + (N1 + N2 - 2)}$$

Paired-samples *t*-test

It is used if there is only one group of people and you collect data from them on two different occasions. Pre-test/post/test experimental designs are an example of situation where this technique is suitable.

- Click on **Analyze** from the menu at the top of the screen. Choose the **Compare Means** and then **Paired Samples T test**.
- Click on the two variables that you want to compare for each subject and move them into the box labeled **Paired Variables** by clicking on the arrow button.
- Click on **OK** or on **Paste** to save o **Syntax Editor**.

Calculating the effect size for paired-samples t-test

IBM SPSS does not provide effect size statistics for *t*-test. There are a number of websites that can let you calculate an effect size statistics. The procedure for calculating eta squared by hand is

$$\text{Eta squared} = \frac{t^2}{t^2 + (N-1)}$$

One-way analysis of variance

If you are interested in comparing the mean scores of more than two groups, you can use analysis of variance (ANOVA).

One way-between-groups ANOVA can be used if you have one independent variable with three or more levels and one dependent continuous variable. It indicates that there is only one independent variable.

One-way between-groups ANOVA with post-hoc tests

- Click on **Analyze** from the menu at the top of the screen. Choose **Compare Means**, then **One-way ANOVA**.
- Click on the dependent (continuous) variable. Move it into the **Dependent List** box by clicking on the arrow button.
- Click on the independent, categorical variable. Move it into the **Factor** box.
- Click the Options button and then **Descriptive, Homogeneity of variance test, Brown-Forsythe, Welch** and **Means Plot**.
- Make sure there is a dot in the option **Exclude** cases analysis by analysis for **Missing values**. Click on **Continue**.
- Click on **Post Hoc**. Click on **Tukey**.
- Click on **Continue** and then **OK** or **paste** to save to **Syntax Editor**.

Calculating the effect size for ANOVA

IBM SPSS does not generate the effect size analysis. The information you need is calculating **eta squared**.

$$\text{Eta squared} = \frac{Sum\ of\ squares\ between\ groups}{Total\ sum\ of\ squares}$$

One-way between-groups ANOVA with planned comparisons

If you are interested in only a subset of the possible comparisons it makes it is good to use planned comparisons, rather than post-hoc tests. The information on the coefficient for each of your groups is required in **contrasts** section of the IBM SPSS.

- Click on **Analyze** from the menu at the top of the screen. Choose Compare Means and the **One-way ANOVA**.
- Click on the dependent (continuous) variable. Click on the arrow to move this variable into the box **Dependent List**.
- Click on the independent, categorical variable. Move this into the box **Factor**.
- Click the **Options, Descriptive, Homogeneity of variance test, Brown-Forsythe, welch** and **Means Plot**.
- Make sure there is a dot in the option **Exclude** cases analysis by analysis for **Missing Values**. Click on **Continue**.
- Click on the Contrasts button. Type the coefficient for the first group in the Coefficient box. Click on **Add**. Type in the coefficient for the second group. Click on **Add**. Type in the coefficient for the third group. Click on **Add**. The Coefficient Total down the bottom of the table must be 0 if you entered all the coefficients correctly.
- Click on **Continue** and then **OK** or paste to save to **Syntax Editor**.

One-way repeated measures ANOVA

In one-way repeated measures ANOVA, each subject is exposed to two or more different conditions. It may be measured on the same continuous scale on three or more occasions. It may be used to compare responses to two or more different questions or items.

- Click on **Analyze** from the menu at the top of the screen, then **General Linear Model**, then **Repeated Measures**.
- Type in a name that shows your independent variable in the **Within Subject Factor Name** box.
- Type the number of levels or groups in the **Number of Levels** box.
- Click **Add**.
- Click on **Define**.
- Choose the three variables that show your repeated measures variable. Click on the arrow button. Move them into the **Within Subjects Variables** box.
- Click on the **Options** box.

- Tick the **Descriptive Statistics** and **Estimates of effect size** boxes in **Display**. Choose your independent variable name in the **Factor and Factor Interactions** section and move in into the **Display Means for** box if you want to ask for post-hoc tests. Tick **Compare main effects**. Click on the down arrow and select the second option **Bonferroni** in the **Confidence interval adjustment**.
- Click on **Continue** and **OK** or **Paste** to save to **Syntax Editor**.

Two-way between –groups ANOVA

It explores two-way, between-groups analysis of variance. Two-way means we have two independent variables, and between-groups shows different people are in each of the groups. We need three variables, two categorical independent variables and one continues dependent variable.

- Click on **Analyze** from the menu at the top of the screen. Choose **General Linear Model**, then **Univariate**.
- Click on the dependent, dependent variable and click on the arrow to move in into the box **Dependent variable**.
- Click on two independent, categorical variables and move them into the **Fixed Factors**.
- Click on the **Options** button, **Descriptive Statistics**, **Estimates of effect size** and **Homogeneity tests**, and then **Continue**.
- Click on the **Post Hoc** button. Select the independent variable(s) that you want from the **Factors** on the left-hand side. Click on the arrow button to move it into the **Post Hoc Tests for** section. Select the test you want to use. Click on **Continue**.
- Click on the **Plots** button. Put the independent variable that has the most groups in the **Horizontal** box.
- Put the other independent variable in the **Separate Lines**.
- Click on **Add**.
- See your two variables in the **Plots** section.
- Click on **Continue** and then **OK** or **paste** to save to **Syntax Editor**.

Mixed between-within subjects analysis of variance

In some situations you want to combine one independent variable being between –subjects and the other a within-subjects variable.

- Click on **Analyze** from the menu at the top of the screen. Choose **General Linear Model** and then **Repeated measures**.
- Type a name that describes the within-subjects factor in the **Within-Subject Factor Name**.
- Type the number of levels that this factor has in the **Number of Levels**.
- Click on the **Add** and then **Define** button.

- Click on the variables that show the **within-subjects variables** box.
- Click on your between-subject variable. Click on the arrow to move this variable into the **Between-Subjects Factors** box.
- Click on the **Options** button. Make sure there is a tick for **Descriptive statistics, Estimates of effect size, Homogeneity tests** in the **Display** box. Click on **Continue**.
- Click on the **Plots** button.
- Click on the within-groups factor and move it into the **Horizontal Axis**.
- Click on the between-groups variable in the **Separate Lines** box.
- Click on Add.
- Click on **Continue** and then **OK** or **Paste** to save to **Syntax Editor**.

Multivariate analysis of variance

Multivariate analysis of variance (MANOVA) is an extension of analysis of variance which can be used when you have more than one dependent variable. These dependent variables should be related in some way. It means there should be some conceptual reason to consider them together. MANOVA has some assumptions. **Sample size** (you need to have more cases in each cell than you have dependent variables) , **Normality,** (through Mahalanobis distances) **Outliers** (data points or scores that are different from the remainder of the scores) , **Linearity** (the presence of a straight-line relationship between each pair of your dependent variables), **Homogeneity of regression** (having some theoretical or conceptual reason for ordering your dependent variables) , **Multicollinearity and singularity** (correlation among dependent variables), and **Homogeneity of variance-covariance matrices** (using Box's M Test of Equality of Covariance Matrices). Before MANOVA analysis, you should test your data to conform the mentioned assumptions.

Performing MANOVA

- Click on **Analyze** from the menu at the top of the screen and choose **General Linear Model,** then **Multivariate**.
- Enter each of your dependent variables in the **Dependent Variables** box.
- Enter your independent variable in the **Fixed Factors** box.
- Click on the **Model** button. In the **Specify Model** box, make sure that the **Full factorial** button is chosen.
- Down the bottom in the **Sum of squares** box, **Type III** should be shown. Click on **Continue**.
- Click on the **Options** button. Click on the independent variable in the **Factor and Factor interactions**. Move it into the box **Display**

Means for. Put a tick in the boxes for **Descriptive Statistics**, **Estimates of effect size** and **Homogeneity tests** in the **Display** section of this screen.

- Click on **Continue** and then **OK** or on **Paste** to save to **Syntax Editor**.

Analysis of covariance

Analysis of covariance is the extension of analysis of variance. It lets you explore differences between groups while statistically controlling for an additional (continuous) variable. The additional variable is called a covariate which you expect might be influencing scores on the dependent variable.

ANCOVA

ANCOVA is used if you have a two-group pre-test/post-test design to compare the impact of two different interventions, taking before and after measures for each group.

One-way ANCOVA

One way ANCOVA involves one independent, categorical variable with two or more levels or conditions, one dependent continuous variable, and one or more continuous covariates.

- Click on Analyze from the menu at the top of the screen. Choose **General Linear Model**, then **Univariate**.
- Put your dependent variable in the **Dependent Variables** box.
- Put your independent or grouping variable in the **Fixed Factor** box.
- Put your covariate in the **Covariate** box. Click on **Continue**.
- Click on the **Model** button then on **Full Factorial** in the **Specify Model** section. Click on **Continue**.
- Click on the **Options**.
- Click on your independent variable in the top section **Estimated Marginal Means**.
- Click on the arrow to move it into the **Display Means for** box.
- Select **Descriptive statistics**, **Estimates of effective size** and **Homogeneity tests** in the bottom **Display** section.
- Click on **Continue** and then **OK** or **paste** to save to **Syntax Editor**.

Two-way ANCOVA

Two-way ANCOVA has two independent, categorical variables with two or more levels or conditions, one dependent continuous variable and one or more continuous covariates.

- Click on **Analyze** from the menu at the top of the screen. Choose **General Linear Model**, then **Univariate**.

- Click on the dependent variable and move it into the **Dependent Variables** box.
- Click on your two independent or grouping variables and move them into the **Fixed Factor** box.
- Put your covariate(s) in the **Covriate** box.
- Click on the **Model** button and then **Full Factorial** in the **Specify Model** section. Click on **Continue**.
- Click on the **Options** button. Click on your two independent variables in the top section, **Estimated Marginal Means**. Click on the arrow to move them into the **Display** means for box. Click on the extra interaction term and move it into the box. Click on **Descriptive statistics, Estimates of effect size** and **Homogeneity tests** in the bottom section. Click on **Continue**.
- Click on the **Plots** button. Highlight the first independent variable. Move it into the **Horizontal** box. Click on the second independent variable. Move it into the **Separate Lines** box. Click on **Add**.
- Click on **Continue** and then ok or **paste** to save to **Syntax Editor**.

Note: For more information turn to Pallant (2013) or go to www.openup.co.uk/spss.

CHAPTER EIGHT
Sample Proposals and Articles

Introduction

University instructors receive many requests from students wishing to see examples of successful proposals.

These samples are provided for your use as *examples* of what a successful proposal is all about. You can use the samples to learn what a good needs statement contains, to see what goals and objectives are and how the activities relate to those goals/ objectives, and to see how an evaluation plan is designed.

While using proposal samples consider the following points.

- A successful proposal is one that has been locally planned and designed. You must meet the needs of *your* community.

- The guidelines your proposal should follow may not be the same as the ones around which the sample proposals were written. You must match your proposal to the exact guidelines given by the one for whom you are writing your proposal.

- No proposal is perfect - not even those that are successful. You may inadvertently choose to copy something from one of the samples that was not quite as strong as it could have been.

A review of sample proposals allows you to see new ideas for using tables and graphs. You may see a component in one of the proposals that you may not have thought of but that would make your project even stronger. If that is the case, be certain that you tailor the idea specifically to *your* project and your community.

217

A Sample Proposal

Iran University of Science and Technology
Department of Foreign Languages

MA Proposal of English Language Teaching

Subject:
The effect of using translation from L1 to L2 as a teaching technique in the improvement of Iranian EFL learners' linguistic accuracy— focus on form

Proposal Advisor:
Shahin Vaezi, PhD

Consulting advisor:
Hossein Farhady, PhD

By:
Mehdi Mirzai
2006-2007

1. Introduction

The debate over whether English language classrooms should include or exclude students' native language has been a contentious issue for a long time (Brown, 2000, p. 195). Although the use of mother tongue has been banned since the emergence of Direct Method, there are still figures who advocate the use of L1 in the classroom. According to Cook (2001) "bringing the L1 back from exile may lead not only to the improvement of existing teaching methods but also to innovations in methodology. In particular, it may liberate the task-based learning approach so that it can foster the students' natural collaborative efforts in the classroom through their L1 as well as their L2" (p. 189).

Dörnyei and Kormos (1998) report that the L1 is used by L2 learners as a communication strategy to compensate for deficiencies in the target language. Auerbuch (1993) not only acknowledges the positive role of the mother tongue in the classroom, but also identifies the following uses for it: classroom management, language analysis and presenting rules that govern grammar, discussing cross-cultural issues, giving instructions or prompts, explaining errors, and checking for comprehension.

Obviously, one of the noticeable aspects of L1 use is translation which can serve as a teaching technique. Cook (2001) asserts that the word 'translation' has so far been avoided as much as possible because of its negative implication in teaching. "Translation as a *teaching technique* is a different matter from translation as a goal of language teaching" (p. 200).

On the other hand, focus on form, in its communicative sense, is defined by Richards and Schmidt (2002) as any focusing of attention on the formal linguistic characteristics of language, as opposed to a pure focus on meaning in communication. In a more technical sense, focus on form has been defined as "a brief allocation of attention to linguistic form as the need for this arises incidentally, in the context of communication" (p. 205). The significance of focus on form has been well appreciated by Ellis (2002) who claims that "there is by now ample evidence to show that form-focused instruction (FFI) has a positive effect on second language (SL) acquisition. That is, by and large, learners seem to learn the grammatical structures they are taught" (p. 225).

Similarly, this research study tries to utilize an instrument which would lead to the reinforcement of focus on form whose chief object is to enhance linguistic accuracy. The instrument which is used in this study for such a purpose is translation from L1 to L2. The idea of using translation as a teaching method has also been supported in the literature. Duff (1989) states that "translation does not have to be a lone, pointless struggle between student and text. Many other approaches are possible. Translation can be introduced purposefully and imaginatively, into the language learning program. If we can find a way to offset the weak points and make the best use of its assets, translation as a teaching technique can be used to help students learn a second language more thoughtfully and effectively" (p. 6).

1.1. Statement of the Problem

This study is an attempt to examine whether using translation from L1 to L2 has any effect in the improvement of a group of Iranian EFL learners' linguistic accuracy—focus on form—or not.

1.2. Research Question

The research question formulated for the purpose of this study is as follows: Does the use of translation from L1 to L2 have any effect in the improvement of Iranian EFL learners' linguistic accuracy—focus on form?

1.3. Statement of Hypothesis

The null hypothesis of the present study is:
Using translation from L1 to L2 has no effect on the improvement of Iranian EFL learners' linguistic accuracy—focus on form.

1.4. Significance of the Study

The significance of this study is appreciated from two respects. Firstly, this study signifies the role that mother tongue can play in second language learning. In effect, although the use of learners' first language has been banned since the immergence of Direct Method at the end of the nineteenth century (Cook, 2001), it has recurrently been noted that mother tongue is a rich resource which can help one to improve his/her second language learning. "While the English Only paradigm continues to be dominant in communicative ELT, research into teacher practice reveals that the L1 is used as a learning resource in many ESL classes" (Auerbach, 1993, p. 15). Therefore, translation, as an obvious feature of L1 use, is used in this study to lay emphasis on the focus on form whose chief goal is to enhance linguistic accuracy.

Secondly, another feature of communicative language teaching, which is nowadays widely used, is the fact that in CLT gives more prominence to fluency than accuracy. As a result of this mere focus on meaning and deemphasizing accuracy in CLT classes, the present study aims at using a teaching technique to improve linguistic accuracy-- focus on form-- of Iranian EFL learners. In other words, this study tries to investigate the efficiency of a teaching technique— namely translating from L1 to L2—in enhancing Iranian intermediate learners' focus on form by means of using particular grammatical structures. As Duff (1989) puts it, "Translation as a teaching technique can be used to help students learn a second language more thoughtfully and effectively" (p. 6). Although focus on form can be achieved through different techniques, the present study aims at introducing an alternative technique-- translation from L1 to L2-- to reach the same goal.

In fact, the idea of this research has been primarily inspired by the contribution of both the researcher's area of interest and the learners' feedback after experiencing this technique. In other words, the mentioned technique has been employed in the researcher's own classes and, surprisingly, it has gained favor with the learners in most cases. Receiving such a positive feedback from the learners in this respect was a strong motivation for carrying out this study.

1.5. Definition of Key Terms

Explicit focus on form: Explicit focus on form refers to the time when an error is explicitly referred to, and the learner is directly told that *it is not X but it is Y*. This kind of focus on form could be done through explicit or direct strategies which again involve explicitly drawing the attention of learners to the error with or without rule explanation. Further, Doughty and Williams (1998) state that explicit focus on form "is to *direct* learners' attention to *exploit pedagogical the grammar* in this regard" (p. 232).

Focus on form: Focus on form has been defined as "a brief allocation of attention to linguistic form as the need for this arises incidentally, in the context of communication" (Richards and Schmidt, 2002, p. 205). Moreover, focus on form, in contrast to focus on formS, "consists of an occasional shift of attention to linguistic code features—by the teacher and/ or one or more students—triggered by perceived problems with comprehension or production" (Long& Robbins, 1998, p. 23).

Focus on formS: "Refers to the kind of focus on one form (or rule) at a time that one finds in a language course where there is a "structure of the day", usually specified by the teacher or the textbook" (Richards and Schmidt, 2002, p. 205).

Translation: The process of rendering written language that was produced in one language (the source language) into another (the target language), or the target language version that results from this process.

2. Review of Related Literature

2.1. Introduction

In this chapter, some key issues related to the justification of using the mother tongue in EFL classrooms, the significance of using translation as a teaching technique in teaching a foreign language, and the importance and aspects of focus on form in EFL contexts will be elaborated on.

2.2. The Role of Mother Tongue in Second Language Learning

The debate over whether English language classrooms should include or exclude students' native language has been a contentious issue for a long time (Brown, 2000, p. 195). Although the use of mother tongue has been banned since the emergence of Direct Method, there are still figures who advocate the use of L1 in the classroom. According to Cook (2001) "bringing the L1 back from exile may lead not only to the improvement of existing teaching methods but also to innovations in methodology. In particular, it may liberate the task-based learning approach so that it can foster the students' natural collaborative efforts in the classroom through their L1 as well as their L2" (p. 189).

Dörnyei and Kormos (1998) find that the L1 is used by L2 learners as a communication strategy to compensate for deficiencies in the target language. Auerbuch (1993) not only acknowledges the positive role of the mother tongue in the classroom, but also identifies the following uses for it: classroom management, language analysis and presenting rules that govern grammar, discussing cross-cultural issues, giving instructions or prompts, explaining errors, and checking for comprehension. Furthermore, "when the native language *is* used, practitioners, researchers, and learners consistently report positive results" (Auerbach, 1993, p. 18).

Moreover, Cook (1999) claims that "Treating the L1 as a classroom resource opens up several ways to use it, such as for teachers to convey meaning, explain grammar, and organize the class, and for students to use as part of their collaborative learning and individual strategy use. The first language can be a useful element in creating authentic L2 users rather than something to be shunned at all costs" (p. 185).

Although the provision of maximum L2 exposure to the learners seems essential, L1 can be used alongside L2 as a complement. In this regard, Turnbull (2001) states that "for me, maximizing the target language does not and should not mean that it is harmful for the teacher to use the L1. A principle that promotes maximal teacher use of the target language acknowledges that the L1 and target language can exist simultaneously" (p. 153). As Stern (1992, p. 285) suggests, use of L1 and target language should be seen as complementary, depending on the characteristics and stages of the language learning process.

On the other hand, overuse of L1 will naturally reduce the amount of exposure to L2. Therefore, attempt should be made to keep a balance between L1 and L2 use. Turnbull (2001) believes that using the L1 can save time in the EFL/ ESL classroom. He adds that "I agree that it is efficient to make a quick switch to the L1 to ensure that students understand a difficult grammar concept or an unknown word. However, it is crucial for teachers to use the TL as much as possible in contexts in which students spend only short periods of time in class on a daily basis, and when they have little contact with the TL outside the classroom" (p. 160).

2.3. Using Translation as a Teaching Technique in L2 Teaching

Obviously, one of the noticeable aspects of L1 use is translation which can serve as a teaching technique. Also, the idea of using translation as a teaching technique has been supported in the literature. Cook (2001) asserts that the word 'translation' has so far been avoided as much as possible because of its pejorative overtones in teaching. "Translation as a *teaching technique* is a different matter from translation as a goal of language teaching" (p. 200).

Similarly, Duff (1989) states that "translation does not have to be a lone, pointless struggle between student and text. Many other approaches are possible. Translation can be introduced purposefully and imaginatively, into the language learning program. If we can find a way to offset the weak points and make the best use of its assets, translation as a teaching technique can be used to help students learn a second language more thoughtfully and effectively" (p. 6).

A number of scholars view the two extreme positions of pure translation and forbidding translation in the classroom as unnecessary extremes and instead, advocate for a balanced approach in which teachers strategically use L1 in order to promote foreign language acquisition. Stibbard (1994) analyzed the use of oral translation as a L2 teaching activity. He suggested that translation may play a valuable role in L2 teaching. Moreover, he asserted that translation should be an integral part of the language-learning program. Levenston (1985) presented an overview of the role of translation in foreign language teaching and learning. He argued that translation is useful for: (1) practicing grammatical structures, (2) explaining vocabulary items, (3) testing at all levels, and (4) developing communicative competence. He recommended translation be taught as a skill in its own right.

According to Chellapan (1982), we should not simply eliminate translation but we should absorb translation into a larger creative process of learning. He points out; "Translation can make the student come to closer grips with the target language. A simultaneous awareness of two media could actually make the student see the points of convergence and divergence more clearly and also refine the tools of perception and analysis resulting in divergent thinking" (p. 60).

A significant benefit of translation in language teaching is that teachers can use translation as an effective means of explaining particular aspects of language, such as cultural differences, grammatical rules and syntactic structures with which the students have difficulty. In this regard, Chellapan (1982) explains that this way of using translation involves a conscious process of learning. Through translation, a learner can be aware of the distinctiveness of similar structures in the two languages, and also of the different processes used in conveying the same message. "Deliberate translation," as he calls it, focuses on lexical items, where the contrasts in the two languages vary, but it should be done in a larger context. This will help the students learn the different distributions in the two languages and also show that the meaning of any item is part of the total environment of the text in the two languages.

Another benefit of using translation is that it helps to develop the learners competence and to improve performance. According to Chomsky (1965), there is a clear distinction between competence (the knowledge of a language) and performance (the actual use of language in a concrete situation). In Chomsky's view, the learners' ability to perform is based on his/her competence, which is entirely linguistic. Hymes (1972), on the contrary, proposes a broader notion of competence, that of communicative competence. He claims that the learners' performance reflects both knowledge of grammatical rules and knowledge of how these rules are used to communicate meaning, knowledge of when, where, and with whom to use the rules. Hymes stresses that the learners ability to perform needs to be understood in terms of communicative competence rather than linguistic competence.

For translation to be whether linguistic or both linguistic and communicative is not the focus of this study; rather, the main concern is to argue that translation can be used effectively to help learners acquire the most important linguistic ability, that is the ability "to understand and to produce utterances which are grammatical as well as appropriate to the context in which they are made" (Campbell and Wales, 1970, p.247).

As for the students' knowledge of linguistic rules, the translation method can be used very successfully to teach grammar and structural patterns. It helps point out and clarify the differences between the grammatical system and syntactic structures in the target and the native languages. As mentioned, translation, more than other methods of instruction enables students to understand more clearly how various grammatical features are used.

2.4. Focus on Form

Focus on form, in its communicative sense, is defined as any focusing of attention on the formal linguistic characteristics of language, as opposed to a pure focus on meaning in communication. In a more technical sense, focus on form has been defined as "a brief allocation of attention to linguistic form as the need for this arises incidentally, in the context of communication" (Richards and Schmidt, 2002, p. 205). The significance of focus on form has been well appreciated by Ellis (2002) who claims that "there is by now ample evidence to show that form-focused instruction (FFI) has a positive effect on second language (SL) acquisition. That is, by and large, learners seem to learn the grammatical structures they are taught" (p. 225).

In a research to investigate the effect of focus on form on the quality of instruction, M. Lightbown and Spada's (1994) observations of the intensive program classes revealed that overall the instruction focused on meaning-based activities, and teachers gave little attention to grammar or accuracy. Their observations also indicated, however, that some teachers responded to learners' errors more often than others and that, in some cases, this response appeared to be related to the achievement of higher levels of accuracy.

Research into focus on form (Nunan, 1989) and into the practices of good language learners (Naiman, Frohlich, Stern, & Todesco, 1996) reveals the importance of metalinguistic explanation in adult second language learning, particularly when learning involves abstract notions. Some of this explanation, however, must be done in the L1 if it is to be understood by lower level learners.

Norris and Ortega (2000) in a meta-analysis of 49 Focus on Form Instruction studies found that not only did focus on form make a difference but also that it made a very considerable difference. Their analysis also found that explicit instruction was significantly more effective than implicit instruction and that the effects of focus on form were durable. Moreover, Ellis (2001) claims that "language acquisition can be speeded by explicit instruction" (p. 145).

Ellis (2002) comments that "there is a general agreement and strong empirical evidence to show that focus on form can affect explicit knowledge. It seems reasonable to conclude that it is easier to teach explicit knowledge than implicit knowledge" (p. 234).

Moreover, Robinson and Long (1998) assert that "code switching could also be added to teacher techniques such as recast, which aim at drawing learners' attention to errors performed during communicative activities. The use of L1 could be considered then as a strategy helping to introduce a 'focus on form' in the foreign language classroom" (p. 56).

3. Method

This chapter deals with the different components of the methodology which includes the participants, instrumentation, and procedure.

3.1. Participants

In order to achieve the objectives of this study, 120 participants studying at Paniz Language Institute and City Training Center (Eshragh Branch) and Kish Language Institute will take part in the first phase of the research. The participants are male intermediate learners of English and their age range from 13 to 20 years old. They will be given a test which tests their control over certain structures. Having collected data from this test, 60 of the participants who proved to lack the required knowledge about the intended structures will be selected for the second phase of the study. Then, they will be divided into two groups of 30— one the experimental group, and a control group.

3.2. Instrumentation

In order to carry out the study, a teacher-made achievement test, which comprises the newly introduced structures of *New Interchange 2* course book, is developed in multiple-choice format. In fact, the reason for developing such a test is to make sure that the participants do not have any familiarity with the specific structures under study. It is worth mentioning that three items for each intended structure is used so as to discriminate the participants who have knowledge about the selected structures from those who do not. In other words, those participants who cannot answer any or just one of the items form each intended structure would prove to have lack of control on those specific structures and therefore are suitable for the study.

The instrument used for the treatment is a series of Farsi sentences which are developed in accordance with the structures which have already been taught in each session. The participants have to translate these sentences into English using the specific structure they have learnt in that session.

Finally, another teacher-made achievement test will be used after implementing the treatment to both experimental and control group to find out to what extend the teaching technique used in this study was effective.

3.3. Procedure

This study requires 60 homogeneous learners who also have no familiarity with the following grammatical structures namely **used to do** (along with question and negative forms), **passive voice** (with simple present, present continuous, simple past, past continuous, future with *'going to'* and *'will'*) **conditional type 1 and type 2** and **present perfect**.

To select such a population, 100 intermediate learners who have not studied *New Interchange 2* course book yet are given a multiple- choice test which includes questions testing the learners' knowledge of the mentioned grammatical structures. There will be 3 items which test each of these structures. The reason for this is to discriminate the participants who have knowledge about the selected structures from those who do not. Consequently, those participants who cannot answer any of the items related to each intended structure or can answer only one of them will be selected for the study. In fact, such a test will help the researcher identify those suitable for the study have no control over those structures which are going to be worked on in the study.

The next step would be to select 60 of the participants who were qualified in the first phase; that is, those who did not have knowledge about the structures to be worked on in the study. These participants will be divided into two groups— one comparison group and the other one the experimental group. The experimental group will receive the treatment in the following way: having taught the new structures—namely *used to do, passive voice, conditional type 1 and type 2* and *present perfect* — in each session, the participants will be given 7 sentences in Persian which are developed in accordance with the structures which have already been taught in that session. The participants have to translate these sentences into English, individually, using the specific structure they have learnt in that session.

The participants should do the task inside the classroom and individually. After that, the teacher will check the participants' answers and correct their linguistic mistakes in terms of *accurate* use of the specific structure under study.

However, the control group will receive the placebo in the form of the exercises available in their course book which are done monolingually. In other words, the placebo will be the tasks and the exercises that the participants perform as directed in the course book.

Having finished teaching all the structures, the final step is to give a post-test to investigate the effectiveness of the teaching technique used for the experimental group. The test will be given to both experimental and control group and the results from both groups will be compared and will show whether this technique was effective in enhancing linguistic accuracy of the experimental group.

References

Auerbach, E. (1993). Reexamining English only in the ESL classroom. *TESOL Quarterly 27*, (1), 9–32.

Brown, H. (2000). *Principles of language learning and teaching.* Longman: San Francisco.

Campbell, R., & Wales, R. (1970). The study of language acquisition. In John Lyons (Eds.), *New Horizons in Linguistics*, 242—293. Harmonswort: Penguin Books.

Chellapan, K. (1982). Translanguage, translation and second language acquisition. In F. Eppert (Eds.), *Papers on Translation: Aspects, Concepts, Implications* (pp.57—63). Singapore: SEMEO Regional Language Centre.

Chomsky, N. (1965). *Aspects of the theory of syntax.* Cambridge: M.I.T. Press.

Cook, V.J. (1999). Going beyond the native speaker in language teaching. *TESOL Quarterly, 33*, (2), 185-209.

Cook, V.J. (2001). Using the first language in the classroom. *Canadian Modern Language Review, 57*, (3), 184-206.

Dörnyei, Z. and J. Kormos. (1998). Problem-solving mechanisms in L2 communication: A psycholinguistic perspective. *Studies in Second Language Acquisition, 20*, (3), 349–385.

Doughty, C., & Williams, J. (1998). Pedagogical choices in focus on form. In C. Doughty, & J. Williams (Eds.), *Focus on form in classroom second language acquisition,* (pp.197-261). Cambridge: Cambridge University press.

Duff, A. (1989). *Translation.* Oxford: Oxford University Press.

Ellis, R. (2001). Investigating form-focused instruction. *Language Learning, 51*(1), 1-46

Ellis, R. (2002). Does the form-focused instruction affect the acquisition of implicit knowledge? *Studies in Second Language acquisition. 24*, (2), 223-36.

Hymes, D. (1972). On communicative competence. In JB Pride & J. Holmes (Eds.), Sociolinguistics. Harmondsworth, England: Penguin Books.

Levenston, E. A. (1985). The place of translation in the foreign language classroom. *English Teachers' Journal, (32)*, 33–43.

Lightbown, P., & Spada, N. (1994). An innovative program for primary ESL students in Quebec. *TESOL Quarterly, 28*(3), 563–80.

Long, M., & Robinson, P. (1998). Focus on form: Theory, research, and practice. In C. Doughty, & J. Williams (Eds.), **Focus on form in second language acquisition, (pp.15-41).** Cambridge University Press.

Naiman, N., Frohlich, M., Stern, H., & Todesco, A. (1996). *The good language learner.* Clevedon: Multilingual Matters.

Norris, J.M., & Ortega, L. (2000). Effectiveness of L2 instruction: A research synthesis. and quantitative meta-analysis. *Language Learning, 50,* 417-528.

Nunan, D. (1989). *Designing tasks for the communicative classroom.* London: Cambridge University Press.

Richards. J. C, & Schmidt, R., (2002). *Longman dictionary of language teaching and applied linguistics* (2nd ed.). Essex: Longman Group.

Stern, H. H. (1992). *Issues and options in language teaching.* Oxford: Oxford University Press.

Stibbard, R. (1994). The use of translation in foreign language teaching. *Perspectives: Studies in Translatology, (1),* 9-18.

Turnbull, M. (2001). There is a role for the L1 in second and foreign language teaching, But ... *Canadian Modern Language Review, 57,* (4), 150-16.

A Sample Article
The Effect of Using Translation from L1 to L2 as a Teaching Technique on the Improvement of EFL Learners' Linguistic Accuracy - Focus on Form

Shahin Vaezi, Iran University of Science and Technology
Mehdi Mirzai, Iran University of Science and Technology

Abstract

The present study was conducted to examine the effect of using translation from L1 to L2 as a teaching technique on the improvement of EFL learners' linguistic accuracy—focus on form. To fulfill the purpose of the study, 72 pre-intermediate learners were chosen by means of administering an achievement test. This test, which also functioned as the pre-test, was designed in a way that the participants who did not have familiarity with the four aimed structures of this study, i.e. *Passive voice, Indirect reported speech, Conditional type 2,* and *Wish+ simple past,* were identified. Based on the pretest, the experimental and comparison groups were formed. The experimental group underwent the treatment, i.e. translating Persian sentences into English using the newly learned structures. Nonetheless, the comparison group received the placebo—grammar exercises in the course book. Both groups were posttested through another achievement test. The results of the post-test—through *t*-test analysis—demonstrated that the experimental group outperformed the comparison group in terms of accuracy. It is concluded that this technique can be used by teachers to reinforce new structures.

Keywords: 1. accuracy 2. focus on form 3. translation

Introduction

The debate over whether English language classrooms should include or exclude students' native language has been a controversial issue for a long time (Brown, 2000). Although the use of mother tongue was banned by the supporters of the Direct Method at the end of the nineteenth century, the positive role of the mother tongue has recurrently been acknowledged as a rich resource which, if used judiciously, can assist second language teaching and learning (Cook, 2001). Therefore, this research study tries to open up a new horizon for English instructors to find a thoughtful way to use learners' mother tongue in second language teaching.

The technique in which L1 was used in this study was translation from L1 to L2; a technique which is rarely used systematically by EFL teachers. Atkinson (1987) is one of the first and chief advocates of mother tongue use in the communicative classroom. He points out the

229

methodological gap in the literature concerning the use of the mother tongue and argues a case in favor of its restricted and principled use, mainly in accuracy-oriented tasks. In his article, Atkinson (1987) clearly states that translation to the target language which emphasizes a recently taught language item is a means to reinforce structural, conceptual and sociolinguistic differences between the native and target languages. In his view, even though this activity is not communicative, it aims at improving accuracy of the newly learned structures. Similarly, this research aimed at investigating the effect of translation from L1 to L2 on the accurate use of the structures.

The arguments in supports of using the learners' mother tongue in L2 instruction clearly reveal that not only doesn't the use of first language have a negative impact on L2 learning, but it can be factor to help students improve the way they learn a second language. Although the 'English Only' paradigm continues to be dominant in communicative language teaching , research into teacher practice reveals that the L1 is used as a learning resource in many ESL classes (Auerbach, 1993). Auerbach adds that when the native language is used, practitioners, researchers, and learners consistently report positive results. Furthermore, he identifies the following uses of mother tongue in the classroom: classroom management, language analysis and presenting rules that govern grammar, discussing cross-cultural issues, giving instructions or prompts, explaining errors, and checking comprehension.

Professionals in second language acquisition have become increasingly aware of the role the mother tongue plays in the EFL classroom. Nunan and Lamb (1996), for example, contend that EFL teachers working with monolingual students at lower levels of English proficiency find prohibition of the mother tongue to be practically impossible. Cook (2001) in support of the role of L1 states that "bringing the L1 back from exile may lead not only to the improvement of existing teaching methods but also to innovations in methodology" (p. 189). Furthermore, Brooks and Donato (1994, cited in Cook, 2001) argue that the use of mother tongue is a normal psycholinguistic process that facilitates L2 production and allows the learners both to initiate and sustain verbal interaction with one other.

Prodromou (2001) in an online article draws an analogy between the mother tongue in EFL classroom and a skeleton in the cupboard— "something most people have, in one form or another". This metaphor makes sense since "we have for a long time treated the mother tongue as a 'taboo' subject, a source of embarrassment and on the part of teachers, a recognition of their failure to teach properly, i.e. using 'only English'". In spite of this negative view toward using the first language of learners in the classroom, most nonnative speaker teachers of English have quietly been using the L1, to a lesser or greater extent; "the skeleton has been there all the time, we just haven't wanted to talk about it". He believes that the reason for such treatment of the first language lies in the fact that the psycholinguistic or pedagogic framework which justifies the place of mother tongue in L2 instruction does not exist yet. Smith (1994) in support for bilingual education states that providing children quality education in their first language gives them two things: knowledge and literacy. The knowledge that children get through their first language helps make the English they hear and read more comprehensible. "Literacy developed in the primary language transfers to the second language. The reason is simple: Because we learn to read by reading—that is, by making sense of what is on the page" (p. 55).

L1 can have various uses in L2 classroom; Auerbuch (1993) suggests the following uses for the first language of learners: language analysis and presenting rules that govern grammar, classroom management, giving instructions or prompts, explaining errors, discussing cross-cultural issues, and checking comprehension. Moreover, Cook (1999) asserts that treating the L1 as a classroom resource opens up a number of ways to use it, such as for teachers to convey meaning, explain grammar, and organize the class, and for students to use as part of their collaborative learning and individual strategy use. "The first language can be a useful element in creating authentic L2 uses rather than something to be shunned at all costs" (p. 185).

Although the provision of maximum L2 exposure to the learners seems essential, L1 can be used alongside L2 as a complement. In this regard, Turnbull (2001) states that maximizing the target language use does not and should not mean that it is harmful for the teacher to use the L1. "A principle that promotes maximal teacher use of the target language acknowledges that the L1 and target language can exist simultaneously" (p. 153). Similarly, Stern (1992) states that "the use of L1 and target language should be seen as complementary, depending on the characteristics and stages of the language learning process" (p. 285). On the other hand, overuse of L1 will naturally reduce the amount of exposure to L2. Therefore, attempt should be made to keep a balance between L1 and L2 use. In this regard, Turnbull (2001) acknowledges that although it is efficient to make a quick switch to the L1 to ensure, for instance, whether students understand a difficult grammar concept or an unknown word, it is crucial for teachers to use the target language as much as possible in contexts in which students spend only short periods of time in class, and when they have little contact with the target language outside the classroom.

Surely there is a difference between judicious and principled use of L1 and an absolute leeway in using the mother tongue of the learners. For example, Duff and Polio (1990) examined the quantity of input to which students were exposed in foreign language classes at an English-speaking university. They reported that the 13 teachers' L2 use ranged from 10% to 100% of the time observed. The authors noted that "there seems to be a lack of awareness on the part of the teachers as to how, when, and the extent to which they actually use English in the classroom" (p. 320).

Bawcom (2002, cited in Krajka, 2004), in her study on using L1 in the classroom, found out that in the group of learners under investigation, 36% used the mother tongue for affective factors (e.g. sense of identity, security, social interaction); 41% as a way of implementing learning strategies (e.g. checking comprehension, going over homework); for 18% of learners it was an example of expediency (e.g. translation of directions for activities and passive vocabulary), while the remaining 5% was unintelligible. Cook (1992) argues that all second language learners access their L1 while processing the L2. She suggests that "the L2 user does not effectively switch off the L1 while processing the L2, but has it constantly available" (p. 571). She also maintains that when working with ESL learners, teachers must not treat the L2 in isolation from the L1. In fact, according to Cook, one cannot do so because "the L1 is present in the L2 learners' minds, whether the teacher wants it to be there or not. The L2 knowledge that is being created in them is connected in all sorts of ways with their L1 knowledge" (p. 584). One might suppose that using L1 in L2 instruction will lead to negative interference. However, Beardsmore (1993) believes that although it may appear contrary to common 6sense, maintaining and developing one's native language does not interfere with the developing of the second language proficiency. To him experience shows that many people around the world become fully bi- and multilingual without suffering interference from one language in the learning of the other.

Another benefit of using the L1 in L2 teaching is psychological values. Contrary to reasons put forth as to why students should be encouraged to use only the target language in class, informal translation in the class can become a form of peer support for the learners. According to Atkinson (1987) one reality of the classroom is that the students bring their own L1 strengths into the class and it is not possible to create a class where all the students are of equal abilities because some students have stronger listening skills than others and some have better comprehension of syntax or lexical items.

Lucas and Katz (1994) put more emphasis on the psychological value of using the mother tongue by asserting that "using native language in EFL classroom has psychological benefits in addition to serving as a practical pedagogical tool for providing access to academic content, allowing more effective interaction, and providing greater access to prior knowledge" (p. 539). If the native language of learners is used and valued in schools and classrooms, it will support and enhance the students' learning because they themselves are indirectly valued.

The use of students' native language can also increase their openness to learning by reducing the degree of language and culture shock they are encountering (Auerbach, 1993). He adds that because "relations of power and their affective consequences are integral to language acquisition" (p. 16), students' learning can also be enhanced by integrating students' native language into their educational experiences, thus giving their language a status more comparable to that of English. Finally, Harbord (1992), in support for using L1 in the classroom as a humanistic treatment of learners, states that eliminating or limiting the use of mother language does not guarantee better acquisition, "nor does it foster the humanistic approach that recognizes learners' identities as native speakers of a valuable language that is as much a part of them as their names" (p. 351).

Another issue addressed by this paper is translation. Translation is obviously one of the noticeable aspects of using L1. The role of translation in the ESL and EFL classroom has and will continue to be a highly debatable issue. The use of the students' first language (L1) in the foreign language classroom has been an issue of argument for linguists and teachers alike since the fall from grace of Grammar- Translation as a teaching method. It is also assumed that translation does not belong in the classroom because it does not embody making full use of the target language.

Even though translation is still widely used throughout the world, no teaching methodology exists that supports it and many speak out against it (Richards & Rodgers, 1986). Atkinson (1987) claims that because there is not much positive literature on the use of translation in the classroom, and the negative treatment it receives by the experts, teachers have been cautious of experimenting with it or doing research on it.   However, to some experts, translation can constructively be used in L2 teaching and it can also serve as a teaching technique. Cook (2001) asserts that the word 'translation' has so far been avoided as much as possible because of its negative implication in teaching. "Translation as a *teaching technique* is a different matter from translation as a goal of language teaching" (p. 200). Moreover, translation has been viewed, in Oxford's (1990) view, as a learning strategy. Despite the traditionally negative view of translation, Atkinson (1993, p. 53) claims that by raising one's consciousness of the nonparallel nature of languages, the learning process becomes richer; translation not only "allows learners to think comparatively," but it is also "a real life activity" because students who learn English for their jobs will probably need to know something about translation. Similarly, Duff (1989) states that translation does not have to be an aimless struggle between the learner and the text. However, many other approaches are possible which introduce purposeful and imaginative use of translation in language learning programs. "If we can find a way to offset the weak points and make the best use of its assets, translation as a teaching technique can be used to help students learn a second language more thoughtfully and effectively" (p. 6).

The two extreme positions of pure translation . and forbidding translation in the classroom are unnecessary extremes and instead a balanced approach in which teachers strategically use L1 in order to promote foreign language acquisition seems to be logical. Stibbard (1994) analyzed the use of oral translation as a L2 teaching activity. He suggested that translation may play a valuable role in L2 teaching. Moreover, he asserted that translation should be an integral part of the language learning program. In addition, Levenston (1985) presents an overview of the role of translation in foreign language teaching and learning. He argues that translation is useful for: (1)

practicing grammatical structures, (2) explaining vocabulary items, (3) testing at all levels, and (4) developing communicative competence. He recommended translation be taught as a skill in its own right. Contrary to what many might think translation is not a passive activity which lacks communication. According to Duff (1989) translation is a kind of communicative activity which is practiced within a meaningful context. He adds that "it enhances interaction between the teacher and the students and among the students themselves due to the fact that rarely is there any absolute right rendering of the text" (p. 55).

A significant benefit of translation in language teaching is that teachers can use translation as an effective means of explaining particular aspects of language, such as cultural differences, grammatical rules and syntactic structures with which the students have difficulty. In this regard, Chellapan (1982) explains that this way of using translation involves a conscious process of learning. Through translation, a learner can be aware of the distinctiveness of similar structures in the two languages, and also of the different processes used in conveying the same message. Deliberate translation, as he calls it, focuses on lexical items, where the contrasts in the two languages vary; therefore, it should be done in a larger context which will help the students learn the different distributions in the two languages and also shows that the meaning of any item is part of the total environment of the text in the two languages.

Atkinson (1987) suggests that activities that involve some translation promote guessing strategies amongst students and help reduce the word-for-word translation that often occurs and which results in inappropriate L2 use. Similarly, Harbord (1992) admits that some translation work teaches students to work towards transferring meaning "rather than the word-for-word translation that occurs when the learner's unconscious need to make assumptions and correlations between languages is ignored" (p. 354). Moreover, focus on form is the last issue dealt with in this paper. Focus on form, in its communicative sense, is defined by Richards and Schmidt (2002) as any focusing of attention on the formal linguistic characteristics of language, as opposed to a pure focus on meaning in communication. The significance of focus on form has been valued by Ellis (2002) who claims that "there is by now ample evidence to show that form-focused instruction (FFI) has a positive effect on second language (SL) acquisition. That is, by and large, learners seem to learn the grammatical structures they are taught" (p. 225). Therefore, today, one can claim that the current trend in language teaching has shifted attention to focus on form and improving accuracy (See Celce-Murcia, 1991).

Although new teaching methods give more prominence to fluency rather than accuracy, many research studies support the idea that accuracy is, at least, as important as fluency, and they should be used integrally in L2 teaching. For example, in a research to investigate the effect of focus on form on the quality of instruction, Lightbown and Spada's (1990, cited in Muranoi, 2000) observations of the intensive program classes revealed that the major portion of instruction focused on meaning-based activities, and teachers gave little attention to grammar or accuracy. Their observations also indicated; however, that some teachers responded to learners' errors more often than others and, in some cases, this response appeared to be related to the achievement of higher levels of accuracy. In another study, Leeman, Arteagoitia, Fridman, and Doughty (1995, cited in Muranoi, 2000) compared focus on form instruction and focus on meaning instruction. The participants consisted of two groups of US college students in advanced Spanish classes, one of which received focus on form instruction, the other of which received focus on meaning instruction. Post-tests revealed that those students who received focus on form instruction were more accurate in their production of Spanish verbs than were those who received focus on meaning instruction. As a result of this need to pay attention to the structural aspect of language in language teaching, the present study aims at using a teaching technique to improve linguistic accuracy of Iranian EFL learners. In other words, this study tries to investigate the efficiency of a teaching technique— namely translating from L1 to L2—in enhancing Iranian intermediate learners' focus on form by means of using particular grammatical structures.

The purpose of the study

To achieve the purpose of this study, the following research question was proposed:

> *Does the use of translation from L1 to L2 have any effect on the improvement of Iranian EFL learners' linguistic accuracy—focus on form?*

Based on the research question, the following null hypothesis was formulated:

> *Using translation from L1 to L2 has no effect on the improvement of Iranian EFL learners' linguistic accuracy—focus on form.*

Methodology

Participants

To accomplish the objectives of this study, 70 male and 85 female (i.e. 155 participants, altogether) Iranian pre-intermediate learners of English between the age of 13 to 24 studying in Paniz Language Institute, Eshragh Cultural Center, and Parsiyan Language Institute were given a pre-test. 124 learners met the necessary condition (i.e., lack of familiarity of the aimed structures in the study to enter the second phase. In the second phase, 72 participants, out of 124, with scores one standard deviation below and above the mean on the normal distribution curve of the pretest were chosen for the final phase of the study. On the basis of their pretest scores, they were randomly put into two similar groups; one group as the experimental group, and the other as the comparison group.

Instruments

In order to carry out this study, a number of learners were required who had almost no familiarity with certain structures under study. Therefore, two main points had to be kept in mind; firstly, some structures had to be selected to be worked on in the research; and secondly, a number of participants had to be selected who had almost no familiarity with those structures. Consequently, in order to have a sound justification for the choice of the structures to work on, a structured questionnaire was designed to find out which structures are more difficult to master for pre-intermediate and intermediate learners of English. To do so, *New Interchange* textbooks were chosen and according to the table of specification of these books, the list of structures which were taught in these books was produced. Therefore, the questionnaire included the list of structures existing in the mentioned textbooks. The questionnaire was answered by 50 EEL teachers and they were asked to determine the structures which seemed to them to be more difficult to master for the learners of *New Interchange* textbooks.

Having gathered the data - through the calculation of the frequency of the marked structures - 4 structures, from the first 6 structures which were found out to be the more complicated ones to be mastered than others, were selected. The selection of these 4 structures was mainly due to the fact that they were all presented in one book; that is, *New Interchange 2;* hence, such a selection made the study considerably more manageable to be carried out. The most frequently marked structures in the questionnaire were: *Passive voice*: 80%; *Indirect reported speech*: 78%; *Conditional type 2:* 68%; and *Wish* 70%; *Conditional sentences type 3:* 84%; *Causative:* 82%. The next step was to construct a test to identify the participants who did not have familiarity with the aimed structure. Therefore, an achievement test was designed which included three main types of items: 1) 20 teacher-made achievement items based on *New Interchange Intro & New Interchange1* (since the aimed structures of the study were introduced in *New Interchange 2* course book). It is worth mentioning that these items were prepared according to the table of specifications of the mentioned books which contribute to the content validity of the test. 2) 20 items of the aimed structures of the study: *Passive voice*: 5 items, *Indirect reported speech*: 5 items, *Conditional type 2:* 5 items, and *Wish+ simple past* 5 items. 3) 10 items which had not yet been studied by the participants.

Moreover, after reviewing and rewriting the items, the test was piloted with 30 similar learners to determine item characteristics, i.e., item facility and item discrimination. After applying necessary changes to the questions, the final version of the test was ready to be administered. Also, a time allocation of 60 minutes was decided for the final version of the test to be appropriate. In addition, the reliability of the test was calculated through

KR-21 method which turned out to be 0.80. The treatment used in this study was the Persian sentences which had to be translated by the participants in the experimental group into English within 16 sessions. For each structure under study in this project, that is, *Passive, Wish+ simple past, Conditional type 2,* and *Indirect reported speech*, 24 Persian sentences were distributed among the participants to translate into English within 4 sessions; that is, 6 sentences each session.

The last instrument used in this study was the post- test which was designed in a way that had a similar format and content as the pre-test; hence, the difficulty level was kept the same. Also, this test was piloted with 30 participants in order to be checked in terms of item characteristics; that is, item facility, item discrimination and choice distribution.

Procedure

This study required 72 homogeneous learners who also had almost no familiarity with four grammatical structures namely *Passive, Wish+ simple past, Conditional type 2,* and *Indirect reported speech.* To do so, twenty items (i.e., five items for *conditional type 2* sentences, five items for *wish,* five items for *passive,* and five items for *indirect reported speech*) were added to the test. It is worth mentioning that the participants who incorrectly answered at least 3 items out of the 5 items designed for each structure were selected for the final phase of the study. In other words, those who answered 3 or more items of each aimed structure correctly were omitted from the study. This procedure made it possible for the researcher to make sure that in the beginning of the treatment, the participants had almost no familiarity with the aimed structures in the study.

The test was first piloted with 30 learners and after applying the necessary changes and calculations to achieve item characteristics, i.e., item facility and item discrimination, as well as reliability, 155 learners took the test, out of whom 124 learners met the necessary condition (i.e., lack of familiarity with the aimed structures) to enter the second phase.   In the second phase, 78 participants, out of 124, with scores one standard deviation below and above the mean on the normal distribution curve were chosen for the final phase of the study (since 6 participants did not take part in the whole steps of the study, the number of participants decreased to 72). On the basis of their pretest scores, they were randomly put into two similar groups, each containing 36 participants; one group as the experimental group, and the other as the control group.

Regarding the treatment of the study, as discussed in the Instrumentation section, Persian sentences were used to be translated into English. For this purpose, for each structure under study in this project; that is, *Passive, Wish+ simple past, Conditional type 2,* and *Indirect reported speech*, 24 Persian sentences were distributed among the participants to translate into English within 4 sessions; that is, 6 sentences each session. Therefore, the whole project took 16 sessions of instruction. In other words, after presenting each of the mentioned structures to the participants in the experimental group, 24 Persian sentences, which were supposed to be translated into English using the same structure which had been taught, and with the same difficulty level as the ones which were presented in the textbook, were given to the participants to be translated into English. After the participants' translating the sentences individually as an exercise, the last step was to translate and discuss the sentences by the teacher—in terms of correct use of structures. This important part of the treatment was accompanied by grammatical explanations on the part of the teacher.

Regarding the comparison group, everything was similar to that of the experimental group, except that there were no Persian sentences to be translated into English. Instead, they received the same amount of grammar exercises but from their course book and some similar ones which were provided by the teacher, not to mention, in English. Consequently, contrary to the experimental group, the control group received no exercise which included Persian language. The two groups were posttested through another achievement test—similar in content with the pretest— in order to make sure that the difference in the scores of the aimed structures is due to the function of treatment. Of course, only the twenty items which included the aimed structures were significant to the researcher. In other words, the comparison was made only between the scores of the items which addressed the aimed structure. Therefore, contrary to the pretest scores which were calculated out of 50 items, the posttest scores were calculated out of 20, i.e. the number of items of the aimed structures, in order to see whether the application of treatment improved participants' knowledge in the specific area of the structures under study.

Data Analysis

To delve into the purposes of the study certain statistical procedures were utilized to analyze and interpret the data elicited by the study. The main statistical procedure employed in this study was t-test in order to compare the means of the experimental and comparison groups of the study to determine whether the application of the treatment had any considerable effect on the linguistic accuracy of the experimental group.

Results and discussion

The first step in the statistical procedures of the research pertained to the selection of a homogeneous group. Therefore, a population of 72 participants with scores one standard deviation above and below the mean with the following descriptive information (Table 4.1) were selected.

Table 4.1 Descriptive Analysis of the Pretest

	N	Mean	Std. Dev.
Comparison	36	17.44	4.19
Experimental	36	16.66	3.52

In order to determine if the difference between the means of the scores of the two groups were significant on the pre-test, an independent t-test was conducted between the scores of the participants in both groups. The observed t-valve of the df= 70 was 0.85, which is a smaller than the critical t-value that equals 2.00 at the same degree of freedom (df= 70). Therefore, it can be concluded that the difference between the means of the pre-test scores in the two groups was not significant, i.e. the two groups performed fairly similar to each other in the pre-test. Of course, the purpose of t-test was twofold: to determine whether the two groups under study were homogenous, and to compare participants' performance in the pre-test and the post-test. The result of the independent *t*-test for the pre-test scores is shown in Table 4.2.

Table 4.2. Independent Sample t-test for Pre-test Scores

	t-test for Equality of Means		
	T	df	Sig. (2-tailed)
Comparison & Experimental	0.85	70	0.39

In order to find out the effectiveness of using translation from L1 to L2 on the improvement of the linguistic accuracy—focus on form—of the experimental group and compare their improvement with their counterparts' in the control group, both groups took part in a post-test which enjoyed similar content and format as the pre-test. It is worth mentioning that in the posttest only the scores of the items which corresponded to the aimed structures of this study were of significance to the researcher. Therefore, the scores of the participants in this test are calculated from 20. The descriptive analysis of the post-test is presented in Table 4.3.

Table 4.3. Descriptive Analysis of the Post-test

	N	Mean	Std. Dev.
Comparison	36	10.69	2.84
Experimental	36	12.69	3.87

After administering the post-test to both groups, an independent t-test between the scores of the participants in the experimental and the control groups was conducted to determine the significance of the mean difference between the scores of the two groups. As shown in the Table 4.4. below, the observed t-value for the post-test was 2.49 (df=70), which is greater than 2, i.e. the critical t-value at the same degree of freedom (2.49>2; df=70).

Table 4.4. Independent Sample t-test for Post-test Scores

	t-test for Equality of Means		
Comparison &	T	df	Sig. (2-tailed)
Experimental	2.49	70	0.015

From the t-test table (i.e. Table 4.4), it is quite obvious that the effect of using translation from L1 to L2 on the improvement of the linguistic accuracy —focus on form— has been significant since the *t*-observed value is greater than the set value of *t* critical. Therefore, as a result of the above-mentioned analyses reveal, the hypothesis formulated in this study can be rejected with caution. In other words, it is concluded that using translation from L1 to L2 improves the linguistic accuracy of Iranian EFL learners.

Consequently, the results of the statistical analyses of this research manifested that translation from L1 to L2 as a teaching technique plays a major role in improving learners' linguistic accuracy. The results obtained from the t-test analysis and the obtained value of *t*- observed is high enough to claim that the null hypothesis has been rejected. In other words, the findings obtained in this research suggest that the experimental group which received treatment in the form of translation from L1 to L2 using specific structures outperformed the control group which received the placebo.

The findings of this study support Cook's (2000) idea who believes that translation is a *teaching technique* which can promote learners' accuracy as well as fluency. The results also support Atkinson's (1987) statements who introduces translation from L1 to L2 as a means of improving the accuracy of the newly learned structures:

> *An exercise involving translation into the target language of a paragraph or set of sentences which highlight the recently taught language item can provide useful reinforcement of structural, conceptual and sociolinguistic differences between the native and target languages. This activity is not, of course, communicative, but its aim is to improve accuracy. (p. 244)*

The findings of this research are also in line with Duff's (1989) belief: "translation as a teaching technique can be used to help students learn a second language more thoughtfully and effectively" (p. 6). As for the role of L1 and the significance of translation, this research project supports Nunan (1999) who states that:

> *In some cases it is inevitable that language learners use their dominant languages (L1) as a resource. Indeed it is a kind of individual learning style for some students. They need to be able to relate lexis and structures of target language into their equivalents in their mother tongue. Therefore, sound pedagogy should make use of this learning style. (p. 52)*

Conclusions and pedagogical implications

Conclusions

Based on the results obtained from the statistical analyses in the study, it was discovered that the idea of the effectiveness of using translation from L1 to L2 as a teaching technique to improve a group of Iranian EFL learners' linguistic accuracy was supported. Therefore, it can be concluded that translating form L1 to L2, using specific structures, can enhance learners' linguistic accuracy within the scope of those structures. It also manifests that learners' mother tongue is not a useless element in second or foreign language learning. In other words, mother tongue, if used purposefully and systematically, can have a constructive role in teaching other languages. In effect, the purpose of the present study was to join the three vertices of the triangle i.e., first language, translation, and focus on form.

Moreover, it can be claimed that translating sentences form L1 to L2, if selected purposefully, can push learners to use specific structures accurately when producing utterances in the second language. This mental practice in transforming an idea from mother language to the second language helps the learner tackle the psycho-linguistic challenge they have to face in producing second language in real life situations. Nevertheless, when utilizing this teaching technique, the learners should be bewared about the structural differences existing between languages which may cause negative interference from their L1. In other words, learners should be warned that there is not always a structural correspondence between their first language and the language they are learning. To make it short, translation from L1 to L2 is a kind of practice which makes the learners use specific L2 structures *accurately* in order to express L1 ideas. This transformation—mental translation from L1 to L2—is a natural and sometimes inevitable process which is mostly experienced by the learners of lower levels. Consequently, as discussed above, the technique used in this study is a means through which learners can practice producing L2 grammatically correct sentences which enables them to perform accurately in communicative situations.

Implications for Teaching and Teacher Training

Translation from L1 to L2 is not a strange process; nonetheless, it might not have been dealt with through systematic and research-based studies yet. Although the word 'translation' and even 'mother tongue' has been abominated by many so-called innovatory-oriented teachers, this study demonstrated that there are judicious ways in which language teachers can use mother tongue, in general, and translation from L1 to L2, in particular, in their instruction with the purpose of improving learners' proficiency. In addition, mother tongue *is* truly a very rich source of linguistic knowledge with which any L2 learner is already equipped, and it does not seem reasonable to deprive our learners from using this recourse at the expense of exercising an English-only atmosphere in our classrooms.

Therefore, it can be suggested that teachers be familiarized with advantages of using learners' mother tongue in EFL/ESL classrooms and they should be reasonably given enough leeway to use this resource constructively. In particular, language teachers can use the technique presented in this study, i.e. using translation from L1 to L2, as a communicative *task* to promote their learners' linguistic accuracy. Therefore, it seems reasonable to allocate some time to the training of teachers in this regard.

Implications for Materials Development

One of the challenges and responsibilities of materials developers has always been to design grammar sections for the books. There are a variety of methods for presenting grammar; however, materials developers can also make use of the findings of this study and design sections of grammar in which the learners have to translate sentences from L1 to L2 with the newly learned structures in English. This activity can be introduced to be done as a task and learners can also do it collaboratively and in groups. Therefore, it is recommended that materials developers include exercises and activities in their materials which require the learners to translate texts from Persian to English using accurate grammatical sentences.

Limitations and Delimitations of the Study

1. This project was limited to study the effect of using translation from L1 to L2 to improve the participants' linguistic accuracy; however, other aspects of language learning such as fluency and communicative use of language were not taken into account.
2. The participants of the study were in the age range of 13 to 24, therefore; the results might not be generalized to learners out of this age range.
3. In this study the practice of translation from L1 to L2 was done in written form; nevertheless, translation in spoken mode was not practiced.
4. In this study, Persian language was used in the form of translation from L1 to L2; however, other forms of using mother tongue in L2 teaching were not taken into account.
5. Among the participants who took part in this study, 6 out of 78 participants did not go through all the steps of the study.

References

Atkinson, D. (1987). The mother tongue in the classroom: A neglected resource? *ELT Journal, 41*(4), 241-247.

Auerbach, E. (1993). Reexamining English only in the ESL classroom. *TESOL Quarterly, 27*(1), 9-32.

Beardsmore, H. (1993). The European school model. In H. Beardsmore

(Eds.), *European models of bilingual education*, 21-54. Clevedon, England: Multilingual Matters.

Brown, H. D. (2000). *Principles of language learning and teaching*. San Francisco: Longman.

Celce-Murcia, M. (1991). Grammar pedagogy in second and foreign language teaching. *TESOL Quarterly, 25*(3), 459-480.

Chellapan, K. (1982). Translanguage, translation and second language acquisition. In F. Eppert (Eds.), *Papers on Translation: Aspects, Concepts, Implications*, (pp. 57-63). Singapore: SEMEO Regional Language Centre.

Cook, V. J. (1992). Evidence for multicompetence. *Language Learning, 42*(4), 557591.

Cook, V. J. (1999). Going beyond the native speaker in language teaching. *TESOL Quarterly, 33*(2), 185-209.

Cook, V. J. (2001). Using the first language in the classroom. <u>*Canadian Modern Language Review*</u>, *57*(3), 184-206.

Duff, A. (1989). *Translation*. Oxford: Oxford University Press.

Ellis, R. (2002). Does the form-focused instruction affect the acquisition of implicit knowledge? *Studies in Second Language Acquisition. 24* (2), 223-236.

Harbord, J. (1992). The use of the mother tongue in the classroom. *English Language Teaching Journal, 46*(4), 350-356.

Krajka, J. (2004). Your mother tongue does matter! Maria Curie Sklodowska University, Poland. Published in the <u>Teaching English withTechnology-</u> Volume 4, Issue 4, October 2004. Retrieved August 17, 2006, from <u>http://www.iatefl.org.pl/call/j_review19.htm</u>

Levenston, A. (1985). The place of translation in the foreign language classroom. *English Teachers' Journal, (32)*, 33–43.

Lucas, T., & Katz, A. (1994). Reframing the debate: The role of native languages in English-only programs for language minority students. *TESOL Quarterly, 28*(3), 537-561.

Muranoi, H. (2000). Focus on form through interaction enhancement: Integrating formal instruction into a communicative task in EFL classrooms. *Language Learning, 50*(4), 617-673.

Nunan, D., & Lamb, C. (1996). *The self-directed teacher*. Cambridge: Cambridge University Press.

Oxford, R. (1990). *Language and learning strategies: What every teacher should know*. New York: Newbury House.

Polio, C., & Duff, P. (1994). Teachers' language use in university foreign language classrooms: a qualitative analysis of English and target language alternation. *Modern Language Journal, 78*(3), 311-326.

Prodromou, L. (2001). From mother tongue to other tongue. Retrieved July 14, 2006, from <u>http://www.thrace-net.gr/bridges/bridges5</u>

Richards, J. C., & Rodgers, T. (1986). *Approaches and methods in language teaching*. Cambridge: Cambridge University Press.

Richards, J. C., & Schmidt, R. (2002). *Longman dictionary of language teaching and applied linguistics* (2nd ed.). Essex: Longman Group.

Smith, F. (1994). *Understanding reading: A psycholinguistic analysis of reading and learning to read* (5th ed.). Hillsdale, New Jersey: L. Erlbaum.

Stern, H. (1992). *Issues and options in language teaching.* Oxford: Oxford University Press.

Stibbard, R. (1994). The use of translation in foreign language teaching. *Perspectives: Studies in Translatology, (1)*, 9-18.

Turnbull, M. (2001). There is a role for the L1 in second and foreign language teaching, but ... <u>Canadian Modern Language Review</u>, *57*, (4), 150-163.

References

Allwight, D. (2005). Developing principles for practitioner research: the case of exploratory practice. *Modern Language Journal* 89(3), 353-66.

Ary, D., Jacobs, L.c., & Razavieh, A. (2010). *Introduction to research in education* (8th ed.). Orlando, FL: Harccourt Braca College Publishers.

Bachman, L. F. (1990). *Fundamendal considerations in language testing.* Oxford: Oxford University Press.

Bagheri, M. S., & Haghighat, Z. (2011). *A practical guide to writing proposals, articles, theses and dissertations.* Islamic Shiraz Azad University Press.

Bartol, K. M. (1981). *Survey results from editorial board members: Lethal and nonlethal errors.* Los Angeles, CA.

Brown, J. D. (1995). *Understanding research methods in applied linguistics.* Cambridge: Cambridge University Press.

Brown, J. D., & Rodgers, T.S. (2002). *Doing second language research.* Oxford, UK: Oxford University Press.

Dörnyei, Z. (2003). *Questionnaires in second language research.* Mahwah, NJ: Lawrence Erlbaum Associates.

Dörnyei, Z. (2003). *Questionnaires in second language research: Construction, administration, and processing.* New York: Lawrence Erlbaum Associates.

Dörnyei, Z. (2011). *Research methods in applied linguistics.* Oxford: Oxford University Press.

Farhady, H. (2002). *Research methods in applied linguistics. Tehran:* Payame Noor University Press.

Gall, M. D., Borg, W. R., & Gall, J. P. (1996). *Educational research: An introduction.* White Plains, NY: Longman.

Gall, M. D., Gall, J. P., & Walter, R. P. (2006), *Educational research: An introduction* (8th ed.) White Plains, NY: Longman.

Hatch, E., & Farhady, H. (1981). *Research design and statistics for applied linguistics.* Rowley, Massachusetts: Newbury House.

Jalilifar, A. R. (2009). *Research articles in applied linguistics: A genre-based writing guide.* Ahvaz : Ahvaz University Press.

Johnson, D. (1992). *Approaches to research in second language learning.* New York: Longman.

Kazemi, A. , & Zarei, L. (2014). *Language teaching practicum.* Yasuj: Islamic Azad University, Science and Research Branch of Kohkilouyeh and Boyerahmad.

Lester, J. D. (1994). *Writing research papers: A complete guide* (6th ed). Austin, TX: Harper Collins Publishers Inc.

Mckay, S. L. (2006). *Researching second language classrooms.* New Jersey: Lawrence Erlbaum Associates, Inc.

Mousavi, S.A. (1997). *A dictionary of language testing.* Tehran: Rahnama Publications Press.

Nunan, D. (1997). *Research methods in language learning.* Cambridge: Cambridge University Press.

Paltridge, B., & Starfield, S. (2007). *Thesis and dissertation writing in a second language*: A Handbook for Supervisors. London: Routledge

Pallant, J. (2007). *A step-by-step guide to data analysis using SPSS version 15: SPSS survival manual.* Berkshire: Mcgraw-Hill.

Pallant, J. (2013). *A step by step guide to data analysis using IBM SPSS: Survival manual* (5th ed). Berkshire: Mcgraw-Hill.

Patton, M.Q. (1990). *Qualitative evaluation and research methods.* Newbury Park, CA: Sage.

Publication manual of the American Psychological Association (6th Edition). (2010). Washington, DC: American Psychological Association.

Razmjoo, A., & Sahragard, R. (2006). *Fundamental considerations of research methods in applied linguistics.* Shiraz: Sandbad

Riazi, A. M. (1991). *A dictionary of research methods: Quantitative and qualitative.* Tehran: Rahnama Publications.

Riazi, A. M. (2000). *How to write research propsals.* Tehran Rahnama Publications Press.

Riazi, A. M. (2002). *Writing academic papers in English.* Shiraz: Shiraz University Press.

Richards, K. (2003). *Qualitative inquiry in TESOL.* Basingstoke: Palgrave Macmillan.

Ruiying, Y. , & Allison, D. (2004). *English for specific purposes,* 23(3), 264-279.

Seliger, H. W., & Shohamy, E. (1989). *Second language research methods.* Oxford: Oxford University Press.

Swales, J. M. (1990). *Genre analysis: English in academic and research settings.* Cambridge, UK: Cambridge University Press.

Swales, J. M. (2004). *Research genre: Explorations and applications.* Cambridge: Cambridge University Press.

Vaezi, S., & Mirzai, M. (2007). The Effect of Using Translation from L1 to L2 as a Teaching Technique on the Improvement of EFL Learners' Linguistic Accuracy - Focus on Form. *Humanising Language Teaching, volume* 5. Retrieved from http://www.hltmag.co.uk/sep07/mart03.htm on 20/02/2013.

Yamini, M., & Rahimi, M. (2007). *A guide to statistics and SPSS for research in TEFL, linguistics and related disciplines.* Shiraz: Koshamher.

Yin, R. K. (2003). *Case study research design and method.* Thousand Oaks, CA: Sage.

Internet resources

http:// Understanding Descriptive and Inferential Statistics
http://www.wikihow.com/Conduct-Academic-Research
https://statistics.laerd.com/statistical-guides/descriptive
http://www.investopedia.com/terms/n/null_hypothesis.asp
http://www.ehow.com/how_8459002_calculate-stanine-scores
k12grants.org/samples

http:// www.davidmlane.com/hyperstat/A18652.html
http:// www.mathsisfun.com/data/pie-charts.html
http://www.give2all.org/pdf/barchart/8.pdf
s://statistics.laerd.com/statistical-guides/standard-**score**
https://owl.english.purdue.edu/
http://psychology.about.com/
http://psych.athabascau.ca/
http://www.professorbwisa.com/
http://www.wikihow.com/Conduct-Scientific-Research
http://www.wikihow.com/Establish-a-Research-Topic
http://www.wikihow.com/Write-a-Research-Paper
http://www.wikihow.com/Research-for-a-Historical-Essay/Paper
http://www.wikihow.com/Do-Internet-Research
http://www.wikihow.com/Begin-Writing-a-Research-Paper
http://www.wikihow.com/Do-Your-Dissertation-Research-Productively
http://explorable.com/writing-a-discussion-section

Appendixes

Appendix 1

Tables | T-11

Table entry for p and C is the critical value t* with probability p lying to its right and probability C lying between −t* and t*.

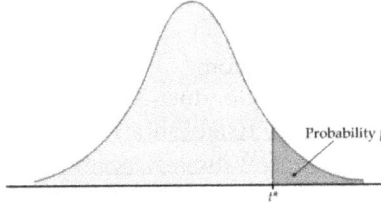

Probability p

t distribution critical values

df	Upper-tail probability p											
	.25	.20	.15	.10	.05	.025	.02	.01	.005	.0025	.001	.0005
1	1.000	1.376	1.963	3.078	6.314	12.71	15.89	31.82	63.66	127.3	318.3	636.6
2	0.816	1.061	1.386	1.886	2.920	4.303	4.849	6.965	9.925	14.09	22.33	31.60
3	0.765	0.978	1.250	1.638	2.353	3.182	3.482	4.541	5.841	7.453	10.21	12.92
4	0.741	0.941	1.190	1.533	2.132	2.776	2.999	3.747	4.604	5.598	7.173	8.610
5	0.727	0.920	1.156	1.476	2.015	2.571	2.757	3.365	4.032	4.773	5.893	6.869
6	0.718	0.906	1.134	1.440	1.943	2.447	2.612	3.143	3.707	4.317	5.208	5.959
7	0.711	0.896	1.119	1.415	1.895	2.365	2.517	2.998	3.499	4.029	4.785	5.408
8	0.706	0.889	1.108	1.397	1.860	2.306	2.449	2.896	3.355	3.833	4.501	5.041
9	0.703	0.883	1.100	1.383	1.833	2.262	2.398	2.821	3.250	3.690	4.297	4.781
10	0.700	0.879	1.093	1.372	1.812	2.228	2.359	2.764	3.169	3.581	4.144	4.587
11	0.697	0.876	1.088	1.363	1.796	2.201	2.328	2.718	3.106	3.497	4.025	4.437
12	0.695	0.873	1.083	1.356	1.782	2.179	2.303	2.681	3.055	3.428	3.930	4.318
13	0.694	0.870	1.079	1.350	1.771	2.160	2.282	2.650	3.012	3.372	3.852	4.221
14	0.692	0.868	1.076	1.345	1.761	2.145	2.264	2.624	2.977	3.326	3.787	4.140
15	0.691	0.866	1.074	1.341	1.753	2.131	2.249	2.602	2.947	3.286	3.733	4.073
16	0.690	0.865	1.071	1.337	1.746	2.120	2.235	2.583	2.921	3.252	3.686	4.015
17	0.689	0.863	1.069	1.333	1.740	2.110	2.224	2.567	2.898	3.222	3.646	3.965
18	0.688	0.862	1.067	1.330	1.734	2.101	2.214	2.552	2.878	3.197	3.611	3.922
19	0.688	0.861	1.066	1.328	1.729	2.093	2.205	2.539	2.861	3.174	3.579	3.883
20	0.687	0.860	1.064	1.325	1.725	2.086	2.197	2.528	2.845	3.153	3.552	3.850
21	0.686	0.859	1.063	1.323	1.721	2.080	2.189	2.518	2.831	3.135	3.527	3.819
22	0.686	0.858	1.061	1.321	1.717	2.074	2.183	2.508	2.819	3.119	3.505	3.792
23	0.685	0.858	1.060	1.319	1.714	2.069	2.177	2.500	2.807	3.104	3.485	3.768
24	0.685	0.857	1.059	1.318	1.711	2.064	2.172	2.492	2.797	3.091	3.467	3.745
25	0.684	0.856	1.058	1.316	1.708	2.060	2.167	2.485	2.787	3.078	3.450	3.725
26	0.684	0.856	1.058	1.315	1.706	2.056	2.162	2.479	2.779	3.067	3.435	3.707
27	0.684	0.855	1.057	1.314	1.703	2.052	2.158	2.473	2.771	3.057	3.421	3.690
28	0.683	0.855	1.056	1.313	1.701	2.048	2.154	2.467	2.763	3.047	3.408	3.674
29	0.683	0.854	1.055	1.311	1.699	2.045	2.150	2.462	2.756	3.038	3.396	3.659
30	0.683	0.854	1.055	1.310	1.697	2.042	2.147	2.457	2.750	3.030	3.385	3.646
40	0.681	0.851	1.050	1.303	1.684	2.021	2.123	2.423	2.704	2.971	3.307	3.551
50	0.679	0.849	1.047	1.299	1.676	2.009	2.109	2.403	2.678	2.937	3.261	3.496
60	0.679	0.848	1.045	1.296	1.671	2.000	2.099	2.390	2.660	2.915	3.232	3.460
80	0.678	0.846	1.043	1.292	1.664	1.990	2.088	2.374	2.639	2.887	3.195	3.416
100	0.677	0.845	1.042	1.290	1.660	1.984	2.081	2.364	2.626	2.871	3.174	3.390
1000	0.675	0.842	1.037	1.282	1.646	1.962	2.056	2.330	2.581	2.813	3.098	3.300
z*	0.674	0.841	1.036	1.282	1.645	1.960	2.054	2.326	2.576	2.807	3.091	3.291
	50%	60%	70%	80%	90%	95%	96%	98%	99%	99.5%	99.8%	99.9%

Confidence level C

Appendix 2

t Table

cum. prob	$t_{.50}$	$t_{.75}$	$t_{.80}$	$t_{.85}$	$t_{.90}$	$t_{.95}$	$t_{.975}$	$t_{.99}$	$t_{.995}$	$t_{.999}$	$t_{.9995}$
one-tail	0.50	0.25	0.20	0.15	0.10	0.05	0.025	0.01	0.005	0.001	0.0005
two-tails	1.00	0.50	0.40	0.30	0.20	0.10	0.05	0.02	0.01	0.002	0.001
df											
1	0.000	1.000	1.376	1.963	3.078	6.314	12.71	31.82	63.66	318.31	636.62
2	0.000	0.816	1.061	1.386	1.886	2.920	4.303	6.965	9.925	22.327	31.599
3	0.000	0.765	0.978	1.250	1.638	2.353	3.182	4.541	5.841	10.215	12.924
4	0.000	0.741	0.941	1.190	1.533	2.132	2.776	3.747	4.604	7.173	8.610
5	0.000	0.727	0.920	1.156	1.476	2.015	2.571	3.365	4.032	5.893	6.869
6	0.000	0.718	0.906	1.134	1.440	1.943	2.447	3.143	3.707	5.208	5.959
7	0.000	0.711	0.896	1.119	1.415	1.895	2.365	2.998	3.499	4.785	5.408
8	0.000	0.706	0.889	1.108	1.397	1.860	2.306	2.896	3.355	4.501	5.041
9	0.000	0.703	0.883	1.100	1.383	1.833	2.262	2.821	3.250	4.297	4.781
10	0.000	0.700	0.879	1.093	1.372	1.812	2.228	2.764	3.169	4.144	4.587
11	0.000	0.697	0.876	1.088	1.363	1.796	2.201	2.718	3.106	4.025	4.437
12	0.000	0.695	0.873	1.083	1.356	1.782	2.179	2.681	3.055	3.930	4.318
13	0.000	0.694	0.870	1.079	1.350	1.771	2.160	2.650	3.012	3.852	4.221
14	0.000	0.692	0.868	1.076	1.345	1.761	2.145	2.624	2.977	3.787	4.140
15	0.000	0.691	0.866	1.074	1.341	1.753	2.131	2.602	2.947	3.733	4.073
16	0.000	0.690	0.865	1.071	1.337	1.746	2.120	2.583	2.921	3.686	4.015
17	0.000	0.689	0.863	1.069	1.333	1.740	2.110	2.567	2.898	3.646	3.965
18	0.000	0.688	0.862	1.067	1.330	1.734	2.101	2.552	2.878	3.610	3.922
19	0.000	0.688	0.861	1.066	1.328	1.729	2.093	2.539	2.861	3.579	3.883
20	0.000	0.687	0.860	1.064	1.325	1.725	2.086	2.528	2.845	3.552	3.850
21	0.000	0.686	0.859	1.063	1.323	1.721	2.080	2.518	2.831	3.527	3.819
22	0.000	0.686	0.858	1.061	1.321	1.717	2.074	2.508	2.819	3.505	3.792
23	0.000	0.685	0.858	1.060	1.319	1.714	2.069	2.500	2.807	3.485	3.768
24	0.000	0.685	0.857	1.059	1.318	1.711	2.064	2.492	2.797	3.467	3.745
25	0.000	0.684	0.856	1.058	1.316	1.708	2.060	2.485	2.787	3.450	3.725
26	0.000	0.684	0.856	1.058	1.315	1.706	2.056	2.479	2.779	3.435	3.707
27	0.000	0.684	0.855	1.057	1.314	1.703	2.052	2.473	2.771	3.421	3.690
28	0.000	0.683	0.855	1.056	1.313	1.701	2.048	2.467	2.763	3.408	3.674
29	0.000	0.683	0.854	1.055	1.311	1.699	2.045	2.462	2.756	3.396	3.659
30	0.000	0.683	0.854	1.055	1.310	1.697	2.042	2.457	2.750	3.385	3.646
40	0.000	0.681	0.851	1.050	1.303	1.684	2.021	2.423	2.704	3.307	3.551
60	0.000	0.679	0.848	1.045	1.296	1.671	2.000	2.390	2.660	3.232	3.460
80	0.000	0.678	0.846	1.043	1.292	1.664	1.990	2.374	2.639	3.195	3.416
100	0.000	0.677	0.845	1.042	1.290	1.660	1.984	2.364	2.626	3.174	3.390
1000	0.000	0.675	0.842	1.037	1.282	1.646	1.962	2.330	2.581	3.098	3.300
z	0.000	0.674	0.842	1.036	1.282	1.645	1.960	2.326	2.576	3.090	3.291
	0%	50%	60%	70%	80%	90%	95%	98%	99%	99.8%	99.9%
					Confidence Level						

Appendix 2

Oxford University Press
and
University of Cambridge Local Examinations Syndicate

Name: ....

Date: ....

quick
placement
test

Version 2

This test is divided into two parts:

Part One (Questions 1 – 40) – All students.

Part Two (Questions 41 – 60) – Do not start this part unless told to do
so by your test supervisor.

Time: 30 minutes
Part 1

Questions 1 – 5

- Where can you see these notices?
- For questions **1** to **5**, mark **one** letter **A**, **B** or **C** on your Answer Sheet.

1

You can look, but don't touch the pictures.	A in an office
	B in a cinema
	C in a museum

2

Please give the right money to the driver.	A in a bank
	B on a bus
	C in a cinema

3

NO PARKING PLEASE	A in a street
	B on a book
	C on a table

4

CROSS BRIDGE FOR TRAINS TO EDINBURGH	A in a bank
	B in a garage
	C in a station

5

KEEP IN A COLD PLACE	A on clothes
	B on furniture
	C on food

Questions 6 – 10

- In this section you must choose the word which best fits each space in the text below.
- For questions **6** to **10**, mark **one** letter **A**, **B** or **C** on your Answer Sheet.

THE STARS

There are millions of stars in the sky. If you look **(6)** .... the sky on a clear night, it is possible

to see about 3000 stars. They look small, but they are really **(7)** .... big hot balls of burning

gas. Some of them are huge, but others are much smaller, like our planet Earth. The biggest stars are

very bright, but they only live for a short time. Every day new stars **(8)** .... born and old stars

die. All the stars are very far away. The light from the nearest star takes more **(9)** .... four

years to reach Earth. Hundreds of years ago, people **(10)** .... stars, like the North star, to know

which direction to travel in. Today you can still see that star.

6	**A**	at	**B**	up	**C**	on
7	**A**	very	**B**	too	**C**	much
8	**A**	is	**B**	be	**C**	are
9	**A**	that	**B**	of	**C**	than
10	**A**	use	**B**	used	**C**	using

Questions 11 – 20

- In this section you must choose the word which best fits each space in the texts.
- For questions **11** to **20**, mark **one** letter **A**, **B**, **C** or **D** on your Answer Sheet.

Good smiles ahead for young teeth

Older Britons are the worst in Europe when it comes to keeping their teeth. But British youngsters

(11) .... more to smile about because **(12)** .... teeth are among the best. Almost

80% of Britons over 65 have lost all or some **(13)** .... their teeth according to a World

Health Organisation survey. Eating too **(14)** .... sugar is part of the problem. Among

(15) .... , 12-year olds have on average only three missing, decayed or filled teeth.

11	**A** getting	**B** got	**C** have	**D** having
12	**A** their	**B** his	**C** them	**D** theirs
13	**A** from	**B** of	**C** among	**D** between
14	**A** much	**B** lot	**C** many	**D** deal
15	**A** person	**B** people	**C** children	**D** family

Christopher Columbus and the New World

On August 3, 1492, Christopher Columbus set sail from Spain to find a new route to India, China and Japan. At this time most people thought you would fall off the edge of the world if you sailed too far. Yet sailors such as Columbus had seen how a ship appeared to get lower and lower on the horizon as it sailed away. For Columbus this (16) .... that the world was round. He (17) .... to his men about the distance travelled each day. He did not want them to think that he did not (18) .... exactly where they were going. (19) ...., on October 12, 1492, Columbus and his men landed on a small island he named San Salvador. Columbus believed he was in Asia, (20) .... he was actually in the Caribbean.

16   A   made   B   pointed   C   was   D   proved

17   A   lied   B   told   C   cheated   D   asked

18   A   find   B   know   C   think   D   expect

19   A   Next   B   Secondly   C   Finally   D   Once

20   A   as   B   but   C   because   D   if

Questions 21 – 40

- In this section you must choose the word or phrase which best completes each sentence.
- For questions **21** to **40**, mark **one** letter **A**, **B**, **C** or **D** on your Answer Sheet.

21   The children won't go to sleep .... we leave a light on outside their bedroom.

   A except   **B** otherwise   **C** unless   **D** but

22   I'll give you my spare keys in case you .... home before me.

   A would get   **B** got   **C** will get   **D** get

23   My holiday in Paris gave me a great .... to improve my French accent.

   A occasion   **B** chance   **C** hope   **D** possibility

24   The singer ended the concert .... her most popular song.

   A by   **B** with   **C** in   **D** as

25   Because it had not rained for several months, there was a .... of water.

   A shortage   **B** drop   **C** scarce   **D** waste

26   I've always .... you as my best friend.

   A regarded   **B** thought   **C** meant   **D** supposed

27   She came to live here .... a month ago.

   A quite   **B** beyond   **C** already   **D** almost

28   Don't make such a ....! The dentist is only going to look at your teeth.

   A fuss   **B** trouble   **C** worry   **D** reaction

29   He spent a long time looking for a tie which .... with his new shirt.

   A fixed   **B** made   **C** went   **D** wore

30   Fortunately, ... from a bump on the head, she suffered no serious injuries from her fall.

   A other   **B** except   **C** besides   **D** apart

31 She had changed so much that .... anyone recognised her.

    A almost   **B** hardly   **C** not   **D** nearly

32 .... teaching English, she also writes children's books.

    A Moreover   **B** As well as   **C** In addition   **D** Apart

33 It was clear that the young couple were .... of taking charge of the restaurant.

    A responsible   **B** reliable   **C** capable   **D** able

34 The book .... of ten chapters, each one covering a different topic.

    A comprises   **B** includes   **C** consists   **D** contains

35 Mary was disappointed with her new shirt as the colour .... very quickly.

    A bleached   **B** died   **C** vanished   **D** faded

36 National leaders from all over the world are expected to attend the .... meeting.

    A peak   **B** summit   **C** top   **D** apex

37 Jane remained calm when she won the lottery and .... about her business as if nothing had happened.

    A came   **B** brought   **C** went   **D** moved

38 I suggest we .... outside the stadium tomorrow at 8.30.

    A meeting   **B** meet   **C** met   **D** will meet

39 My remarks were .... as a joke, but she was offended by them.

    A pretended   **B** thought   **C** meant   **D** supposed

40 You ought to take up swimming for the .... of your health.

    A concern   **B** relief   **C** sake   **D** cause

Part 2

Do not start this part unless told to do so by your test supervisor.

Questions 41 – 50

- In this section you must choose the word or phrase which best fits each space in the texts.
- For questions **41** to **50**, mark **one** letter **A**, **B**, **C** or **D** on your Answer Sheet.

CLOCKS

The clock was the first complex mechanical machinery to enter the home, **(41)** .... it

was too expensive for the **(42)** .... person until the 19th century, when

(43) .... production techniques lowered the price. Watches were also developed, but

they **(44)** .... luxury items until 1868 when the first cheap pocket watch was designed

in Switzerland. Watches later became **(45)** .... available and Switzerland became the

world's leading watch manufacturing centre for the next 100 years.

---

41 A despite   **B** although   **C** otherwise   **D** average

42 A average   **B** medium   **C** general   **D** common

43 A vast   **B** large   **C** wide   **D** mass

44 A lasted   **B** endured   **C** kept   **D** remained

45 A mostly   **B** chiefly   **C** greatly   **D** widely

Dublin City Walks

What better way of getting to know a new city than by walking around it?

Whether you choose the Medieval Walk, which will **(46)** .... you to the Dublin of

1000 years ago, find out about the more **(47)** .... history of the city on the Eighteenth

Century Walk, or meet the ghosts of Dublin's many writers on the Literary Walk, we know you will

enjoy the experience.

Dublin City Walks **(48)** .... twice daily. Meet your guide at 10.30 a.m. or 2.30 p.m. at

the Tourist Information Office. No advance **(49)** .... is necessary. Special

(50) .... are available for families, children and parties of more than ten people.

46 A introduce   B present   C move   D show

47 A near   B late   C recent   D close

48 A take place   B occur   C work   D function

49 A paying   B reserving   C warning   D booking

50 A funds   B costs   C fees   D rates

Questions 51 – 60

- In this section you must choose the word or phrase which best completes each sentence.
- For questions **51** to **60**, mark **one** letter **A, B, C** or **D** on your Answer Sheet.

51 If you're not too tired we could have a .... of tennis after lunch.

   A match   **B** play   **C** game   **D** party

52 Don't you get tired .... watching TV every night?

   A with   **B** by   **C** of   **D** at

53 Go on, finish the dessert. It needs .... up because it won't stay fresh until
   tomorrow.

   A eat   **B** eating   **C** to eat   **D** eaten

54 We're not used to .... invited to very formal occasions.

   A be   **B** have   **C** being   **D** having

55 I'd rather we .... meet this evening, because I'm very tired.

   A wouldn't   **B** shouldn't   **C** hadn't   **D** didn't

56 She obviously didn't want to discuss the matter so I didn't .... the point.

   A maintain   **B** chase   **C** follow   **D** pursue

57 Anyone ...... after the start of the play is not allowed in until the interval.

   A arrives   **B** has arrived   **C** arriving   **D** arrived

58 This new magazine is .... with interesting stories and useful information.

   A full   **B** packed   **C** thick   **D** compiled

59 The restaurant was far too noisy to be .... to relaxed conversation.

   A conducive   **B** suitable   **C** practical   **D** fruitful

60 In this branch of medicine, it is vital to .... open to new ideas.

   A stand   **B** continue   **C** hold   **D** remain

Alte level	Paper and pen test score		Council of Europe Level
	Part 1 score out of 40	Part 1 score out of 60	
0 beginner	0-15	0-17	A1
1 elementary	16-23	18-29	A2
2 lower intermediate	24-30	30-39	B1
3 upper intermediate	31-40	40-47	B2
4 advanced		48-54	C1
5 very advanced		54-60	C2

STUDENT: ....

LANGUAGE TEST

Choose the answer and write a cross in the appropriate box

	A	B	C	D
1				
2				
3				
4				
5				
6				
7				
8				
9				
10				
11				
12				
13				
14				
15				
16				
17				
18				
19				
20				
21				
22				
23				
24				
25				
26				
27				
28				
29				
30				
31				
32				
33				
34				
35				
36				
37				
38				
39				
40				
41				
42				
43				
44				
45				
46				
47				
48				
49				
50				

	A	B	C	D
51				
52				
53				
54				
55				
56				
57				
58				
59				
60				

www.ingramcontent.com/pod-product-compliance
Lightning Source LLC
Chambersburg PA
CBHW062058090426
42741CB00015B/3270